MODERN TEACHING OF MATHEMATICS

MODERN TEACHING OF
MATHEMATICS

Manpal Singh

ANMOL PUBLICATIONS PVT. LTD.
NEW DELHI - 110 002 (INDIA)

ANMOL PUBLICATIONS PVT. LTD.
H.O.: 4374/4B, Ansari Road, Darya Ganj,
New Delhi-110 002 (India)
Ph.: 23278000, 23261597
B.O.: No. 1015, Ist Main Road, BSK IIIrd Stage
IIIrd Phase, IIIrd Block,
Bangalore - 560 085 (India)
Visit us at: www.anmolpublications.com

Modern Teaching of Mathematics

PRINTED IN INDIA

Printed at Mehra Offset Press, Delhi.

Contents

Preface

Education is a vast discipline and Teachers' Training is a vital part of it. The responsibilities of the educationists and educators are focused on the task of providing better training to the future teachers for their better learning and proper development. Needless to say that this responsibility can only be exercised, if the trainers are equipped with the required knowledge of the subject concerned. That's why it becomes essential for making adequate provisions for each course to the student-teachers or teacher trainees. The present series is designed for providing a solid workable base for all course-papers. It has been prepared strictly according to the syllabus of the B.Ed class, prescribed by the UGC for different universities.

No doubt, there are so many other books on the subject, available in the market, written by worthy authors. However, every writer has his or her own style and way of presentation. The present work also has its own features and characteristics.

In preparation of this series of texts, the editor had to refer to the works of other authors and information sources. The editor feels a deep sense of gratitude for incorporating their ideas in the text. Hopefully, this series would serve as a 'ready to refer' tool for all teachers, teacher-students and others.

—Editor

1
Introduction

Mathematics is a very important subject. Therefore, before imparting and transmitting its knowledge, it is necessary to understand, that, 'what is Mathematics?' Why its knowledge is given? and 'What is its nature? No one definition of mathematics is universally accepted. Generally, there are many definitions of Mathematics for example, some define mathematics as a science of calculation, some as a science of space and numbers and some as a science of measurement, magnitude and direction. Infact, the meaning of the word mathematics is—'The science in which calculations are prime.' In this way on the basis of these assumptions of mathematics, we can say that mathematics is the science of numbers, word , sign, etc. with which we can know about magnitude, direction & space. It is also highlighted in National Policy on Education (1986), as follows—

"Mathematics should be visualised as the vehicle to train a child to think, reason, analyse, articulate logically. Apart from being a specific subject it should be treated as a concomitant to any subject involving analysis and meaning."

Mathematics has originated from Numbers and Number System is a special field of it, by which other branches of Mathematics are developed.

The Concept

In Hindi, Mathematics is known as 'GANITA' meaning there by— 'The science of Calculations'. The term Mathematics can be defined in numerous ways to quote oxford dictionary

"Mathematics is the science of measurement, quantity and magnitude." Some definitions of mathematics are as follows—

Marshal H. Stone—According to Stone, "Mathematics is the study of abstract system built of abstract elements. These elements are not described in concrete fashion."

Bertrand Russell—According to him, "Mathematics may be defined as the subject in which we never know what we are talking about nor whether what we are saying true."

Benjamin Peirce—He emphasised that, "Mathematics is the science that draws necessary conclusions."

Prof. Voss—According to Voss, "Our entire civilization depending on the intellectual penetration and utilization of nature has its real foundation in the mathematical sciences.

Galileo—"Mathematics is the language in which God has written the universe."

Locke—"Mathematics is a way to settle in the mind of children a habit of reasoning."

On the basis of above definitions, we can say or conclude that—

1. Mathematics is the science of space and number.
2. Mathematics is the science of calculations.
3. Mathematics is the science of measurement, quantity and magnitude.
4. Mathematics is a systematised, organised and exact branch of science.
5. It deals with quantitative facts and relationships.
6. It is the abstract form of science.
7. It is a science of logical reasoning.
8. It settles in the mind a habit of reasoning.
9. It is an inductive and experimental science.
10. Mathematics is the science which draws necessary conclusions.

The Format

What is Mathematics and how does it grow are the basic questions which all the students of Mathematics must understand. In school, those subjects which are included in the curriculum must have certain aims and objectives on the basis of which its nature is decided. Mathematics holds a strong and unbreakable position as compared to other school subjects.

With this reason, mathematics is more stable and important than other school subjects. The way in which the structure of a subject becomes weak, its truthfulness, reliability and prediction also decreases in the same manner. On the basis of this specific structure, the nature of each subject is determined and placed in the school curriculum.

It is not necessary that all subjects have same nature. Mathematics has its unique nature thus on the basis of which we can compare it with other subjects. The basis of comparison of two or more subjects is their nature. We can understand the nature of Mathematics on the basis of following features—

1. Mathematics is a science of space, numbers, magnitude and measurement.
2. Mathematics has its own language. Language consists mathematical terms, mathematical concepts, formulae, theories, principles and signs, etc.
3. Mathematics is a systematised, organised and exact branch of science.
4. Mathematics involves conversion of abstract concepts in to concrete form.
5. Mathematics is the science of logical reasoning.
6. Mathematics does not leave any doubt in the mind of learner about theories, principles concepts etc.
7. Mathematics helps to develop the habit of self-confidence and self reliance in children.

8. Mathematics helps in the development of sense of appreciation among children.
9. Mathematics helps in developing scientific attitude among children.
10. The study of Mathematics gives the training of scientific method to the children.
11. Mathematical knowledge is based on sense organs.
12. It gives accurate and reliable knowledge.
13. Mathematical knowledge is exact, systematic, logical, and clear so that once it is captured it can never be forgotten.
14. Mathematical rules, laws and formulae, are universal and that can be verified at any place and time.
15. It develops the ability of induction, deduction and generalisation.
16. Mathematical language is well defined, useful and clear.
17. It draws numerical infrences on the basis of given information and data.
18. Mathematical knowledge is applied in the study of science and in its different branches; for example physics, chemistry, biology, and other sciences.
19. It is not only useful for different branches of science but also helps in its progress and organisation.

Thus on the basis of above points we can understand the nature of mathematics and draw conclusion that the structure of mathematics is indeed the basis of its nature and is more strong as compared to other school subjects. That is why its study is essential in school education. Roger Bacon has well said that, ***"Mathematics is the gate way and key of all sciences."***

The Significance

Mathematics is an important subject in school curriculum. It is more closely related to our daily life as compared to other subjects. Except our mother tongue there in no other subject which is more closely related to our daily life as Mathematics. Mathematics is considered as father of science. In present days mathematics has been given an important place in school curriculum. In order to give an important place in curriculum, a particular subject must possess the following views—

1. Utility of particular subject in daily life.
2. Whether the subject is helpful in the development of mental discipline or not.
3. The social and cultural importance of particular subject.

Today, Mathematics holds an important place in schools. For giving a place in curriculum there is no special need of evaluation and testing of it. Mathematics also helps to develop the child as social and intellectual citizens, like other subjects. It has its own disciplinary values. In addition to these, mathematics also develops those qualities which can be developed by other subjects. Napoleon also remarked that, "The progress and improvement of Mathematics is linked to the prosperity of the state."

In this context Kothari Commission (1964-66) suggested that "Science and mathematics should be taught on a compulsory basis to all pupils as a part of general education during first ten years of Schooling."

Generally, the children are send to schools for achieving different goals and it is assumed that the child will be able to achieve the following objectives—

1. Acquisition of knowledge and skills.
2. Acquisition of intellectual habits and various powers as discipline etc.
3. Acquisition of desirable attitude and ideals.

Now the question arises that whether the study of Mathematics helps the student in achieving the above goals or not? If it is so, then only it is valuable in educational system and is an important part of education. Indeed there are many advantages of giving due importance to mathematics and making it compulsory subject.

The importance of mathematics can be expressed in the form of values. There are certain values of teaching mathematics. On the basis of these values we can prove its importance in school curriculum. Mathematics helps in attaining and developing various values amongst the children.

Teaching Norms

Values are regarded as desirable, important and are held in high esteem by the people who live in a particular society. Thus values give meaning and strength to a person's character by occupying a central place in his life. Values are the guiding principles of life which are conducive to all round development. Therefore values reflect one's personal attitudes judgements, decisions, choices, behaviour, relationships, dreams and vision. Napolean also remarked that the progress and improvements, of mathematics is linked to the prosperity of the state. Therefore, mathematics plays an important role in the progress of Society. Mathematics teaching has the following values.

1. Intellectual value.
2. Moral value.
3. Utilitarian or practical value.
4. Disciplinary value
5. Social value.
6. Cultural value.
7. Aesthetic value.
8. Vocational value.
9. Psychological value.
10. Value related to scientific Attitude.
11. International value.

These values of Mathematics teaching can be shown as follows — (fig., Tree of values of teaching Mathematics)

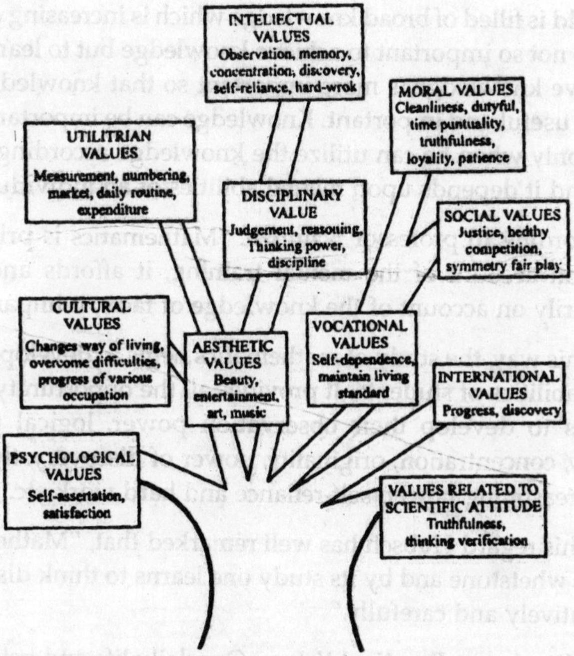

Tree showing Values of Mathematics Teaching

The various values of Mathematics teaching can be explained as follows—

Intellectual Values—Mathematics teaching is very important for intellectual development. There is no other subject in the curriculum like mathematics which make student's brain active. Problem-solving helps us in development of mental faculties. Mental work is needed for solving mathematical problem. As a child, faces a mathematical problem his brain becomes active in solving that problem. Each problem of Mathematics possesses such a sequence which is necessary for constructive and creative process. In this way, all mental abilities of child are developed through mathematics.

Throwing light on intellectual values of mathematics, a great educationist, Plato has said, "Mathematics is the subject which provides an opportunity for training the mind, to close thinking, stirring up a sleeping and unstructured spirit."

World is filled of broad knowledge which is increasing day by day. It is not so important to achieve knowledge but to learn how to achieve knowledge is more important so that knowledge can be more useful and important. Knowledge can be important for a person only when he can utilize the knowledge according to his needs and it depends upon mental abilities of an individual.

According to professor Schultze, "Mathematics is primarily taught on account of the mental training, it affords and only secondarily on account of the knowledge of facts, it imparts."

In this way, the study of mathematics helps to develop all the mental abilities of students. It provides all the opportunity to the students to develop their observation power, logical power, memory, concentration, originality, power of discovery, thinking power, reasoning power, self-reliance and hard work etc.

In this regard Hubsch has well remarked that, "Mathematics is like a whetstone and by its study one learns to think distinctly, consecutively and carefully."

Utilitarian or Practical Value—Our daily life and behaviour is totally dependent on mathematics. We need mathematics in order to classify and to understand every fact. We need its knowledge in our daily routine, house, outside, market, income-expenditure etc. In the absence of mathematical knowledge a person can neither treat his family well nor he can face his social duties. In this way every aspect of our life is concerned with the application of mathematics.

Our daily routine, measures and calculations all are dependent on it. Before sleeping and after awakening, mathematics is must for us. When we have to awaken? When we have to sleep? When we have to work? etc., all these evidences are related to it. Even all natural phenomenon are based on mathematical principles.

Each and every person of society needs mathematical knowledge either he is accepted personality or rejected one. It is not that mathematical knowledge is needed only by engineers, doctors, traders, businessmens etc. but also it is needed to smallest citizen of society, such as labourers, workers, drivers, coolies salesmans, vendors etc. In this context Young, J.W.A. said that, "Wherever we turn in these days of iron, steam and electricity we find that mathematics has been the pioneer. Were its backbone removed, our material civilization would inevitably collapse." Moreover, it is also required to study other school subjects, especially, science subjects. Generally, it is said that the child gets high achievement in mathematics also keeps high achievement in physics because physics also involves various types of calculations like maths. All scientific inventions and instruments which have made our daily life so easy smooth and happy are available only by mathematics. In this support Bacon has also remarked that—

"Mathematics is the gate way and key of all the sciences."

Hence in the age of science and information technology the knowledge of mathematics is very much essential and useful.

Disciplinary Value—Mathematics is not meant only for development of mental abilities but also to develop their personality with some qualities like concentration, truthfulness, seriousness etc. That is why the disciplinary value of Mathematics is also important. A person who is gaining mathematical knowledge is not in favour of working against the rules of under sentimental situations. A child judges about his good or bad with the help of his reasoning power, wisdom, patience, and self-confidence.

Mathematics is the only subject whose knowledge develops the habit of hard work, concentration, well organized and clearity in the students. These are such conditions which enable the students of mathematics to lead seriously, wisdomful, and disciplined life. In this context Locke says," Mathematics is a way to settle in the minds of children, a habit of reasoning."

Mathematical knowledge is exact, real and pure so that a special kind of discipline develops in the child's mind. Its facts are real and definite. Discipline is the only necessary requirement in order to use the acquired knowledge. It develops thinking and reasoning power and demands less from memory.

Moral Value—Morality is the important phase of life which is most effected by time, person, situation and place. Mathematical knowledge is helpful in character and personality development. It develops all those qualities which a person of strong character must possess. Child develops qualities of cleanliness, reality, punctuality, truthfulness, honesty, loyality, justice, dutifulness, self control, self reliance, self-confidence, patience, listens to others and respect them etc. through the study of mathematics. In this way mathematics leads to character development and moral development. It deprives off the feelings of jealous, hate etc.

Explaining the moral value of mathematics Dutton has said," Mathematics does furnish the power for deliberate thought and accurate statements and to speak the truth. Gossip, flattery, slander, deceit all speak from a mind that has not been trained by Mathematics." Thus mathematics is the only subject which really gives the training of self-control to the child and gives advance knowledge.

Social Value—Man is a social animal and human life depends upon the co-operation of each other. In order to live a social life, each other. In order to live a social life, its knowledge is needed because the give and take process, business and industry depends upon the knowledge of mathematics.

The change in the social structure with regards to modern facilities like mode of transport, means of communication and progress in the field of science and technology is due to mathematics only. Ideal education is that which helps to make a child a qualified and useful citizen of society from the beginning. Napolean has accepted the social value of mathematics and said that, "The progress and improvements of mathematics are linked to the prosperity of the state."

In this way mathematics has played an important role in not only understanding the progress of society but also to develop the society. At present our social structure seems to be so scientific and systematic its credit goes to mathematics. In its deficiency, the entire social system will be disturbed.

Cultural Value—The culture of every nation or society has its unique characteristics. It has its own importance. Each nation or society reflects its culture by its living standards rituals, artistic progress, economic, social, and political aspects etc. The history of mathematics presents the image of culture of different nations. The person is said to be cultured if one is well educated and have refined manners of dealing. The person becomes critical observer, logical thinker and proper knowledge of mathematics changes the mind of the person. Thus the person becomes more cultured with the proper knowledge of mathematics. The famous mathematician Hogben has remarked that "Mathematics is the mirror of civilization." In fact mathematical knowledge is indispensable and changes the way of ones living.

Mathematics not only familiarize us with culture and civilization but also helps in preventing, promoting cultural heritage and transmitting it to future generations. Through the application of scientific and mathematical discoveries, our culture and civilization is undergoing constant change. The welfare of our civilization is now almost wholly-dependent upon scientific as well as mathematical progress. It affects view of life and way of living as a result of which it also effects our philosophy of life. Hence the teaching of mathematics plays a vital role in developing our cultural heritage. Young, J.W. has also remarked that, "whenever we turn in these days of iron, steam, and electricity we find that mathematics has been the pioneer. Were its backbone removed, our material civilization would inevitably collapse. Hence mathematics shapes culture as a playback pioneer and has played an important role in bringing him to such an advanced stage of development."

Aesthetic Value—Mathematics is just like a song, beautiful, an art, music and a means of gaining pleasure for those who studies and likes it. But only few people who have not yet studied it have made a belief that mathematics is a dull and boring subject. One gets pleasure in solving mathematical problems, specially when he get the correct answers to his problems. At that moment every child feels pleasure, satisfaction, confidence and self-reliance. Perhaps this is the reason that Pythagorous gave scarification of 100 oxen, when he discovered his theorem. Keats has well remarked that "Truth is beauty." Thus whenever a mathematician discovers some thing new with the help of mathematical laws, facts, theorems and principles, a sense of joy is developed in his mind. He realises the aesthetic aspect of his findings or research. So the child gets encouragement, satisfaction and happiness in attaining remarkable achievements. Indeed a sense of appreciation is developed in the mind of the child.

If mathematics is considered as the creator and nurturer of all arts then it might not be wrong because in the development of all arts such as drawing, painting, art of sculpture, fine art, music, dance etc. mathematics plays an important role. Lebnitz has also said that 'Music is a modern hidden exercise in arithmetic of a mind unconscious of dealing with numbers.'

Moreover day-to-day changes, beautiful, and latest designs of our clothes, beautiful gardens, lawns, even flower pots etc., all these follow the mathematical rules in one or the other way. Various mathematical puzzles and riddles not only entertain the mind of the child but they also produces a sense of joy and appreciation amongst the children. Infact in the mind of the child a feeling of appreciation of mathematical knowledge is developed.

Vocational Value—The main aim of education is to help the children to earn their living and to make them self dependent. To achieve such aim, mathematics is the most important subject than any other. At present the vocational value of engineering, technology, management, information technology has became more important and prestigeous or reputed. The knowledge and training of these vocations is possible only through mathematics. Almost each and every vocation needs the knowledge of mathematics. Even to learn different vocations related to different branches of science require the knowledge of mathematics. Moreover, mathematics plays a very important role in different vocations.

For example—

* An architect cannot become a god designer without the knowledge of geometrical drawing and measurement.
* Official work requires the knowledge of mathematics.
* To become an engineer, accountant, banker etc., there is need of mathematical knowledge.

* Similarly to understand different sciences, knowledge of mathematics is must.

Therefore, it can be said that each and every person needs mathematical knowledge for the earning and to maintain his living standard.

Psychological Value—Mathematics education is also useful from the point of view of psychological aspects. Mathematics fulfills the psychological needs of the children. In mathematics emphasis is given on operations and drill work so that its knowledge becomes more solid as well as durable. The teaching of mathematics follows the various laws and principles of psychology. For example, the child acquires knowledge on the various principles of psychology such as—learning by doing, learning through experiences and problem-solving, etc. Through its knowledge the child develops and satisfies his desires, creative and constructive tendencies, self-satisfaction, self assertion etc.

Value Related to Scientific Attitude—The knowledge of mathematics trains the children in attempting the problems according to a definite and distinct procedure which may be called as the scientific method. Generally scientific method involves the following steps—

* Identification of the problem.
* Defining the problem.
* Collection of data/information regarding the problem.
* Drawing conclusions.
* Verification of the results.

Thus we can reach to the depth of the problem and then select the most appropriate solution to the problem. Scientific attitude involves open-mindness, critical observation, suspended judgement, free from superstition and false belief etc. Thus, the training which a child receives in studying mathematics can be applied to solve the problems arising in new situations.

International Value—Mathematics not only gives the knowledge about the nation and its background but also gives a message of nationality. The progress in the field of mathematics is neither the achievement of a single person, nation, society, cast or religion followers only nor it is the property of a particular nation. Any invention of a nation when crosses its boundaries, it reaches to its international value. This is the reason of the progress in the field of science and mathematics. Now a days it is the requirement of the time that all the scientists, mathematicians, educationists and researchers of the world should work as an integrated nation. These all facts reflect the international value of teaching mathematics.

Hence it is quite clear from the above discussion that mathematics which is so valuable, important, psychologically based and so closely connected with our day-to-day life, is justified to be included in the school curriculum.

Status of the Subject

Curriculum includes all those activities, experiences and environment which the child receives during his educational career under the guidance of educational authorities. Thus curriculum is the total education of the child.

Curriculum touches all the aspects of the life of the pupils—the need and interest of pupils environment which should be educationally congenial to them, ways and manners in which their interest can be kindled and warmed up, the procedures and approaches which cause effective learning among them, the social efficiency of the individual and how they fit in with the community around.

In education, the importance and the place of a particular subject depends on the fact that "to what extent the subject is helpful in achieving the aims of the education". If any subject is more useful for achieving educational objectives then its importance increases accordingly. Since ancient times mathematics has played a vital role in achieving aims of education, as compared to others. Present age is the age of science and information. Whatever, technological and physical progress being made, shall be correspondent to the role of mathematics. Being so important "What place should be given to mathematics in the curriculum?"

in school Kothari Commission has explained about placing mathematics as a compulsory subject upto higher secondary or tenth standard and has said, "Mathematics should be made a compulsory subject for the students of Ist to Xth standard, as a part of general education."

But some people lay more emphasis on making it an optional subject after eight standard, therefore various reasons were framed against this proposal.

1. It is very difficult subject and its learning requires a sharp brain and intelligence, as many children will face difficulties for gaining the knowledge.
2. It is only an imagination that mental abilities, discipline, culture, social and moral developments can be done by mathematics.
3. The numbers of failures in mathematics in high school examination are more as compared to that of other subjects.
4. In higher studies, mathematical knowledge is important for those who keep their main subject as physics, chemistry, or mathematics. Thus it is useless for others.
5. Every student can't become an engineer or a technician, then what is the necessity of mathematics for all.

In this way, the reasons for forbading the compulsion of mathematics upto tenth standard seems to ideological.

All great educationalist like Herbert, Pestolozzi etc. has accepted mathematics as a symbol of human development. Accepting mathematics as a best means of intellectual and cultural developments, these educationists placed mathematics on the top in the curriculum. Thus we can give certain logical points regarding mathematics as a compulsory subject. These are as follows :

1. If mathematics is not given an important place in the curriculum then students would not get any opportunity for mental training and in the absence of which their intellectual development might be affected.

2. For gaining the knowledge of mathematics no innate power is required, which is separate from ability of study of other subject.
3. Training of reasoning, thinking, discipline, self confidence and emotions are developed in students by mathematics.
4. Through mathematics child leans to gain knowledge systematically.
5. It is needed either forwardly or adversely for studying almost all the subjects because it is considered as the basis of science and each and every art.

Thus on the basis of above discussion, we can conclude that mathematics is only subject whose knowledge is needed for the whole life. It can be possible only when every child will study mathematics as a compulsory subject upto tenth standard. Mathematics occupy a prominent place in men's life, from an engineer to technician or labour to finance minister and other businessmen, all needed the help of mathematics according to their requirements. The knowledge of this subject is indefensible and it is bound to grow as the need grows. A mathematical approach is essential for any progress. Any approach devoid of mathematical consideration is likely to lead to failure. If anybody wants to get success in his life, he must have recourse to mathematics.

In America or England the standard of mathematics in X is just equal to that of XII standard of mathematics in India. There the students adapt the easier method for choosing their career through mathematics.

Thus mathematics should be placed on higher level even though it is required for earning. There are some reasons for giving it an important place in school curriculum, some of them are as follows—

Case for Mathematics

Mathematics is the Basis of all Sciences—The different branches of science likewise—physics, chemistry, Astronomy,

Biology, Medical Science, Geology, Astrology etc. are the important subjects which are based on mathematics for e.g.—Area, volume, weight, density, number of atoms and electrons, medicines all are related to mathematical study.

Mathematics is Related to Human Life—Right from getting up in the morning till going to bed we need the help of mathematics. For purchasing, planning our day, each and every aspect involves the use of mathematics. Today in the modern age, the knowledge of mathematics is essential and more important in one form or the other. Engineering, banking and other business which are directly linked with mathematics, for them mathematics works like a foundation brick and the business which are indirectly related to mathematics, also depends totally on it. Besides these. in our daily routine also, we need a general mathematical knowledge.

Mathematics Generates Logical Attitude—Mathematics give training to different faculties of mind. In order to solve a mathematical problem a child has to think logically. Every step is related to other step on the basis of some logic with which child develops his mental abilities and it further effects his intellectual development.

Mathematics Provides a Definite way of Thinking—The children who study mathematics develop attitude with which they learn to work systematically, regularly and properly. Along with this it also develops a logical thinking in them.

Mathematics is an Exact Science—By the study of mathematics child develops the attitude to accept the knowledge of mathematics in an exact form. All mathematical concepts, formulae, facts are related to exactness and thus it removes the feeling of doubt. For example; 2 + 2 = 4. Which cannot be 3 or 5 etc.

1. Mathematics provides opportunity to develop mental abilities of the child.
2. Mathematics helps in character formation as well as morality.

3. It develops the characteristic of discipline.
4. The language of mathematics is universal.
5. Knowledge of mathematics is useful in the study of other school subjects.
6. Mathematics deals with significant, abstracts and consistent structures.
7. Mathematics is the study of sets and structures. Generally mathematics have basically three structures —

The Algebric Structures—In Algebric structures we study operations of addition, multiplication and generalization.

The Topological Structures—The topological structures include different concepts like limit, neighbourhood or nearness etc.

The Order Structure—This type of structures include concepts like greater than and less than etc.

Mathematics is a very important subject. There are several definitions of mathematics. It may be defined as science of space, numbers, measurement, magnitude and direction. Number system is a special field of mathematics by which other branches of mathematics are developed.

Definitions—According to Oxford dictionary mathematics is the science of measurement, quantity and magnitude. Other definitions given by Marshal H. Ston, Bertrand Russell. Peirce, Prof. Voss, Galileo and Locke.

Mathematics' Value

The structure of mathematics is indeed the basis of its nature and is more strong than other school subjects.

* Mathematics is a science of numbers, magnitude, space, measurement, logical reasoning.
* Mathematics has its own language which is well defined, useful and clear.

* It helps to develop-self confidence, reasoning, logical and critical thinking, self reliance, sense of appreciation, scientific attitude.
* It develops the abilities of induction, deduction, analysis, synthesis and generalisation.
* Useful in the study of all sciences, etc.

Significance of the Subject

It is an important subject in school curriculum. It is considered as father of all sciences. Mathematics helps the students in achieving the educational goal and objectives. The importance of mathematics can be expressed in the form of values. It help in attaining and developing various values among the child. There are certain values of teaching mathematics. The values give meaning and strength to a person's character by occupying a central place in his life. Values of teaching mathematics are as follows—

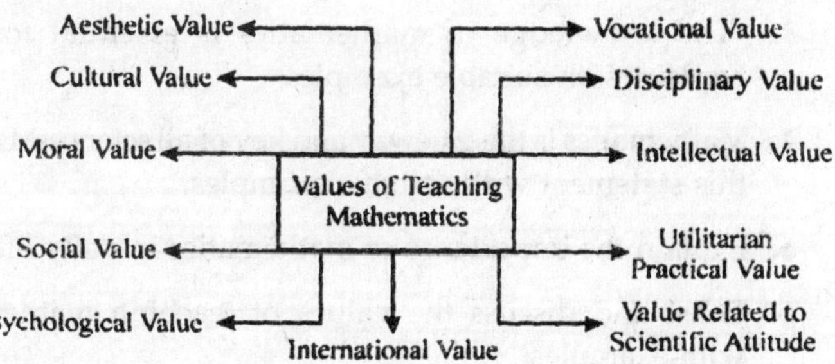

Place of Mathematics in School Curriculum. Curriculum includes all those activities, experiences and environments which the child receives during his educational career.

Curriculum touches all the aspects of the life of the child. In the present age of science and technology whatever, technological and physical progress are being made, all that shall be correspondent to the role of mathematics. In brief mathematics is only subject whose knowledge is needed for the whole life. Thus mathematics should be given in important place in the school curriculum.

Reasons for Keeping Mathematics in School Curriculum

* It is the basis of all sciences and much related to human life.
* It generates logical attitude, provides definite way of thinking.
* It is an exact science, develops the characteristics of discipline, self confidence, reasoning etc.

QUESTION

Essay Type Questions

1. Define mathematics and clarify its Nature.
2. What is the place of mathematics in school curriculum and what is the need of mathematics teaching at secondary stage?
3. "The knowledge of mathematics is essential for all." Explain with suitable examples.
4. Mathematics is the gateway and key of all sciences. Explain this statement with suitable examples.
5. Explain the importance of mathematics in daily life?
6. Enlist and discuss the values of teaching mathematics with examples.
7. Write an essay on need and importance of mathematics at secondary level.
8. Write short notes on following—
   (a) Reasons for keeping ma1thematics in the school curriculum.
   (b) Intellectual value of mathematics teaching.
   (c) Social and cultural value of mathematics teaching.

(d) Nature of mathematics.

9. What are the educational values of teaching mathematics? Discuss.

10. How mathematics can be defined and what is the nature of mathematics.

11. Discuss the place of mathematics in school curriculum.

Objective Type Questions

(A) Multiple Choice

1. The nature of mathematics is—

(a) Ornamental (b) Logical
(c) Difficult (d) Not for common.

2. Who said that, "Mathematics is the science which draws necessary conclusions".

(a) Hogben (b) Locke
(c) Benjamin Peirce (d) None of the above.

3. Mathematics is the science of—

(a) Space (b) Numbers
(c) Calculations (d) All the above.

4. "To appreciate the works of mathematician." Corresponds to which value—

(a) Intellectual (b) Utilitarian
(c) Aesthetic (d) None of the above.

5. According to Hogben, "Mathematics is the mirror of civilization" this statements corresponds to which value of mathematics—

(a) Cultural (b) Social
(c) Disciplinary (d) None of the above.

(B) Fill in the Blanks —

1. According to.................................... Truth is beauty.

2. Mathematics is the.................................of measurement, quantity, and magnitude.
3. Mathematical puzzles and riddles are the examples of .... value of mathematics.
4. According to ....mathematics is the language in which God has written the universe.

2

Interesting Subject

To arouse and maintain the students interest in mathematics is a major problem for the teacher. He knows that loss of interest is one of the major causes of students failure. Action and thought of an individual is related to his interest specially towards particular things. Different students have different ideas and their interest varies from subject to subject. Someone show more interest in learning mathematics while others have fearful thinking about mathematics considering as if it is very difficult subject. Teacher should try to locate the interest of the child. He should try to provide the situation and the contents of the subject matter according to their interest. One can be one a successful teacher if one has ability to motivate and arouse interest in learning specially mathematics which is in general considered to be one of the dull and dry subjects in the school curriculum if the teacher is successful in locating and arousing interest of the child depending upon his mental level, he can help the child to a greater extent in gaining more and more knowledge effectively.

Constant Study

1. By explaining to the child the usefulness of learning mathematics in their daily life and for higher studies.
2. By correlating the contents of mathematics with other school subjects.
3. By removing the fear from the mind of the child that it is not a difficult subject rather very easy and interesting.

4. By giving practical shape to the subject matter in the process of learning and teaching i.e. by stressing upon the idea of learning by doing.
5. By solving some interesting puzzles in mathematics.
6. By Using different methods of teaching.
7. By relating the work and life history of great mathematicians.

Some times due to improper follow up programme of instructions and applications of the learnt material in the subject of mathematics, the aroused interest in the mind of the child starts fading with the passage of time. To keep it lasting for a longer time and workable practically in the everyday life of the child. Teacher should try to maintain the aroused interest for learning mathematics in the mind of the child with following suggestive measures—

By Explaining the Vocational Values of the Subject Matter (Mathematics Subject)—The teacher should not give only bookish knowledge to the child, but teacher should explain the uses of learning mathematics in other vocations so that child may learn vocation of his own interest with the proper use of his mathematical knowledge with proper vocational ability child can become self learner independently.

By Explaining Utilitarian Values of Mathematics—Teacher should try to correlate the theoretical knowledge of the child with some practical values of life. These ideas about the utilitarian values of mathematical concepts can help the teacher to a greater extent in maintaining the aroused interest for learning mathematics in the mind of the child.

By Explaining the Correct Way of Learning Mathematics—Just like other subjects say history, language, social studies mathematics can not be learnt. But learning of the subject is based upon the idea 'practice makes a man perfect'. Teacher should try to inculcate the habit of learning their subject matter by waiting repeatedly so that the learnt material may last for a longer time in the mind of the child. At the same time this habit of learning can help, the child to keep the interest in the subject matter a first and lasting for a longer time.

Handling of material and learning through experimentation should be permitted and arranged as frequently as possible. Practical presentation of matter should always precede its abstract form. Preparation of aids and applications based on mathematical topics should be a regular activity of the learners.

By Correlating Mathematics with other School Subjects— Teacher can help the child to maintain the aroused interest for a longer time by giving correlation of the subject matter, in the process of learning and understanding the other school subjects.

Mathematics has played a very important role in building up modern civilization by perfecting all sciences. It is an efficient and necessary roof which is employed by all these sciences and without which these sciences would not have made much progress. It has been very properly said about mathematics "It is a science of all Sciences and art of all arts". It may be a back-stage performer, but is a vary powerful one.

By Explaining the Historical Aspects—Child's aroused interest can also be maintained by relating the biographies of great mathematicians and their achievements in the life for the welfare of the humanity. A reference to the historical background of different mathematical terms and ideas gives a good start for learning them. The teacher should spare no pains to make the subject matter attractive and pleasant. Students fed encouraged to work harder if accomplishment is accomplishment by pleasure. The cultural values received are generally proportional to the pleasures derived. The students should be kept aware of the nature and the universal applicability of mathematical methods. This will provide strong motivation for study.

By Changing the Method of Teaching—Sometimes due to routine work of teaching and learning, interest of students in learning mathematics starts fading. Teacher should have more knowledge of child psychology so that from time to time he may use the method of teaching according to the need and interest of the child. This change are what to say variety in teaching can help the child to maintain the aroused interest of the child.

Some Psychological Condition for Study to be Followed for Maintaining Interest in Mathematics—

Principle of Change—Monotony should not be allowed to settle over the classroom atmosphere A topic should not be continued for too long a period. No aid or device should be employed over and over again.

The unnecessary distractions and interruptions should be avoided.

The concentration should be cultivated by giving a student quiet room, well lighted and ventilated, with chair a and table for convenient work.

The mind should be kept alert and the thoughts may be clarified by writing.

The fundamentals should be learned accurately and **self confidence** should be developed.

The work must be proceeded systematically and thoroughly by giving practical critical thinking.

The above maintained some of the conditions, if provided and enforced will surely lead to better results.

By Making Learning More Meaningful—Some principles of meaningful learning are as follows—

(i) It is necessary that the students should be motivated before they are made to learn anything. A strong interest should be aroused and whole hearted attention to the extent of concentration should be secured.

(ii) The aim and objective of every topic should be made definite and clear. If the students come to relies in the very beginning that the material to be learnt will find wide applications, then their learning will be need-based and more meaningful,

(iii) Motivation is the basic activity for creating interest. Various means such as aids, relationships, historical references, anecdotes, possible application, games can be adopted to provide motivations to the child.

(iv) Heuristic and problem solving attitudes are basic to meaningful learning. When such attitudes are developed from the very beginning the students enjoy learning mathematics. To them mathematics would never appear dull and dry subject.

(v) When correlations of mathematical knowledge with daily life, sciences, social sciences, and other activities is stressed, the pupils can appreciate the meaningfulness of their learning.

(vi) Proper use of mental faculties pays to exercise the thinking and reasoning powers of the learners. The learning becomes meaningful if it is saved from mechanical process and blind creaming, memorization and retention.

(vii) In the learning of mathematics there is need for regular and persistent practice. Students should never loose their patience, hope and self confidence. Thus their learning will become more meaningful solid and fruitful for them. In order to make learning meaningful, it is necessary that the pupil should be motivated before they learn.

(viii) By Setting up of Mathematics Club—Organisation of mathematics club gives a wider aspect of mathematics as a subject. It provides an excellent means of stimulating and fostering mathematical study. Such clubs offer excellent opportunities for free consideration of matter of special interest to the members without the necessity of having any particular sequence of topics. The programmes of mathematics clubs may cover a wide range of topics. The students also get opportunities of mathematical hobbies, mathematical projects, mathematical games, puzzles, discussions and debates. The club will be a medium of developing pupils' interest in the mathematics. Various activities of club will relate the knowledge acquired with other activities and daily life experiences.

Maintaining the Pace

The students can gain interest in mathematics if various activities and games related to the subject are carried in the class. For example—"Guess My Rule". This kind of game can be used to solve basic problems related to Algebra. In this the teacher is given first number 'X' by one student that number can have a pair like (X, Y) Teacher has a rule in his mind and using that rule he gives the number Y to the student. That rule can be of type Y = MX or Y = MX + B. Then other students give the teacher next number 'X ' and he gives then the number Y till the students have guessed the rule for finding Y. If the student gives the correct answer then he becomes the leader of the next round. Hence "Guess My Rule" is one of he best way of arousing interest in mathematics.

Field of Probability is also a very interesting field to arouse interest in mathematics. One of the example is given below—

3 cards are there in a box, these are similar in all respect except the colour, one is black on both the sides, one is white on both the sides and one is white on one side and black on the other one student takes out one card from the box and shows it to the class. If students see the black side of the card the tell the probability of the opposite side leaving white.

It is assumed that the other side of the card may be black or white Hence the answer is ½; But the answer is not ½ but 1/3. Hence this answer will result in various arguments among the class.

Card 1	Card 2	Card 3
W_1	B_1	W_3
W_2	B_2	B_3

When the class sees the black side of the card they are actually seeing either B_1, B_2, or B_3,

Hence

Showing	**Other side**
B_1	B_2
B_2	B_1
B_3	W_3

Hence : out of 3 once the side will see white and the answer is 1/3.

There are still many ways of arousing interest in mathematics like songs, poems can be used in the subject. Problems of social science, rules for sports, graphs etc. can be collected from the various newspapers which arouse interest in the students.

Maintaining the Interest

When the interest for mathematics have been aroused in the students then the question arrises of how to maintain it ? To maintain the interest for longer duration the main thing is success. We know that everyone wants success and the enjoyment which comes along with it. Both success and enjoyment forms the part of a cycle. Hence the teacher should provide students with successful experiences and these successful experiences help to develop the Realistic Achievement level in the students. Hence a teacher should help the students to get success. This is possible only by asking various types of questions from the students.

Example—How many triangle or squares and Rectarg les are there in the following figures.

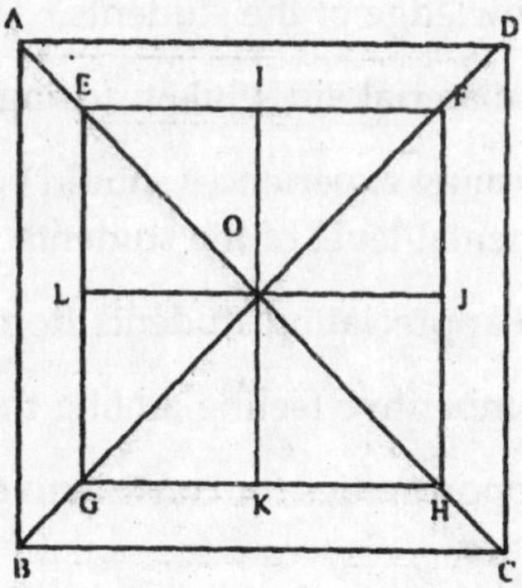

In such questions each and every student gets involved in the discussion and represent the student giving correct answer to the question. Every student will answer according to his capabilities.

Another way of maintaining interest in mathematics is providing the knowledge and training for handling the various instruments used in the class. Hence it is essential to provide practical knowledge to the students. They may be asked to measure the length, breath and height of the class room. With the help of 6 inch scale, one feet scale and one yard/ meter scale. Are there any differences between the scales? Why? Which scale is best to measure the about variables. This keeps the students involved in the subject matter.

Many times teachers uses complicated and expensive material aid in the class which arouse interest in the students but is not able to maintain it longer hence it is better to ask students to prepare easy and small models based on the subject. Black board is a readily available device that enables the teacher to involve the students in active way. Students may be asked to solve problems on the blackboard. The students will participate readily, work hard and experience positive feelings towards mathematics. Hence in order to maintain and arouse interest in mathematics following points should be kept in mind—

1. Teaching should be child centered.
2. New knowledge and experiences should be linked with previous knowledge of the students.
3. Use of right material aid while teaching.
4. Choice of learning experiences should be according to the needs and mental level of the students.
5. Praising and appreciating students from time to time.
6. To arouse competitive feeling among the students.
7. Providing opportunities for constructive & creative work in mathematics.

8. Dealing the students with affection, sympathy and helping them.
9. While teaching, innovative and child-certed methods should be used.
10. The teacher should keep an eye on the pace of the lesson.
11. The lesson should not be drag, when a lesson moves crisply and flows smoothly, students remain interested.
12. Teacher should encourage his students to guess more, rather than less.
13. The teacher must be able to stimulate the pupils to participate actively in the discovery of mathematics.
14. Mathematics teacher should strengthen positive feelings toward mathematics and try to change or at least ameliorate, the negative feelings.

Speed and Accuracy both are interlinked terms used in Mathematics. Speed without accuracy is of no use. An expert teacher is he who is able to solve the problems with the wink of an eye. So in teaching learning process, firstly the students are taught how to solve the problems correctly and then they are learnt to enhance their Speed by drill and practice speed and accuracy plays a vital role in every work of life not single in mathematics, e.g., a typist first learn identification of letters in key-board and then he types them slowly. After regularly practice, he gains speed with no faults in typing. His fast typing is speed and typing correctness is accuracy. Hence, term speed and accuracy runs altogether in every field where value is the main aims. Value refers to quality here. Hence same principle is applied to the engineers who prepare softwares. The engineers can only when be said skilled in their field, if their product out put serves both speed and accuracy, their product will be appreciated and soon well bring a good name. Similarly, teachers, doctors, Bankers, engineers, customers, shopkeepers etc. and even housewives should have both speed and accuracy in mathematical skills. For example if a mathematical teacher is unable to solve the problems in the class with speed and accuracy, he cannot be an effective teacher for his students. Generally, housewives go for shopping and they have to calculate whether the price and total cost of bought things are correct or not speedily and accurately because if they take more time to calculate, then the shopkeeper might get busy with other customers and then after it is not possible to realize his mistake despite of nagging. Thus speed and accuracy is in mathematics are important every where.

If a child solves a problem with speed but not accurately then it is of no use. Therefore, priority should be given to accuracy and then through drill and practice speed should be increased. Speed and accuracy are the symbol of intellectual abilities and capacities. Hence, increase in speed and accuracy develop the intellectual abilities of an individual. In this support Locke has well remarked that, "Mathematics is a way to settle in the mind of the children a habit of reasoning. Thus, speed and accuracy occupy a very important place in mathematics as well as in our daily life. So a mathematics teacher should try to train his students in acquiring both speed and accuracy."

Reasons Behind Dropping in Speed and Accuracy — For better result or output fully devotion to anything is the must thing. This can only when be gained if we are not falling victim of distraction. Distracting attention from real aim will certainly drop both the speed and accuracy. It is obvious that fast speed falls somewhat accuracy, but these both can be maintained if whole attention is to the aim to which we are involved. In job work, a machinist pays full attention to job, all distracting elements are kept away from him to gain speed and accuracy both. There are several reasons for a lack of speed and accuracy in mathematics. Some of the reasons are as follows —

* Untimely accomplishment of the work
* Lack of imagination and power of memorization
* Lack of capacity to take quick decision
* Negative attitude towards maths

* Readiness and concentration deficiency
* Less ability to analyse the problem
* Weakness in calculation skills
* Weakness in oral work
* Overwriting and cutting in calculation work
* Wear blinkers while examining the work
* Not to represent rough work in right manner
* No chance to improve faults
* Lack knowledge of fundamental operations, rules and formulas of mathematics
* Wrong representation of digits and numbers on black board and answer sheets
* Want of alertness towards mathematics
* Untimely observation and unfit direction to students work
* No encouragements to students at right work
* Lack of self confidence and self dependability.
* From the above points we can conclude that mathematics is such subject that needs both speed and accuracy to give outcomes in better proportion. Both the teacher and student are responsible to maintain it.

Means Adopted to Develop Speed — We have known speed and accuracy both are urgent necessity to bring better gain of anything. If one is legging, it influences the result worse; but due to vast curriculum prevailed in schools in present time forces the teacher to complete the syllabus within time maintaining accuracy also. Hence it becomes a major problem before teachers how to develop speed. A mathematics teacher has to pay attention to all the students who learn in a group as they are different in mental status. A good teacher while teaching mathematics keeps all aspects—"standard of student, time factor, accuracy" in view and completes syllabus within time and brings the result better. Below are given some suggestions, adopting them a mathematics teacher can bring desired output—

* Giving the child oral work
* By giving assignment fixing the date of submission
* Developing in the student habit of readiness and concentration
* Developing in the child habit of taking quick decision
* Observing the work according to student's ability and mental status
* By making language brief while solving mathematical problems
* Teaching the students by short-cut-method and method of judging the right answer of the problem
* Helping the students in washing away their doubts and checking their mistakes
* Providing the students a lot of practice work
* Developing in students positive attitude towards mathematics
* Making the students alert physically, mentally and emotionally
* By bring the work in daily routine and being self-active and making the students the same also to work
* By. Creating interest in child towards mathematics and using necessary material to bring variety in teaching
* By endangering the child for future benefits.

Means Adopted to Develop Accuracy in Mathematics—One things can do nothing it is common fact. Great men have also shared their experiences saying that, "It takes two to make quarrel." Then in mathematics, what does alone speed can do? Same is the case in life or universe, it needs couple to bring necessary change with speed, accuracy is also necessary to bring a change. If there is no change, there is no progress. If a person is on in his action, but he gain no quality or accuracy in work, his gain is considered useless. Specially in mathematics accuracy has the major place in every step as to create good interest in completion of the work. Below are given important suggestions adopting them a teacher can serve his purpose and desired output can also be obtained.

1. Encouraging a child to make exact calculations.
2. Developing a child habit of verifying result.
3. Discouraging the students on wrong calculation and removing their mistakes.
4. Providing the students remedial teaching finding their faults.
5. Teaching the child to write correct words, numbers and sentences.
6. Examining the students in fundamental operations, rules and formulas to develop their mechanical skills.
7. Applying diagnostic approach to determine students faults.
8. Developing in students the habits of analyzing and grasping the problem.
9. Developing in students the habit to write down or to copy on from the black board.
10. Clarifying the students that what is given? What is to determine? And how is it to be determined? In a question, before solving it.
11. Emphasizing the students for drill work.
12. Suggesting the students to write the method of calculation as to find the committed fault of any.
13. Developing in students habit to draw figures and diagrams head in mathematics.

14. Giving more emphasis on accuracy than speed.
15. Developing in students habit to grasp question exactly them to solve.

From the above discussion it is clear that purpose of teaching in mathematics can only when be served, if a mathematics teacher knows all the measures how to develop speed and accuracy. Undoubtedly, speed and accuracy in mathematics can bring system of teaching-learning to a great height and thus, present increasing burden of study can be served by taking speed and accuracy together.

Special Library

A place or room in the institution where teaching martial like books, journals, magazines, reference books, news papers are kept is known as general library. In the library there are different sections of different subjects. Teaching material related to specific subject is arranged separately in an right manners. The side in the room where books or literature related to the knowledge of mathematics is kept, is called mathematics section of library. Sometimes in some institutions in different department of different subjects, sperate rooms are made where books and related literature to the specific subject is placed. As for example in the department of mathematics a room where books and literature concerning to the knowledge of mathematics is placed, is called mathematics library on departmental library.

Importance—Library is the mirror of the school and holds very important place in the field of education.

1. Learning material in the form of books, journals, magazines can be perceived for future reading.
2. It develops good hobby of reading in leisure time.
3. Thirst of knowledge can be quenched by reading books of self interest.
4. Habit of self study and self education can be developed.

5. I helps to supplement the knowledge learnt in the classroom.
6. Students can improve their general knowledge by reading general books, magazines, newspaper etc.

Organizations of Library—If there is no provision of departmental library, there should be separate section in the central or say general library of the school for mathematics. The whole section of mathematics library can be divided into following parts—

(a) Text books.

(b) General books.

(c) Reference books.

(d) Inspirational books.

(e) Practical books.

(f) Back ground books.

(g) Popular mathematics books.

(h) Mathematical magazines and Journals.

Text Books—For any subject the text book is very important. There should be provision of all the text books related to mathematics for each class of the school according to prescribed syllabus.

General Books—Books giving general informations related to the subject matter e.g. book of general knowledge containing information of day to day happening and discoveries.

Reference Books—The books which are directed for further study. Tables of constants, logarithms, Books containing mathematical terms in other languages, mathematics dictionaries etc.

Inspirational Books—The books which inspires for teaching and learning. For example wonder of mathematics, puzzles in mathematics, tricks in mathematics, magic of mathematics etc.

Practical Books—Books which provide with the detailed information of experiments. For example books containing particular utility of learnt mathematical facts, figures and principles.

Back Ground Books—It gives the information about the historical development of notation system, metric system. Historical development of different branches of mathematics biographies of the great mathematicians.

Popular Mathematics Books—Popular mathematics containing latest ideas about the discoveries and invention in the field of mathematics.

Mathematics Magazines and Journals—These are very important in mathematical library to develop the thirst of knowledge of mathematics in the students.

Moreover, there should also be a collection of puzzles and game books for the students to enjoy their leisure time. These activities may be basically a series of games, puzzles and experiments. The corners of library might be furnished with several chairs and tables where the pupils can sit right down and read. Definite rules should be set up as to when pupils can use the various activities and how they are to be checked out.

Special Laboratory

The mathematics laboratory provides our opportunity for individualized instructions, an introduction to the use of calculators and computers. It is a setting with in which students can develop their independent study programmes. The literal meaning of the word laboratory is a room where a group of pupils learns the subject matter actually performing experiments. Dr. D.S. Kothari has emphasized that "To learn science is to do science. There is no other way of learning science." The concept of laboratory is not new. E.H. moore, prof. of mathematics, University of Chicago, make statement in his address before the American mathematical society in 1902—"Would it not be possible for the children in the grades to be trained in the power of observation and experiment and selection and deduction so that always their mathematics should be directly connected with matters of a thoroughly concrete character ?......This program of reform calls for the development of a thorough going laboratory system of instruction in mathematics and physics......"

The laboratory approach embodies the concepts of active learning, pupils involvement and participation and relevance. It is a demonstration of the concept of an activity oriented mathematics programme. Nowadays laboratory approach to mathematics instruction is being used effectively with all pupils.

The Significance

Mathematics laboratory in a school is very important and useful. The importance of mathematics laboratory is discussed under following points—

1. Habit of critical thinking and logical reasoning can be developed.
2. Complex theoretically concepts can be made clear by performing sintable experimenters.
3. Learning of subject matter can be given a practical shape.
4. Practical mindedness is developed among the students.
5. Interest in learning mathematics can be developed.
6. Scientific attitude or temperament is developed among the students.
7. Bookish knowledge of the students can be correlated practically with their daily life.
8. Sense of keen or sharp observation of the child can be developed.
9. Problem solving attitude can be developed in pupils.

Various Components for a Mathematics Laboratory

Staffing—The mathematics teacher or head of the department and his staff must be ready and willing to incorporate the mathematics laboratory, Initially establishment of mathematics laboratory requires only one or two members of the department but the development of the laboratory as a mathematical learning centre is dependent upon total staff involvement.

Physical Facilities—New school should include a specific area for a mathematics laboratory. It is recommended that the laboratory be located adjacent to another mathematics classroom and separated from it buy a movable partition, so that a large group instruction area can then be made available when desired.

Furniture—The following furniture is required—calculatery center, measurement center, Game center, Reading center, Diagnostic and tutorial center, Total number of chair and tables, Filing cabinets, Shelving, A storeroom and one large, permanent screen.

Equipments—Equipment such as—calculating equipments, Measuring equipments, Audio-visual aids, Equipment related with games and puzzles etc.

Instructional Materials—Instructional materials; such as: computational skills development materials (e.g. work books, calculator etc.), Individual students records of diagnostic and progress reports, Problem-solving materials (e.g. collection of real life problems, other commercial material), instruments that will assist in diagnosing students needs, weaknesses and in determining the level of performance, an evaluative procedures to accompany each developmental stage, essential and abbreviate audio-visual aids (e.g. charts and models, geometrical figures, tape recorder, improvised and commercially developed materials, materials related with recreational mathematics (e.g. various games and puzzles).

The Arrangement : Before ranging needed equipments, instruments or apparatus to be used in the process of teaching and learning mathematics practically in the mathematical laboratory, a proper provision should be made for a spacious room having Almirahs side shelves. Demonstration tables etc.

Essential Instruments

1. Black Board
2. Demonstration table in the front of Black Board.
3. Tracing material: Graph papers, Tracing papers, Carbon papers, Coloured pencils, Inks, Brushes, Drawing board, Drawing papers etc.
4. Reference material: Reference books, Text books, Magazine, books containing old and latest literature related to subject meter.
5. Drawing instruments like a pencil, chalk, foot rule, Compass, Divider, Set Squares etc.
6. Projective aids: like sound projector, Step projected, Slide projector, Epidea scope, over head projector etc.
7. Laboratory material: Logarithm tables, Ready recliners, Tables of constants.
8. Computer, electronic calculators etc.
9. Measuring instruments i.e., measuring tape, metre rode, sextants balances, weighing machine etc.
10. Teaching Aids: Like sound projector, charts, models of solid figures like cube, cuboid, cylinder, cone, sphire etc.

Conclusion

* Arousing and maintain interest in mathematics
* Giving interest in mathematics
* Speed and accuracy in mathematics
* Reasons behind dropping in speed and accuracy in mathematics
* Means adopted to develop speed in mathematics
* Means adopted to develop accuracy in mathematics
* Mathematics Library

* Importance of mathematics Library
* Organisation of Library
* The mathematics Laboratory
* Importance of mathematics Laboratory
* Various components for a mathematics laboratory
* Arrangement of mathematics laboratory
* List of the Instruments/Apparatus/Instruction material.

QUESTIONS

(A) Essay Type Items

1. What do you mean by speed and accuracy in mathematics ? Discuss the reasons for lessening speed and accuracy ?
2. What means would you adopt to secure speed & accuracy in matters.
3. What is the importance of speed and accuracy in mathematics ? How it can be developed among students of mathematics ?
4. Write an essay on "speed and accuracy in mathematics".
5. How speed and accuracy in mathematics can be developed ? Discuss.
6. How can interest by gained in mathematics ? Illustrate with example.
7. How a mathematics teacher can arouse and maintain interest for learning mathematics.
8. What devices can possibly be used to arous the students' interest in mathematics.
9. Mathematics is becoming increasingly unpopular among the high school students. Discuss some of the ways in which the teaching of mathematics may be made more interesting.
10. Discuss the role of mathematics laboratory in the teaching of mathematics at secondary level.

11. As a teacher of mathematics how would you set up a mathematics laboratory in your school to teach mathematics to the students of secondary schools ? Explain.
12. What is the utility of mathematics library in schools ? How would you organize mathematics library in you school ? Explain.

(B) Objective Type Items

Write True for correct and false for incorrect statement—

(i) For maintaining interest in mathematics unnecessary distinctions and interruptions should be avoided.

(ii) Motivation is the basic activity for creating interest in mathematics.

(iii) Through drill and practice speed can not be increased.

(iv) Speed and accuracy can be increased by creating interest in child toward mathematics.

(v) Mathematics library is helpful in developing the hobby of Reading in leisure time.

(vi) That books which are directed for further study are called text books.

(vii) The mathematics laboratory embodies the concept of passive learning.

(viii) The mathematics laboratory helps in developing critical, scientific and problem solving attitude.

3

Status of the Subject

According to Webster's new dictionary of English language correlation means "The act of correlating or "the state of being correlated" or "mutual relation of two or more things, or parts." Thus the word 'correlation means the reciprocal relationship between various subjects of the curriculum. In other words whenever two variables 'a' and 'b' are so related that a change in one is accompanied by change in the other in such a way that an increase in the one is accompanied by an increase or decrease in the other, then variables are said to be correlated. If two variables vary in the same directions, the correlation is said to be positive, on the other hand if two variables vary in opposite directions, the correlation is said to be negative.

In isolation the child cannot learn the various subjects of curriculum because the child is interested to learn the things which are related to his experiences and previous knowledge. According to the principles of correlation, knowledge cannot be acquired in piece meals. Therefore, the knowledge of various study subjects must be integrated and provided to the child in the form of whole or unit

In such a way knowledge of mathematics may be more interesting and realistic. Hence, the problems of mathematics must be related with day to day experiences of the children.

Concept and Meaning

Ferguson—"Correlation is concerned with describing the degree of relation between variables."

Lathrop— "Correlation indicates a joint-relationship between two variables."

On the basis of above definitions it is clear that correlation is the reciprocals relationship between various study subjects of the school curriculum. Therefore, the knowledge of various study subjects must be integrated and related with the daily life of the child.

Different Dimensions

There are two types of correlation is mathematics—

(i) Incidental correlation
(ii) Systematic correlation

Incidental Relationship

There teacher plays a prominent role. In incidental correlation, the correlation of two or different subjects is not predecided. Thus to establish this type of correlation, a teacher must have versatile knowledge of basic elements of different subjects. Without having sufficient knowledge of different subjects a teacher cannot establish incidental correlation in mathematics. For example—If a mathematics teacher has versatile knowledge of Physics, Chemistry, Zoology etc., he can establish incidental correlation easily. Hence, the teacher of mathematics should have versatile knowledge of other study subjects also.

Systematic Relationship

To establish systematic correlation is the responsibility of curriculum constructors or farmers the content of different subjects is arranged in a particular sequence or order. Here, attention is paid towards the application of the facts, principles and laws of mathematics or one subject to other subject areas. Thus the knowledge becomes more meaningful, interesting, realistic and natural.

Nature of Correlation. The correlation in mathematics is extended in four directions viz—

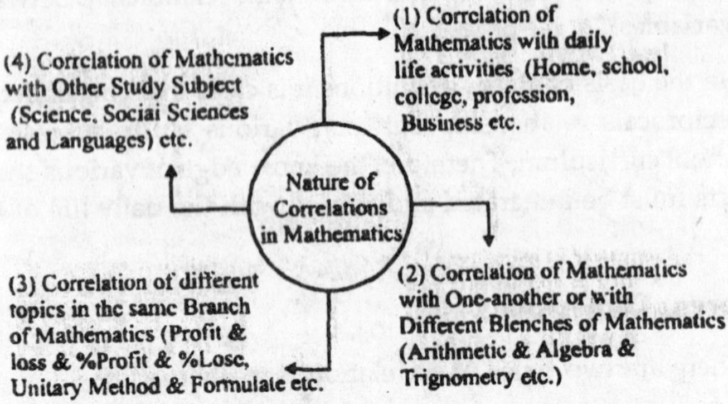

1. Correlation of mathematics with daily life activities (Home, school, college, profession, business etc.)
2. Correlation of mathematics with one-another or with different branches of mathematics (Arithmetic & algebra, algebra & trigonometry etc.)
3. Correlation of different topics in the same branch of mathematics (Profit & loss & % profit & loss, unitary method & formulae etc.)
4. Correlation of mathematics with other study subject (Sciences, Social sciences and languages etc.)

Application to Daily Life

It is true that in each and every sphere of our daily life mathematics provides us its help and patronage without which we can not do anything. The knowledge of mathematics is very versatile and required in all the day to day life activities beginning from awakening to sleep in night. Thus we can say that in our daily life mathematics is as mixed as the oxygen in the air. Every dealing of our life begins and ends with the mathematical thinking and reasoning. For example; daily house hold problems, food, clothing, idea of quantity and quality, daily account of income and expenditure, allocation of funds etc. Such type of day to day problems cannot be solved without the knowledge of mathematics. Young J.W.A. has remarked that "whenever we turn in these days of iron, steam and electricity we find that mathematics has been the pioneer were its backbone removed, our material civilization would inevitably collapse." Create mathematician Hubsch has also emphasised that, "Mathematics is like a wheatstone and by its study one learns to think distinctly, consecutively and carefully."

Hence without the proper knowledge of mathematics literate as well as illiterate people cannot solve their daily life problems. Thus knowledge of mathematics is required in every profession be it a cobbler, a vegetable seller a merchant, a driver, a carpenter, a cashier, a labour etc. To conclude we can say that knowledge of mathematics is closely correlated with our day to day life activities. Each and every individual needs the knowledge of mathematics at every movement.

Application to Different Branches

Mathematics has a well established correlation within the different branches of mathematics. It can be broadly divided into three basic structures—Algebric, Topological and Order structure. All these structures are inter related with each other. Mathematics deeply concerned with the phenomenon of correlation between its various branches. Such as—one cannot learn the four fundamental rules of arithmetic and algebra with out having knowledge of integers, without having elementary knowledge of arithmetic, algebra and geometry, one cannot solve the problem of statistics. Similarly to learn trigonometry one requires the knowledge of arithmetic, algebra and geometry; integral and differential calculus, geometry and dynamics etc., all these branches are interrelated with each other. No one can understand, in isolation of any one branch of mathematics. Thus each and every branch of mathematics is interdependent to each other. Hence, to make the knowledge of mathematics more useful and meaningful, the mathematics should be taught by establishing correlation between different branches of mathematics. Therefore, all the branches of mathematics must be integrated with one-another.

Correlation of Different Topics in the Same Branch. Mathematics plays a vital role in establishing relationship between the numerous topics in the same branch of mathematics. For example; Profit and loss is closely related to the banking and percentage, linear and simultaneous equations can be correlated easily.

Similarly so many examples can be given in support of this types of correlation. Thus the teacher of mathematics should try to establish correlation between the different topics of the same branch. So that pupil can learn the content in a systematic way by interrelating the various topics of the same branch of mathematics. Hence, there must be a logical sequence or continuity in the different topics of same branch. The different units must be so correlated as to bring out clearly the object of teaching the whole subject-matter.

Relationship with Other Subjects

Mathematics and Sciences—Mathematics is the pivot of all sciences. It has been very well said that mathematics is a science of all sciences and art of all arts. In this respect 'Roger Bacon' has remarked that, "Mathematics is the gateway and key of all sciences." The correlation of mathematics with different branches of science is as follows—

Mathematics and Physics—Mathematics and Physics are very closely related and has a very well established correlation. Each rule and principle in physics takes mathematical form and mathematics gives final shape to the rules, laws and principles of physics. For example—

* The laws of motion, friction, expansion of solids, liquid pressure are dependent on mathematics.
* The measurement unit in physics is employed as frequently as in mathematics.
* The coefficient of linear expansion of deferent metals, cubical expansion of liquids, Charles' law of expansion of gases, conversion of the scales, principle of working of lenders, are based on mathematic knowledge.

Mathematics and Chemistry—Mathematics and chemistry are also correlated. All the chemical combinations and their equations are based on mathematics. For example—

* The formation of various compounds like H_2S. The formation of H_2S gas is possible only when two atoms of hydrogen are combined with one atom of sulphur. Without this mathematical ratio and proportion, preparation of H_2S is not possible.
* In the estimation of elements of organic compound, the use of percentage, ratio & proportion is needed.
* Molecular weight & number of organic compound, is based on mathematics.
* Balancing of chemical equations and other calculation work is also based on mathematical knowledge.

Correlation of Mathematics with Biology—A biologist must have the sufficient knowledge of mathematics to understand its branches like; biophysics and bio-chemistry. For example—

* The caloric and nutritive values of food articles are based on mathematics.
* The rate of respiration, transpiration, supply of water in connection to all living bodies, is related to mathematics.
* Number of bones, organs etc., it is also mathematical.
* Mathematics can acquire knowledge of heredity, growth, nutrition, maturation, etc.
* Study of living cells, composition of blood, age & category of plants, animals, is possible through mathematical knowledge.

Mathematics and Engineering—Mathematics is the foundation of engineering sciences. As we know that engineering deals with surveying, lending, construction, estimation, designing, measurement, calculation, drafting, drawing etc., all these processes needs knowledge of mathematics. Hence, high level mathematical knowledge is required for study of engineering subjects. Its exaltation is impossible without mathematical knowledge.

Mathematics and Agriculture—The knowledge of mathematics is also very necessary in the field of agriculture. In agriculture we need mathematics knowledge in numerous way viz—

* Investment of money, energy, time and its return.
* Measurement of land, area, production per unit area, rate of seeds, labour cost etc.
* Progress of production can be judged with the help of graph and other statistical techniques.
* Estimation of average production, profit and loss etc.

Correlation with fine Arts & Drawing. Great mathematics Pythagoras has well remarked that, "where, there is money, there are numbers." Mathematics is considered as the science of reality and truthfulness, Keats has also said that, "Truth is beauty." In the study of mathematics the child has to draw and construct various shapes, sketches, figures, graphs etc. These all activity requires the knowledge of drawing and arts. It is evident that good drawing is needed to draw good geometrical figures. Similarly in fine arts, the mathematical knowledge is applied in many ways, e.g..

* Drawing and painting with symmetry.
* Ratio and proportion in drawing, painting, sketching etc.
* Almost all musical notes and systems work or mathematical principles.
* Exactness of a figure, shape etc. can be measured with the help of mathematics.

Here in this support we can also quote leibnitz, he remarked that 'music' is a modern hidden exercise in arithmetic of a mind unconscious of dealing with numbers. Thus, there is a close correlation between mathematics and fine arts and drawing.

Relationship with Economics

Mathematics laws, language, principles and methods are frequently used in describing, interpreting and explaining economic phenomena. According to J.B. say—"Economics is the science which treats of wealth.." Great economist Marshal has well remarked that, " The direct application of mathematical reasoning to the discovery of economic truths has recently rendered great services in the hands of master mathematics." In economics mathematical knowledge is applied in many ways such as—

Collection analysis, calculation, interpretation and presentation of data regarding, population, investment, income, expenditure, production, banking, business, demand and supply etc.

Various mathematical methods are used to economic forecasts regarding trade cycles, trends of export and import, employment, production etc.

Almost all magazines, news papers etc., are full of figures and graphs regarding population, investment, employment, production, crops, marketing etc. All these employ various numerical and statistical procedures.

This is fact that mathematics play prominent role in economics. Hence the correlation between mathematics and economics is very vast.

Correlation with History. The knowledge of history helps in understanding the historical development of mathematics. History and contribution of great mathematicians in the field of mathematics. Similarly mathematical knowledge is applied in history to know the dates, time, days etc., of various historical events. Thus the correlation between history and mathematics is reciprocal.

Correlation with Geography. The knowledge of mathematics is also applicable to the study of geography. For example—shape and size of earth, area, distance of places, height and distance, temperature longitude, time etc. all are based on mathematical calculation. Similarly, to study the rivers, canals, mountains, population, climate, depth, drawing of graphs, and figures, moment of winds, falling of rains etc. in all these, mathematics plays a prominent role. Hence all the geological and geographical studies are not possible without the proper application of mathematics.

Correlation of Mathematics with Commerce. The knowledge of mathematics helps to understand various concepts and branches of commerce. The basis of banking and accountancy is mathematics. It is considered that without having good knowledge and practice of mathematics one cannot become a good accountant. In commerce calculation of interest etc. all are based on mathematical principles and formulae. Shares, debentures, mutual funds, accounting etc. are also based on mathematical calculation. Thus most of the knowledge of commerce requires the application of mathematical knowledge. Many statistical techniques are also used to solve the problems of different branches of commerce.

Correlation with Logic. Logic is the only branch of knowledge in which logical reasoning and laws are applied. The results can be varied with the help of logical reasoning. Logic is the scientific study of condition of accurate thinking and valid influence. In this respect Pascal, a great mathematician, has well said that, 'Logic has borrowed rules from geometry.' 'D' Alombert' also emphasized that, "Geometry is a practical logic because in it rules of reasoning are applied in the most simple and sensible manner." There fore, the aims of mathematician and logicians are the same. In mathematics the symbols can be use logically such as – $a > b$, $b < a$, $a = b$, A Ç B, B Í A etc.

Correlation with Languages. To study mathematics, language plays very important role because no subject can be taught without language. Various principles, laws, formulae are expressed and generalized through the language. It will be very difficult to express the knowledge of mathematics without the medium of language. To convey the correct and exact idea of mathematical facts, concept, laws etc. language is necessary. Language also helps in developing the various mental powers of the child like-memory, imagination, expression, observation etc.

Correlation with Psychology. Learning of mathematics from psychological point of view is also very important. While learning mathematics various psychological principles, laws, theories and concepts are applied to make the learning child centered. Some psychological principles like—learning by doing, learning through experiences, learning by problem-solving, law of readiness, law of exercise etc. all are very useful to understand mathematics. Similarly, various mathematical and statistical techniques are used to collect, to analyses and to interpret psychological data. Experimental psychology is also based on mathematical calculations and applications. In this support we can quote Herbrt, he remarked that, "It is not only possible but necessary that mathematics be applied to psychology."

Role in Recreation

The word 'Recreation' means refreshment after labour. Everyone needs recreation after the tedious work either a child or a grown up person. In other words recreation is to entertain, to gratify, to create again. Thus recreation is the act of relaxing and amusing oneself after work. The main advantage or importance of recreation is that shapes the thinking and imagination power of a person of any age group. That is why recreation is also related to mathematics and involves many problems which can be solved by the application of mathematical knowledge. As far as, the correlation of mathematics with recreation is concerned, recreation in mathematics implies different kinds of mathematical puzzles, riddles and cross word games or puzzles. These all activities are helpful in raising up the mental level of the child and plays a significant role in the development of different mental abilities of the child. While solving such type of games and puzzles the child gives stress to his mind. Thus these activities help in making his thinking and imagination powers more powerful and strong. After solving these mathematical games, puzzles and riddles, a feeling of self appreciation develops in the mind of the child. So that the child becomes more confident and the feeling of competition is also developed in his mind.

Apart from the puzzles and riddles, the children form different groups and play various games which require mathematical knowledge. By playing and performing these games, the children recall there previous knowledge and experiences, so that their mind becomes sharp and mental faculties are developed. Thus the more child indulges himself in these games and develops his mental abilities. The popular saying that, "Practice makes a man perfect" becomes true while performing such type of mathematical puzzles, riddles and games.

Hence, we can conclude that to solve the various puzzles, riddles and mathematical tricks etc., the knowledge of mathematics plays an important role. Therefore, recreation and mathematics are correlated with each-other in various aspects.

In this way correlation of mathematics with some more other study subjects may be explained. Here only few subjects have been discussed. On the basis of above discussion it can be concluded that while teaching mathematics, a mathematics teacher should establish the correlation of mathematics with other study subject. So that the children can understand the importance and utility of mathematics in his life.

Summary

Correlation is the reciprocal relationship between various study subjects of the school curriculum. Therefore, the knowledge of various study subjects must be integrated and related with the daily life of the child.

Types of Correlation. There are two types of correlation—Incidental and systematic correlation.

Nature of Correlation in Mathematics. The correlation in mathematical is extended in four directions— 1. Correlation of mathematics with daily life activities (Home, school, college profession, business etc.); 2. Correlation of mathematics with one another (Arithmetic & Algebra, algebra & trigonometry, etc.); 3. Correlation of different topics in the same branch of mathematics (profit & loss & % profit & loss, unitary method & formulae etc.); 4. Correlation of mathematics with other study subjects (with sciences, social sciences, languages, recreation etc.).

QUESTIONS

A. Essay Type Items

1. Write an essay on 'correlation in mathematics.'
2. What do you mean by correlation in mathematics? Discuss the various types of correlation in mathematics.
3. How should the teaching of mathematics be made more realistic and useful? Discuss with reference to correlation in mathematics.
4. "The teaching of mathematics should be imparted by correlating it with the teaching of other subjects." Discuss this statement.
5. In what ways can the teaching of mathematics be correlated with other school subjects and with daily life? Explain with examples.
6. Write notes on the following—

   (a) Correlation between mathematics and sciences.

   (b) Correlation between social sciences

   (c) Correlation of mathematics with logic & Recreation

   (d) Correlation of mathematics with its different branches and topics of the same branch.

   (e) Correlation of mathematics with fine arts, Psychology and Economics.

   (d) Correlation of mathematics with Physics, Chemistry, logic & Engineering.

B. Objective type items

(I) Note—*Write 'true' for correct statement and 'false' for incorrect statement.*

1. There is very high correlation between physics and mathematics.
2. There in no any correlation between mathematics and politicals science.
3. The teacher plays a main role in systematic correlation.
4. According to Lathrop, correlation indicates a reciprocal relationship between two variables.
5. In isolation the child can learn the various school subjects.
6. In incidental correlation, the correlation of different subjects is not pre-decided.

(II) Multiple Choice Type Items

1. In incidental correlation the main role is, of

   (a) The teacher

   (b) The author

   (c) The planners of curriculum.

2. A teacher should have versatile knowledge of all the subject is necessary for—

   (a) Incidental Correlation

   (b) Systematic Correlation

   (c) None of These

3. Correlation between two variables may be—

   (a) Positive

   (b) Negative

   (c) Both 'a' and 'b'

4. Correlation in mathematics indicates—

   (a) Joint relationship

   (b) Reciprocal relationship

   (c) Both 'a' and 'b'

5. Which of the following subjects, mathematics in highly correlated—

   (a) Chemistry

   (b) Botany

   (c) Physics.

4
The Cultivation

Mathematics represents a high level of abstraction attained by the human mind. In India, mathematics has its roots in Vedic literature which is nearly 4000 years old. Between 1000 A.D. and 1000 B.C. and 1000 A.D. Various treatise on mathematics were authored by Indian mathematicians in which were set forth for the first time, the concept of zero, the techniques of algebra and algorithm, square root and cube root.

1. As in the applied sciences like production technology, architecture and shipbuilding, Indians in ancient times also made advance in abstract science like Mathematics and Astronomy. It has now been generally accepted that the technique of algebra and the concept of zero originated in India.

2. But it would be surprising for us to know that even the rudiments of Geometry, called Rekha-Ganita in ancient India, were formulated and applied in the drafting of Mandalas for architectural purposes. They were also displayed in the geometric patterns used in many temple motifs.

3. Even the technique of calculation, called algorithm, which is today widely used in designing soft ware programs (instructions) for computers was also derived from Indian mathematics.

Birth of Zero

The concept of zero also originated in ancient India. This

concept may seem to be a very ordinary one and a claim to its discovery may be viewed as queer. But if one gives a hard thought to this concept it would be seen that zero is not just a numeral. Apart from being a numeral, it is also a concept, and a fundamental on at that. It is fundamental because, terms to identify visible or perceptible objects do not require much ingenuity.

But a concept and symbol that connotes nullity represents a qualitative advancement of the human capacity of abstraction. In absence of a concept of zero there should have been only positive numerals in computation, the inclusion of zero in mathematics opened up a new dimension of negative numerals and gave a cut off point and a standard in the measurability of qualities whose extremes are as yet unknown to human beings, such as temperature.

In ancient Indian this numeral was used in computation, it was indicated by a dot and was termed Pujyam. Even today we use this terms for zero along with the more current term Shunyam meaning blank. But queerly the term Pujyam also means holy. Pram-Pujya is a prefix used in written communication with elders. In this case it means respected or esteemed. The reason why the term Pujya-meaning blank-came to be sanctified can only be guessed.

Indian philosophy has glorified concepts like the material world being an illusion (Maya), the act of renouncing the material world (Tyàga) and the goal of merging into the void of eternity (Nirvana). Herein could lie the reason how the mathematical concept of zero got a philosophical connotation of reverence.

It is possible that like the technique of algebra; the concept of zero also reached the west through the Arabs. In ancient India the terms used to describe zero included Pujyam, Shunyam, Bindu the concept of a void or blank was termed as Shukla and Shubra. The Arabs refer to the zero as Siphra of Sifr from which we have the English terms Cipher or Cipher. In English the term Cipher connotes zero or any Arabic numeral. Thus it is evident that the term Cipher is derived from the Arabic sifr which in turn is quite close the Sanskrit term Shubra.

Beginning of Algebra

In India around the 5th century A.D. a system of mathematics that made astronomical causation easy was developed. In those times its application was limited to astronomy as its pioneers were Astronomers. As trinomial calculation are complex and involve many variables that go into the derivation of unknown quantities. Algebra is a short-hand method of calculation and by this feature, it scores over conventional arithmetic.

In Ancient India conventional mathematics termed Ganitam was known before the development of algebra. This is borne out by the name-Bijaganitam, which was given to the algebraic form of computation. Bijaganitam means 'the other mathematics' (Bija means 'another' or 'second' and Ganitam means mathematics). The fact that this name was chosen for this system of computation implies that it was recognized as a parallel system of computation, different from the conventional one which was used since the past and was till then the only one. Some have interpreted the term Bija to mean seed, symbolizing origin or beginnings. And the inference that Bijaganitam was the original form of computation is derived. Credence is lent to this view by the existence of mathematics in the Vedic literature which was also shorthand method of computation. But whatever the origin of algebra, it is certain that this technique of computation originated in India and was current around 1500 years back, Aryabhatta an Indian mathematician who lived in the 5th century A.D. has referred to Bijaganitam in his treatise on Mathematics, Aryabhattiya. An Indian mathematician-astronomer, Bhaskaracharya has also authored a treatise on this subject, the treatise which is dated around the 12th century A.D. is entitled 'Siddhanta-Shiromani' of which one section is entitled Bijaganitam.

Thus the technique of algebraic computation was known and was developed in India in earlier times. From the 13 century onwards, India was subject to invasions from the Arabs and other Islamised communities like the Turks and Afghans along with these invader; came chroniclers and critics like Al-beruni who studied Indian society and polity.

The Indian system of mathematics could not have escaped their attention. It was also the age of the Islamic Renaissance and the Arabs generally improved upon the arts and sciences that they imbibed from the land they overran during their great Jehad. The system of mathematics they observed in India was adapted by them and given the name 'Al-Jabr' meaning 'the reunion of broken parts.' 'Al' means the broken parts & 'Jabr' mean 'reunion.' This name given by the Arabs indicated that they took it from an external source and amalgamated it with their concepts about mathematics.

Between the 10th to 13th centuries, the Christian kingdoms of Europe made numerous attempts to reconquer the birthplace of Jesus Christ from its Mohammedan-Arab rules. These attempts called thee Crusades failed in their military objective, but the contacts they crated between oriental and occidental nations resulted in a massive exchange of ideas. The technique of algebra could have passed on to the west at the time.

During the Renaissance in Europe, followed by the industrial revolution, the knowledge received from the east was further developed. Algebra as we know it today has lost any characteristics that betray its eastern origin save the fact that the term 'algebra' is a corruption of the term 'Al jabr' which the Arabs gave to Bijaganitam incidentally the term Bijaganit is still in use in India to refer to this subject.

In the year 1816, an Englishman by the name James Taylor translated Bhaskara's Leelavati into English. A second English translation appeared in the following year (1817) by the English astronomer Henry Thomas Colebruke. Thus the works of this Indian mathematician astronomer were made known to the western world nearly 700 years after he had penned them, although his ideas had already reached the west through the Arabs many centuries earlier.

In the words of the Australian Indologist A.L. Basham (A.L. Basham; The Wonder That was India.)."....the world owes most to Indian in the realm of mathematics, which was developed in the Gupta period to a stage more advanced than that reached by any other nation of antiquity. The success of Indian mathematics was mainly due to the fact that Indians had a clear conception of the abstract number as distinct from the numerical quantity of objects or palatial extension."

Thus Indians could take their mathematics concepts to an abstract plane and with the aid of a simple numerical notation devise a rudimentary algebra as against the Greeks or the ancient Egyptians who due to their concern with the immediate measurement of physical objects remained confined to Mensuration and Geometry.

The chief exponent of this Indo-Arab amalgam in mathematics was Al Khawarazmi who evolved a technique of calculation from Indian sources. This technique which was named by Westerners after Al Khwarazmi as "Algorismi" gave us the modern term Algorithm, which is used in computer software.

Algorithm which is a process of calculation based on decimal notation numbers. This methods was deduced by Khwarazmi's from the Indian techniques geometric computation which he has stied. Al Khwarazmi's work was translated into Latin under the title "De Numero Indica" which means 'of Indian Numerals' thus Betraying its India its Indian origin. This translation which belong to the 12th century A.D. credited to one Adelard who lived in a town called Bath in Britain.

Thus Al Khwarazmi and Adelard could looked upon as pioneers who transmit Indian numerals to the west. Incidents according to the Oxford Dictionary, world algorithm. Which we use in the English language is a corruption of the name Khwarazmi which literally means (a person) from Khawarizm,' which was the name of the town where Al Khwarazmi lived. To day unfortunately, the original Indian texts that Al Khwarazmi studied are lost to us, only the translation are available.

The Arabs borrowed so much from India in the field of mathematics that even the subject of mathematics in Arabic came to known as Hindsa which means from India and a mathematics or engineer be in Arabic is called Muhandis which means 'an expert in mathematics.' The word Muhandis possibly derived from the Arabic term mathematics Viz. Hindsa.

5
Teacher's Role

The teacher plays an important role in the system of education. Teachers are considered to be "builders of nation." On him depends the future of the country and infact the future of mankind. The influence of a teacher never stops. Like a painter creates a painting. Similarly a teacher shapes the personality of the child. So we can say that a teacher has a unique opportunity and a vital role to play in contributing to the overall development of the child.

Students to large extent try to imitate their teachers. So a teacher should try to present himself as an "Ideal Example" to the students and bear some qualities. The just and the foremost quality that a mathematics teacher should possess love and respect for learning and teaching mathematics. He should not teach mathematics just for the heck of it but should feel the call for it because unless a teachers loves his subject he cannot inspire his students for studying it.

As we all know that is a continuous process so of mathematics must be a learner throughout his life. According to Rabindra Nath Tagore— "A teacher can never truly teach unless he is still learning himself." Therefore, any teacher of mathematics can continue to grow and bee effective in his or her work, if he is aware of what is new and changing in the field of mathematics.

A mathematics teacher should have scientific bent of mind. This does not mean that he should have the knowledge of science but he should be systematic and orderly in his method of teaching. He should be practical minded. Because as the saying goes—

"We hear, we forget,
we see, we remember,
but when we do, we understand.

So, he should to try make the education practical oriented. A mathematics teacher should have some knowledge of child psychology so that from time to time he may use the method of teaching according to the need and interest of the child. According to secondary education commission—"the most important factor in the contemplated educational reconstruction is the teacher—his personal qualities, educational qualifications, professional training and the place that he occupies in the school as well as in the community. The reputation of a school and its influence on the life of the community variably depends on the working of the teacher working in it."

Vivekananda once also claimed that, "The true teacher is he who can immediately come down to the level of the student and transfer his soul to the students soul and see through and understand through his mind. Such a teacher can really teach and none else." Therefore, a dynamic teacher is he who can understand the process of education, can relate education to other aspects of life, can eradicate contradictions in educational problems and suggest improvement and reforms in education system.

Qualities and Characteristics

The work of a teacher is not only confined to mental development but also to contribute in his emotional, moral and spiritual development. As, a teacher is considered the builder of nation, foundation stone of educational process, and a lead way to society, so a teacher should necessarily have the following qualities—

* Skills and abilities to understand the children,
* Self-educational and teaching abilities,
* Capacity of adjustment and cooperation with the children,

* Will power to work with,
* Impartial nature,
* Leadership power
* Feelings of common harmony.

Only a dedicated and intelligent teacher can make proper use of content of curriculum, teaching methods and different kinds of aid. He can make this subject much more interesting by his experience, ability and knowledge. He can develop in children the power of thinking, understanding, analyzing, debating etc. Different qualities of a mathematics teacher are as follows—

Classification of Qualities and Characteristics of a Mathematics Teacher

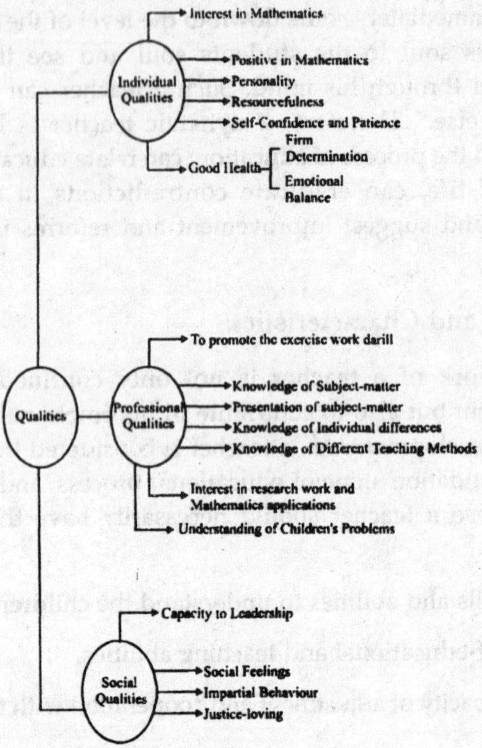

The Qualities for Teaching

Interest in Mathematics—A mathematics teacher should have full command over subject matter. It is possible when he has interest in mathematics.

Positive Attitude towards Mathematics—A mathematics teacher should have positive attitude towards his teaching subject. Because his self attitude directly influences the learning process of the children, the right or positive attitude by introducing them to life history of mathematicians and history of mathematics.

Recourse futures—The teachers who have the qualities of resourcefulness make arrangement of different means timely according to their needs and thus, succeed in making their teaching effective. A mathematics teacher should be creative and imaginative and both the qualities should be well ningled with his activities.

Self-Confidence and Patience—A mathematics teacher should necessarily have self-confidence. For classification and analysing the subject-matter what a teacher needs is self-confidence and patience. Lack of self confidence and patience makes a mathematics teacher a irritative in nature and it costs bad influence on the children. This leads him to failure in his teaching, Patience and self-confidence makes a maths teacher able to solve the problems of his students in very efficient manner.

Good Health—A mathematics teacher should be mentally and physically healthy. He should be refined in character. Generally it is said that a healthy mind lives in a healthy body of health of a teacher is not good, he can not perform teaching work efficiently, because power and activeness bring prompts in teaching. It is not enough that a teacher is physically healthy but awareness is a must thing for him.

Personality—Personality of a teacher influences directly and indirectly to the students. So a mathematics teacher should do his work honestly, patiently and dedicably. A teacher should continue his study. He should always be inspired to gains more and more knowledge with the use of different material aids and different teaching methods. To maintain practical value of mathematics, a mathematics teacher should have experimental and heuristic attitudes. A teacher should firstly know the previous knowledge of the students then he should make efforts to link it with the new knowledge.

Knowledge of subject-matter—A mathematics teacher should have full knowledge of his subject. A little knowledge in subject-matter can not make him trust worthy among students. A teacher can not work with confidence unless he has full command over content. Lack of subject-matter knowledge, puts fear in the mind of a tends 'that tended him to commit repeatedly mistakes.'

Presentation of subject-matter—A teacher should present the subject matter skillfully making interaction with the students, introducing well methods and applying various aids. Every problem should be introduced to the students logically and in a systematic manner. He should first judge nature of the students then he should apply different methods to make his teaching more effective and comprehensive.

Knowledge of Individual Differences—A good teacher is he who has the knowledge to judge individual differences because every student is different in reading and writing, understanding and work speed. He is successful when he makes teaching arrangement according to individual differences. A mathematics teacher should necessarily have knowledge of psychology to make him able to understand interest, ability and capacity of different students and thus, he can guide them properly.

Knowledge of Different Teaching Methods—With a firm grip over subject matter, a mathematics teacher should know different teaching methods. He should clearly know the aims and objectives of mathematics. Thus, required teaching learning situations can be created. He should teach the students by effective teaching methods like—Analysis, Synthesis, Methods, Inductive—Deductive method, Laboratory Methods and Project and Problem Solving method so that the students may get the opportunity of learning by doing and the knowledge they have learned can be more permanent and solid.

Interest in Research work and Mathematics Applications—A mathematics teacher should be good at research work. To give importance to research and experiments in mathematics. A mathematics teacher should apply scientific and discovery methods for the solution of different mathematical problems. Priority should be given to experimental work so that students may be habitual of learning by self doing and hence the teacher can work as a scientist and researcher.

Power to Know the Difficulties of the Students—It is very necessary for a mathematics teacher to know where the students are feeling difficulty in solving problems. The solution of students problems depends upon the ability and capacity of the teacher to grasp them and there by a teacher gains popularity among the students. For a mathematics teacher, knowledge of psychology is also essential that helps him to diagnose the problems of the students.

Inspiration to Drill Work—A mathematics teacher should inspire and motivate the students to drill and practice work through examples understand the basic concept of formulae. This method of learning makes them to be creative and the knowledge received become permanent. He should examine the students both through oral and written test so that different skills and habit of regulating can be developed in the students. So a mathematics teacher should inspire the students to do more and more drill work so that the students may learn through practice.

Social Qualities—With individual and professional qualities, a mathematics teacher should haven social qualities. Man is a social creative and he has to live in society and deal with the society, knowing social qualities are necessary to a mathematics teacher.

Leading Capacity—A mathematics should have capacity to lead the students. Leadership quality in a mathematics teacher is different from other kind teachers. Teacher's leadership is totally based upon his character and personality. If a teacher is sound in character and personality, he can inspire the students to participate in different activities in a group.

Social Feeling—To be a good teacher, he should have some social feelings. He should accept the social traits that help him in class-room teaching and school and community. He should possess high decision power, courage, positive attitude, habit to accept his weakness and feelings of cooperation. Hence, he can establish good relationship wherever he will work, by organizing curricular activities, he can develop in students social feelings.

Impartial Behaviours—A teacher should behave, with all the students equally.

It is injustice and unsocial to have affection with an individual. A teacher should make no difference of rich or poor, weak or intelligent, low or high, familiar or not familiar. His behaviour should be impartial with all students.

Justice-loving—Behaviour of a mathematics teacher should be so, as the students can consider him ideal. So a teacher should be both just-loving and refine in character and thus, he can develop in the students qualities of justice-loving.

Some qualities of a mathematics teacher demands upon his nature. It is said, "Good teachers are inborn not made." But it is underlying fact that training and their self experience also bring a great change in them.

A study was done by Dr. F.L. Clapp in America in 1913. He suggested that to be a good teacher ten qualities are necessary. They are as follow—

(i) Address
(ii) Personal appearance
(iii) Optimism
(iv) Reserve
(v) Enthusiasm
(vi) Fairness of mind
(vii) Sincerity
(viii) Sympathy

(ix) Vitality

(x) Scholarship

Bagle and Keith (U.S.A.) included, three & (more) traits in ten ones as suggested by F.L. Clapp—

(i) Tact

(ii) Capacity for leadership

(iii) Good voice

Significant Role

The image of a school refers to the tendency and reactions of society towards the different programmes of school. Image of a school depends upon leadership of head teacher (Principal), cooperative feelings among teachers, and other staff members and good achievements of the students. Teacher is the essential part of a school. So a teacher contributes a lot to improve the school and makes its image grand. A mathematics teacher may be helpful in improving a school in the following manner—

(i) A mathematics teacher should be punctual so as to make the students punctual. Thus he may enable the students to realise the importance of time.

(ii) He should teach in the class according to the time table.

(iii) He should give the students sufficient class work, home work and drill work and also make time correction and suggestions.

(iv) He should use child centred teaching methods and other different teaching aids while teaching.

(v) He should help the students in solving their personal and social problems.

(vi) He should behave with the students impartially, love them, and cooperate them.

(vii) He should develop in the students the tendency of discipline.

(viii) He should develop in students a feeling of cooperation and competition.

(ix) He should make efforts to develop power of leadership by organizing students committee, mathematics club.

(x) He should try to bring change guardian's attitudes towards the school through the activities of parent-teacher association.

(xi) He should participate in co-curricular activities and inspire the students to do so.

(xii) Parents and guardians should be invited in the various programmes and activities of the school so that they may be enable to know the progress of the school and their children.

Advance Preparations

The mathematics curriculum mainly includes different concepts, formulae, hypothesis theorem and subject-matter based on relations. So the work of a mathematics teacher becomes very difficult, he has to think over deeply while presenting any subject-matter in the class that what is to be taught in a particular class? So it becomes essential duty of a mathematics teacher to prepare the lesson before teaching so as to make his teaching effective. Hence, a mathematics teacher should consider the following points before going to class—

Previous knowledge and Experience of the Children—A mathematics teacher should know well the previous knowledge and experiences of the children before going to the class. Then he should link previous knowledge of the children to their new knowledge.

Selection of Teaching Aids and Required Apparatus—To make his teaching effective, a teacher should select and arrange the different teaching aids and apparatus systematically before going to the class. Thus, he can make the teaching and learning more smooth and effective.

Selection of Appropriate Examples—Before going to the class, a mathematics teacher should well consider that what type and how much examples he has to give in his teaching to make the teaching more simple and effective.

Preparation of Lesson Plan—Lesson plan preparation is further step when he has selected right teaching aids apparatus, right examples and previous knowledge and experience of the children while preparing the lesson plan, a mathematics teacher should know the order of points to be taught in class and well consider the lesson plan that involves all the skills that can be developed in a child. It should contain proper drill work, oral work, written work, home work and evaluation etc.

Importance to Drill Work—After finishing a concept, formulae, method rule and lesson, the teacher should previously determine what kind of questions are to be given in drill work.

A teacher should divide the drill work in three categories—

(i) Simple most that can be solved geniusoly.

(ii) Same difficult problems than can be solved only by the normal average student difficult problems that can be solved by every students of the class.

(iii) Some difficult problems that can only be solved by genius students.

Hence, a teacher of mathematics can teach effectively while considering the above all points and will be able to be a successful teacher amongs his students. So a teacher of mathematics should prepare his lesson plan properly before going to the class.

Professional Growth

The social well being and the future progress of any country demand to a large extent upon that small section of its population that is generally known as professional. In general, a profession is also said to be passed on a body of verified experiences, which enable its practitioners to develop theoretical insight in their work.

When teaching is considered in the light of the foregoing criteria, it may be frankly admitted that it can achieve the professional level. No occupation can be rated as high as teaching because its social value lies in its great contribution to the betterment of living, which ultimately leads to the betterment of society.

It is said, "While no one of the professions is more important to the national welfare than any of the others. It is true that the achievement of all are dependent upon how efficiently a group performs its functions.

Professional growth means developing the new trends in teaching and educational experimentation. A teacher is said no teacher without professional qualities. Hence, for this purpose, he should indulge himself in educational research work, advanced study either in the subject of specialisation or in professional training. It takes two inservice programme and pre-service programme to develop in a teacher the real essence of professional growth. Self-evaluation, membership in professional organisations, provision of school and public libraries, attending concerts. Theatres cultural programmes, contributing articles in publications, planning and preparing curriculum guides, launching educational field trips, excursions and tours and inserting school problems go a long way to help in professional growth.

Professional growth is beneficial for a mathematics teacher from the following points of view—

(i) It helps him to develop an alert, sensitive attitude to the advancing edge of human knowledge.

(ii) It supplies him with facts where by he can improve his own work; and

(iii) It stimulates him to go on beyond existing research findings to discover additional facts for himself.

(iv) It gives a teacher right and high place in society and community.

(v) He can maintain a good standard of living.

(vi) It enables him to alone ensure for him a recognition from society.

(vii) It builds up in him faith to feel pride in his work, dignity of his professional, democratic way of life.

(viii) It enables him to identify himself with work and to fulfil his life mission through hard labour and tort.

(ix) It develops organizations from local to state and national levels.

(x) It rises the standards of education.

(xi) It improves the condition of employment.

(xii) It maintains security and integrity of the professional itself.

Conduct Rules

A profession must have code of ethics. A code of ethics is the basic characteristics of all professions. The formation and enforcement of a code of ethics makes the profession self-regulating and self governing. It is profession code of ethic that develops in a vocation. Professional autonomy and thus makes it very difficult to pass a casual remark upon the quality of teachers and their services. In this way, the code of ethics of a profession also protects its members not to go against the professional conduct rules.

Following are the criteria on which a code of conduct is formed—

(a) Teacher's relation with pupils.

(b) Professional colleagues.

(c) Teacher's professional security and professional conduct.

(d) Terms of employment.

An ethical code of a professional depends upon two factors—

(i) Security and integrity.

(ii) Ideal of service.

Security and Integrity—It services as a basic for professional obligations, rights, privilege, etiquitte and above all competence.

Ideal of Service—A teacher should find satisfaction in serving the children and the adults alike. His masterful teaching must be conjoined with the spirit of service to mankind. Through his knowledge, understanding and unbiased consideration, he should be able to bring about significant changes in the lives of his pupils by guiding their eyes to the things of beauty and perfection.

In community, he should try his best to replace illiteracy remove ignorance by knowledge and understanding and substitute jealousy and selfishness by concern and sympathy for others.

Emerson once remarked, "there are two types of teachers. One types speaks from outsides. He is concerned with facts outside and measurements. The other type speaks from the depth of his soul. He is the prophet inwardness."

The present Indian society needs the teacher education program to produce such trained prospectives who will not only fulfill the manpower requirements but also acquire necessary insight and skill for future shocks. To keep pace with the social, economic and industrial change the teacher must be a good communicator, efficient organiser and democratic group leader. Hence in such changing scenario the role of teacher will be more of a facilitator of learning than importer of learning.

Summary

A dynamic and effective teacher of mathematics is he who can understand the process of education. The reputation of a school and its influence of the life of the community invariably depends on the kind of the teacher working in it.

* Qualities and Characteristics of a Mathematics Teacher
* Individual, Professional and Social Qualities.

* Role of a Mathematics Teacher in Improving the Image of a School
* Proportion of a Mathematics Teacher Before Going to the Class.
* Professional Ethics and Growth of Mathematics Teacher
* Code of Ethics of a Mathematics Teacher

QUESTIONS

(A) Essay Type Question—

1. "Teacher is a nation builder." Prove the statement stating the duties he should perform under the present circumstance.
2. What is the importance of teacher in the school? Describe the qualities of an ideal teacher.
3. What qualities and characteristics should a good mathematics teacher possess?
4. Describe the functions of a school teacher with reference to the N.P.E., 1986.
5. What is the role of mathematics teacher in improving the image of the school?
6. What preparation should be done by the mathematics teacher before going into class? Describe.
7. Write notes on—
   (a) Qualities of a mathematics teacher.
   (b) Professional responsibilities of a mathematics teacher.
   (c) The role of a teacher in improving the image of the school.
   (d) Professional growth of mathematics teacher.
8. "A mathematics teacher requires much more merely the mastery in technique of teaching." Discuss.
9. Explain the professional ethics of a mathematics teacher. Why is it important.

Object Type Question

(B) Multiple choice items—Select the right choice—

1. Which work is not related with a teacher—

   (a) Planning (c) Guidance
   (b) Teaching (d) Budgeting

2. Which point is not included in the professional skills of a teacher—

   (a) Knowledge of self
   (b) Dedication
   (c) To experiment well
   (d) Satisfactory knowledge of social matter

3. "Preponderate of nation" is—

   (a) Guardian (b) School inspector
   (b) Teacher (d) None of these

4. Which is not the characteristics of a successful teacher—

   (a) Practicability
   (c) Partial behaviour
   (b) Non changeability/rigidness
   (d) 'a' and 'b' both

5. Which of the following area related with a teacher is developed is National Policy on Education—

   (a) Finance as (c) Service conditions
   (b) Educational (d) 'a' and 'c' both

(B) True/False Statement

Give the answer by writing 'True' for right statement and 'False' for wrong statement—

(i) School office provides help to the teacher for supervision.

(ii) A teacher is responsible for the arrangement of school building.

(iii) According to National Policy of Education—Service and

income of a teacher should be according to their social and profession responsibilities.

(iv) Dr. clapp has advised of being ten .characteristics in a good teacher.

(v) A teacher must posses creative and imagination power.

(vi) Law of exercise or drill should be followed by a good teacher.

(vii) The quality of justice comes under social qualities of a teacher.

6
Teaching Methods

Method deals with the "How" of mathematics. How the children will learn effectively, depends on the method the teacher adopts. "How to impart mathematical knowledge?" and How to enable the children to learn mathematics?" are the questions to be discussed in this chapter. Methods of teaching have an intimate relationship with teaching and instructional objectives. So the main aim of teaching is to bring about socially desirable behavioural changes in the children. Though teaching is an art. Methods are the way or mode to understand and practice the art. So it is essential that every teacher should be acquainted with different methods of teaching mathematics.

The word 'method' has been derived from Latin which word, means, "Mode" or 'Way". Therefore here it means, method of delivering knowledge and transmitting mathematical skills by a teacher to his pupils and their comprehension and application by them in the process of Learning mathematics.

In a very restricted sense, it means "what to teach?" and "how to teach mathematics?" or "how to approach it?" Hence; "The process of interpreting the world of knowledge to pupils' mind is called the method of teaching." It is just a way to teach. The following figure can make it more clear :

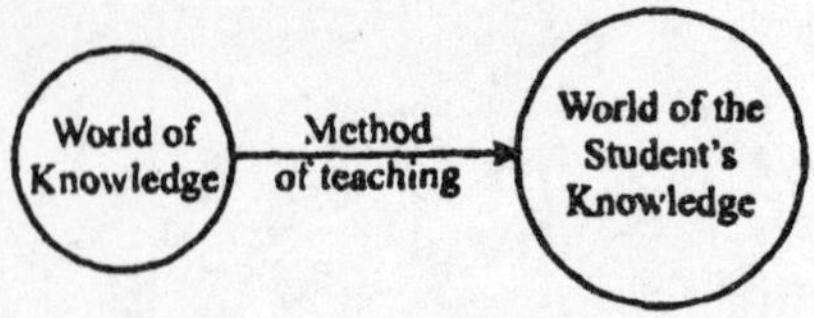

The world of knowledge includes; the knowledge, interest, attitude, skill etc. *i.e.*, all the three domains—cognitive, affective and Psychomotor.

Another approach to define a method of teaching may be as follows: The way is Method

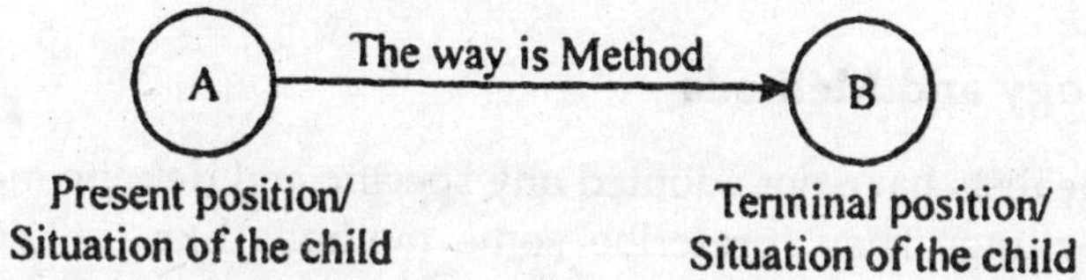

According to Brandy (1963), "Method refers to the formal structure of the sequence of acts commonly denoted by instruction. The word/ term method covers both strategies and techniques of teaching and involves the choice of what is to be taught."

Now which method should be used to teach mathematics, depends upon the abilities and interests of the teacher. But while selecting the method, the teacher should always keep in his mind the aims of teaching mathematics. These aims include the mental, social and moral development of the child. This development is only possible, when methods' of teaching are appropriate and effective. A teacher who does not use suitable method to teach the subject matter according to the requirements of the children, is not suppossed to be a good teacher. Generally, children like that method which makes the subject matter more clear and easily understandable.

However, it is important to note that a method should not become an end in itself but should be used as a means to achieve the determined aims and objectives of teaching mathematics. The teacher is free to use a variety of the teaching methods according to his own abilities, interests and experiences. Following points may be consider while selecting a method:

* What to teach?

* Why to teach?

* Whom to teach?
* How to teach? i.e. What are the various methods?
* What are the problems in using these methods?
* How can we remove those problems?
* Which method is the best.

Ideology and Methods

Idealists have not adopted any specific and definite method of teaching. They 'prescribe some methods like — Lecture, Discussion,

Conversation, Dialogue, Questions answer, Argumentation etc. Realists emphasize scientific and objective method to teaching. They emphasize Heuristic, Experimental, Self-experience, research and correlation method of teaching. Thus they emphasize informal methods of teaching. Naturalists emphasize Learning by doing, Learning by experience and Learning by playing and advocated some methods like-observation, playway. Heuristic, montessori, Dalton plan and kindergarten method of teaching. Pragmatists have also emphasized the principles of Learning by doing, Learning by experience, purposive process of learning and correlation and integration on the basis of these principles. Kilpatric gave birth to the Project method of teaching which is widely accepted and useful in the teaching of science and mathematics.

According to Herbart spencer, methods of teaching should be based on some principles.

These principles are—

(a) From simple to complex

(b) From concrete to Abstract

(c) From known to unknown

(d) From Direct to Indirect

(e) From Definite to Indefinite

(f) From Empirical to Rational

(g) Emphasis on Self-Learning

(h) Method should be Interesting

All the above principles are based on psychological principles because the basis of these principles and their ideology is as same as psychology and shows the influence of Pestalozzi and Froebel.

While selecting a method the teacher should also consider the basic principles of teaching. Some important principles of teaching are as follows—

* Principle of learning by doing.
* Principle of individual differences
* Principle of motivation
* Principle of correlation
* Principle of linking with previous knowledge of the child
* Principle of Distribution
* Principle of Repetition
* Principle of certain objectives
* Principle of evaluation.

Methods and Techniques

According to I.K. Davis "strategies are broad methods of teaching and instruction"

Teaching Method	Teaching Techniques
1. Teaching methods have direct relationship with aims of teaching.	1. Teaching techniques has indirects relationship with aim of teaching.
2. The teaching methods are based on classical theory of human organisation.	2. Based on modern theory of human organisation.

3. In methods emphasis is given on 'How?'	3. In techniques 'with what' or 'whom' is taken into consideration.
4. The criteria for evaluating the teaching method is the mastery on contents.	4. The norm of evaluation is the acquisition of objectives.
5. In teaching method macro approaches are followed.	5. In teaching strategy micro approach is followed.
6. The assumption of teaching method is that teaching is an art.	6. In teaching techniques, the behaviour and relationship are considered important.
7. The main objective of teaching methods is the impressive presentation.	7. The main objection of teaching techniques is to create complete learning situations.
8. In teaching method, the task and its presentation are considered important.	8. In teaching techniques, the behaviours and relationship are considered more important.
9. The direction and speed of teaching is decided.	9. It depends upon the main method of teaching.
10. In teaching method, the teaching objectives are not not considered very important.	10. Teaching objectives are very important. Teaching techniques are selected keeping in view these objectives.

Categories of Methods

Generally, methods of teaching mathematics can be classified in two categories—

* Child-centred methods
* Teacher-centred methods.

Methods for Children

In child-centred methods, the child occupies a central position in the classroom. The whole teaching-learning process is geared to the needs, interests, capabilities and requirements of the child. These are based on psychological principles. The purpose is to develop abilities, skills and discovery attitude amongst the students. These includes: Project, Laboratory, problem-solving, Heuristic, Discussion method etc.

Methods by Teachers

In these Methods, the teacher occupies a central position in the classroom. In these methods focus is given on telling, memorization and recalling informations. The children are just passive recipients and they are in the background of educational process of knowledge. These include: Lecture, Historical and Lecture cum-demonstration method.

Various methods of teaching mathematics are as follows:

1. Lecture method
2. Demonstration method
3. Lecture-cum-Demonstration method
4. Inductive-Deductive method
5. Analytic-Synthetic method
6. Laboratory method
7. Heusistic method
8. Project method
9. Problem-solving method.

Lecture Method

This is a teacher centred method. In this method the teacher is an active participant and the child is a passive learner. This is not a psychological method. In this method the teacher speaks or delivers a lecture on a particular topic and the children listen. It is one way traffic because the teacher gives ideas and the children receive them. This is the method of imparting information through a speech. This is a one man's show because the children remain passive throughout the process. Lecture method is more useful at higher level classes. In this method it is difficult to know the extent to which the student has been able to learn. It is useful in relating some of the historical and mathematical incidents.

When to Use Lecture Method?

* To introduce the new lessons and new topics.
* To develop interest and to motivate the child.
* To give mathematical information.
* To correlate the new knowledge with the previous knowledge
* To give necessary instructions regarding new knowledge.
* To summarize the lesson or content which has been taught.
* To give an illustrative and motivational talk.
* For critical appraisal and to give at random important information.
* To fulfill queries and information.
* To prepare the child mentally to study the new lessons or topics.
* To present interesting and personal experiences.
* To give the information which are not easily available.
* To impart recent mathematical knowledge.
* To give the information regarding historical development of mathematics and contribution of the great mathematicians.
* When a large number of children are to be taught at the same time.

Steps

There are three steps in the process of lecture method—

1. Planning by the teacher

2. Presentation by the teacher
3. Receiving by the learner.

It is clear from above steps that there is no place of pupils's activities. The teacher is active only and the pupil remains a passive learner. He listens the lecture of the teacher. The process of lecture may be shown as follows—

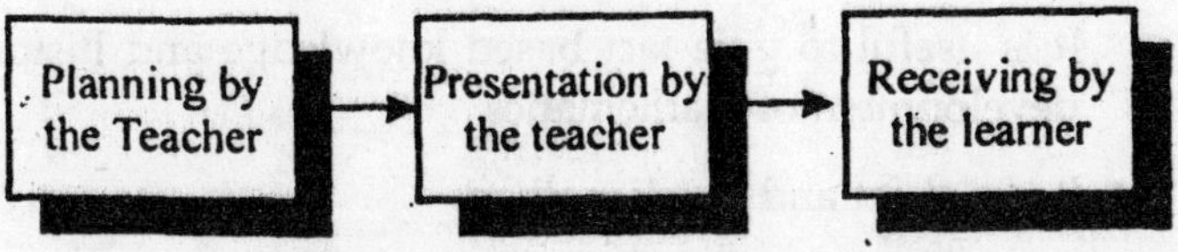

It is a convenient method for the teacher. The teacher is always active. The flow of thought is maintained and the teacher tells about many new things. More information can be given in a short period because it is easy, brief and attractive for teachers. The communication set of lecture can be shown as follows:

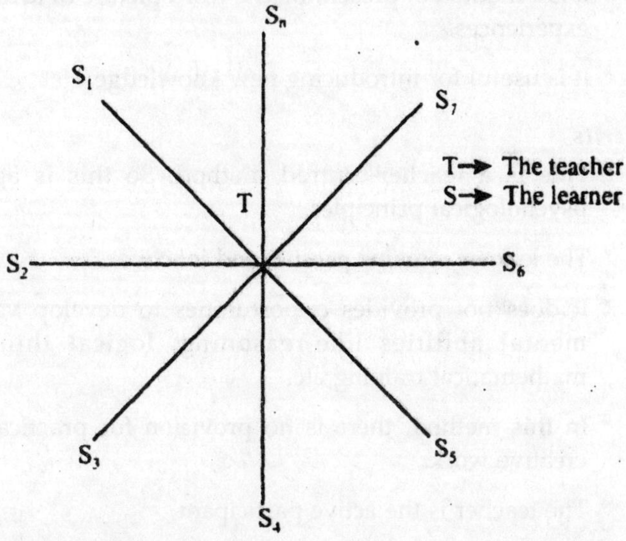

It is clear from the communication set of lecture that there is no direct communication between the students (S_1, S_2, S_3,........................S_n). It is the only teacher who communicates. The feedback channel is also very poor in lecture method. The teacher does not come to know about the extent of success of his communication.

Merits

* This is an easy, attractive and brief method.
* It is economical with respect to time and money.
* It simplifies the work of the teacher.
* It is useful to give fact based knowledge and historical development of mathematics.
* It is a short and quick method.
* A single teacher can teach a large group of students at a time.
* More information may be given in a short time.
* It is more useful for higher classes.
* It is a method of presenting the word picture of ideas and experiences.
* It is useful for introducing new knowledge.

Demerits

* This is a teacher-centred method. So this is against psychological principles.
* The learner remains passive and inactive.
* It does not provides opportunities to develop various mental abilities like-reasoning, logical thinking, mathematical training etc.
* In this method, there is no provision for practical and creative work.
* The teacher is the active participant,
* In this method teacher-taught relationship is neglected.
* The knowledge imparted through lecture/speech is not durable.

* This method is not useful for lower level of education.
* There is no consideration of the intelligence, abilities and interests of the students.
* It is not necessary that the children are attentive and understanding all, what the speaker/teacher is saying.
* Except the sense of hearing no other senses are used in this method.

How to make Lecture Effective and Interesting. To make teaching-learning more effective and interesting, a mathematics teacher should keep the following points in his mind—

* The analysis of the topics/ contents should be done properly and should be presented in a systematic and logical manner.
* Where and whenever required, the teacher should use black-board.
* Teaching points, definitions and other important information should be written on black-board.
* Teacher should present appropriate examples to make teaching-learning process more effective and interesting.
* In order to keep the child active, question should be put up to the students from time to time.
* The language of lecture should be simple, clear and appropriate.
* The voice of the speaker/lecture should be clear and effective but the speed of delevering lecture should be slow.
* At the end of lecture, summary of the lecture should be presented and students should be asked to note down the points.
* While preparing lecture, the previous knowledge of the child should be given due importance.

* To make lecture more interesting teacher should use proper a Audio-visual aids.

If a lecture is properly planned and prepared, it may be helpful in inspiring, stimulating and motivating learners. One of the procedures for preparing a lecture may be as follows—

Aims and objectives of lecture
(why and for what it is planned)

↓

Introduction of the lecture/topic
(Relating with previous knowledge of the learner)

↓

Organisation of the content
(Major points, Development of points, Questions, examples etc.

↓

Presentation of the lecture
(Discussion, Demonstration and Illustration, use of A.V. aids, use of Black-Board, effective voice, use of gestures etc.)

↓

Conclusions & summary
(By asking questions to the students)

Demonstration Method

In the mathematics teaching demonstration method is very important. In this method both the teacher and pupil are active. The teacher makes a theoretical investigation and proves it in the class-room. The teacher performs the experiment while teaching in the class and the pupils acquire knowledge with careful observation of the experiment. Demonstrations may be performed by a single teacher or a group of teachers. The teacher should emphasize major points in the demonstration and preferably should write them on black-board. The teacher should be well-versed in the handling of the apparatus and equipments. While demonstrating teacher should ask some reflective type of questions to stimulate the power of reasoning and interest of students in the classroom.

Merits

1. The teaching becomes effective even if the number of apparatus are less.
2. The pupil develop the power of observation, reasoning and thinking.
3. Demonstration method is appropriate for lower classes.
4. It is less time consuming.
5. The pupil learns by seeing and observing.
6. It is economical method.
7. The sight and hearing sense of children are more active.
8. The pupil can understand the principles/laws/formulae clearly.
9. It is useful where the experiments involve some complex and difficult operations.
10. It is more useful where the apparatus is costly and sensitive to break.

Demerits

1. The pupils do not get a chance to perform experiments. Therefore first hand experience is not possible with the use of this method.
2. It is not based on the principle of Learning by doing.
3. The pupils only observe, what the teacher 'does'?
4. The pupils do not get direct experiences.
5. Some pupils do not observe properly.

Example **: If teacher want to teach various types of polygons and their classification in the class.**

***Solution*—**The procedure to teach this topic may be as follows— The teacher will show 3, 4, 5, 6 sided closed figures to the pupil.

Q. 1. How many sides does each of the figures have?

Ans. The 'pupil will identify the number of sides in each figure.

Q.2. How many sides does have fig. (1)?

Ans. Three.

Q.3. What is the name of this figure?

Ans. Triangle

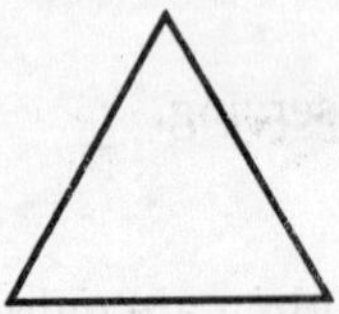

(1)

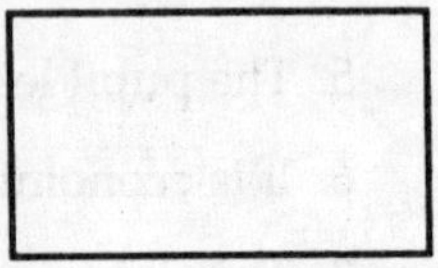

(2)

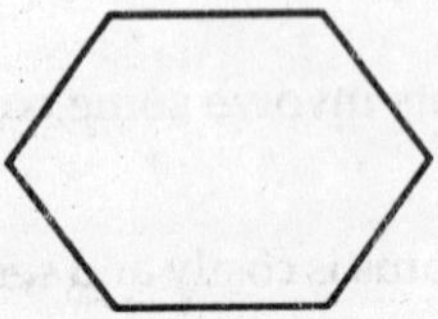

(3)

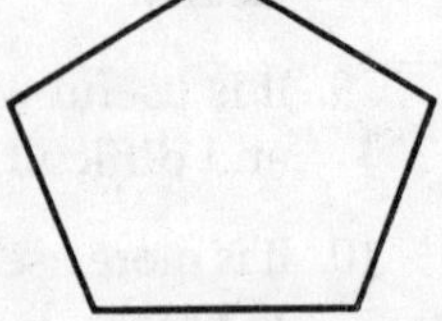

(4)

Q.4. How many sides does have fig. **(2)?**

Ans. Four.

Q.5. What is the name of this figure?

Ans. Rectangle

Q.6. How many sides does have fig. **(3)?**

Ans. Six.

Q.7. What is the name of this figure?

Ans. Hexagon.

Q.8. How many sides does have fig. ?

Ans. Five.

Q.9. What is the name of this figure?

Ans. Pentagon.

Q.10. What is the common name of all these figures?

Ans. Polygons.

Q. 11. How do you define polygons?

Ans. Expected answers.

Teachers' Statement

Polygon is a simple closed plane figure formed by live segments. *Eg.* Triangles, Quadrilateral etc.

Q. 12 What is the basis of classification of polygons?

Ans. Expected answer.

Teachers' Statement

Polygons are classified on the basis of number of sides they have. The teacher will show a chart illustrating the various polygons of different sides and their names as follows—

Different Kinds of Polygons

1. 3 sides — Triangle 
2. 4 sides — Quadrilateral 
3. 5 sides — Pentagon 

4. 6 sides — Hexagon

5. 7 sides — Heptagon

6. 8 sides — Octagon

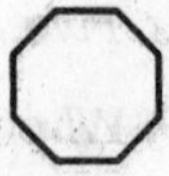

7. 9 sides — Nonagon

8. 10 sides — Decagon

Criteria of a Good Demonstration

1. The purpose of demonstration should be stated before the students clearly.
2. All experiments should be performed infront of the children.
3. The demonstration table should be arranged properly so that all pupils are able to see it properly. The demonstration table should be at a higher level than pupil's table.
4. The equipments required for the demonstration should be kept on the demonstration table.
5. The help of students should be taken while demonstration and experimentation.
6. Doubts of pupils should be cleared simultaneously.
7. The teacher should use easy and simple language.
8. After the completion of demonstration the teacher should discuss the observations and results of the demonstration.
9. Demonstration should be the result of active participation of the teacher and students
10. Demonstration should be speedy and simple.

11. Demonstration should be supplemented with the other audio-visual aids to make it more interesting and effective.

12. The teacher should maintain interest and discipline in the class.

Lecture-cum-Demonstration Method

This is the combination of lecture method and demonstration method. Thus it includes the merits of both the methods. In this method shortcomings/ limitations of lecture method are removed. This method can prove to be one of the best methods if the demonstrations are well planned and effective. It is a economical with regards to both time and money. This method is based on the maxims of teaching proceed from concrete to abstract and simple to complex.

Procedure—In this method the teacher explains the theoretical portion with the help of lecture method makings use of diagrams, figures statements etc., and performs the experiment in the class to make the critical portion more clear. It involves the active participation of children this method does not so involve a one-way communication like lecture method. The children watch the actual apparatus and operations and help the teacher in the demonstration of experiments. During experimentation and demonstration the teacher keeps asking questions from the students. Thus the students observe the demonstration critically. It is helpful in developing observation, reasoning and logical powers.

Therefore, in this method all the limitations of lecture method are removed and it includes all the merits of demonstration method. So merits and demerits of lecture-cum-demonstration method are not discussed here. Please see the merits and demerits of lecture and demonstration method.

There are several criteria as precautions while performing experiments and demonstration in the class room. Please see precautions or criteria of good demonstration.

Inductive Method

Inductive method of teaching and learning methematics is based on induction. Induction means proving a universal truth or theorem by showing that if it is true in any particular case, it will be true in the next case in the same serial order. This is a method of development in which the child is made or led to discover truth for himself. In Inductive method the rules and formula are established after extensive study of experiences, experiments and examples. Inductive method is more useful in lessons where principles, rules, definitions, generalizations and casual connections between facts are to be established.

This method is psychological in nature. The children follow the subject matter with great interest and understanding. The children can understand the whole process in detail. This is motivating and stimulating method of teaching mathematics. It also develops scientific attitude amongst the children. In inductive method child himself attains the knowledge of some formula or principle with the help of facts, examples and experiments. So the knowledge attained by this method becomes solid and durable and different mental powers of the child can also be developed. This method is more useful in arithmetic teaching and learning.

Procedure: In the process of induction, the teacher presents some specific conditions or examples before the children. On the basis of these examples the students reach some specific principles, laws or formulae by logical discussion. In this method we proceed from Particular to General, "specific examples to principles or formulae or universal laws." and then generalize the results. Thus concrete examples are presented and with their help students are asked to arrive at certain conclusions or principles on the basis of concrete facts. For example; if we find that a parrot is green in colour, we find another parrot also green in colour still another parrot green in colour and so on.........., and hence we can say that: all parrots are green in colour. Similarly, the students by measuring the interior angles of a triangle come to the conclusion that the sum of interior angles of a triangle is equal to two right angles i.e. 180°.

Steps. While teaching by this method mainly following steps are used—

(A) Presentation of specific examples

(B) Observation

(C) Generalisation

(D) Testing and verification.

Presentation of Specific Examples. In this step teacher presents many examples of same type before the students and the solutions of those examples are obtained with the help of students. Students are asked to solve the examples with the help of Unitary method.

Observation. After obtaining the solutions of the various examples presented, the students observe these and try to reach to some conclusion with the help of teacher.

Generalisation. After observing the examples presented, the teacher and children decide some common formulae, principle or law by logical mutual discussion.

Testing and Verification. After deciding some common formula, principle or law, children test and verify the laws with the help of other examples or problems. In this way children logically attain the knowledge of inductive method by following above given steps. Therefore, Inductive method is simply a procedure with which some laws, principles, rules and formulae are established by considering the ideas, examples, experiments and experiences.

Application of Inductive Method in Mathematics. The importance & working of inductive method in mathematics can be clarified by following examples.

Problem 1—Establishing a formula for solving simple interest problem.

First Step—The teacher will present many examples related to simple interest before the students and will solve them using unitary method with the help of which the formula for calculating simple interest can be established.

Example—1. Find out S.I of Rs 700 at 8% per annum for 3 years.

Solution—Using Unitary method

... S. I. of Rs 100 for 1 year = Rs. 8

$\therefore$ S. I. of Rs 1 for 1 year = Rs. $\frac{8}{100}$

$\therefore$ S. I. of Rs. 700 for 1 year = Rs. $\left(\frac{8}{100} \times 700\right)$

$\therefore$ S. I. of Rs. 700 for 3 year = Rs. $\left(\frac{8}{100} \times 700 \times 3\right)$

= Rs. (8 × 7 × 3) = Rs. 168

Example 2—Find out S.I. of Rs. 500 at the rate of 5% for 4 years.

Solution— ... S. I. of Rs 100 for 1 year = Rs. 5

$\therefore$ S. I. of Rs 1 for 1 year = Rs. $\frac{5}{100}$

$\therefore$ S. I. of Rs. 500 for 1 year = Rs. $\left(\frac{5}{100} \times 500\right)$

$\therefore$ S. I. of Rs. 500 for 4 year = Rs. $\left(\frac{5}{100} \times 500 \times 4\right)$

= Rs. (5 × 5 × 4) = Rs. 100

Similarly, a number of examples of this type can be presented in the classroom.

Second Step—Students will observe examples with the help of the teacher.

Teacher—What is S.I. for 3 years is in Exp. 1.

Students— S.I. = Rs. $\left(\frac{8}{100} \times 700 \times 3\right)$ = Rs. 168

Teacher—What is S.I. for 4 years in Exp.2.

Students— $$\text{S.I.} = \text{Rs.} \left(\frac{5}{100} \times 500 \times 4\right) = \text{Rs. } 100$$

Similarly by solving other more problems and by observing the process of finding out the interest, the students can arrive at a law or formula.

Third Step—After thorough observation of the given examples children will be able to establish the formula of simple interest For example:

$$\text{In example, 1, S.I. for 3 years} = \left(\frac{8}{100} \times 700 \times 3\right)$$

$$\text{In example, 2, S.I. for 4 years} = \left(\frac{5}{100} \times 500 \times 4\right)$$

Now; the teacher can make the following discussion—

Q. 1. What is 8 and 5 in the given examples?

Ans. 8 and 5 is the rate of interest.

Q.2. What is 700 and 500 in the given examples?

Ans. 700 and 500 is the principal.

Q.3. What is 3 and 4 in the given examples?

Ans. 3 and 4 are years or time. Therefore; we can write;

$$\text{S.I.} = \frac{\text{Rate}}{100} \times \text{Principal} \times \text{Time}$$

or $$\text{S.I.} = \frac{\text{Rate} \times \text{Principal} \times \text{Time}}{100}$$

We can write, $$\text{S.I.} = \frac{\text{Principal} \times \text{Rate} \times \text{Time}}{100}$$

or
$$\boxed{S.I. = \frac{P \times R \times T}{100}}$$

Fourth Step—Students will be able to verify the derived formula by solving other problems of simple interest based on this formula. For example—

Question—find out the S.I. on Rs. 1500 at the rate of 9% yearly for 18 years.

Solution (I)—Using the formula

$$\text{Simple Interest} = \frac{P \times R \times T}{100}$$

$$= \text{Rs. } \frac{1500 \times 9 \times 18}{100}$$

$$= \text{Rs. } 15 \times 9 \times 18 = \text{Rs. } 2430$$

Solution (II) —

$$PRT = \text{Rs. } (1500)$$
$$(9\% \text{ Per Years}) \times (18 \text{ Years})$$

$$= \text{Rs. } 1500 \frac{9}{100} \text{ Per Year} \times 18 \text{ Year}$$

$$= \text{Rs. } 1500 \times \frac{9}{100} \times 18 \text{ Year}$$

$$= \text{Rs. } 15 \times 9 \times 8$$

$$= \text{Rs.}2430$$

In this way children will be able to determine and verify the formula of simple interest with the help of different examples. Similarly with the help of different examples the formula for compound interest and other formula can be determined and generalised in the classroom.

Problem 2—If teacher wants to teach the students that sum of three angles of a triangle is 180°.

Solution—To find the value of sum of three angles of a triangle, the teacher will ask the students to draw triangles of different shapes and sizes. The students will measure their angles of each triangle and find out the sum of these. When students will repeat this process many times then on the basis of their own observation they will certainly be able to draw this conclusion that sum of the three angles of a triangle is 180° or 2 right angles. Also students will be able to generalise this law after testing the truth of this law in different conditions.

Problem-3—To determine the area of four walls of a room.

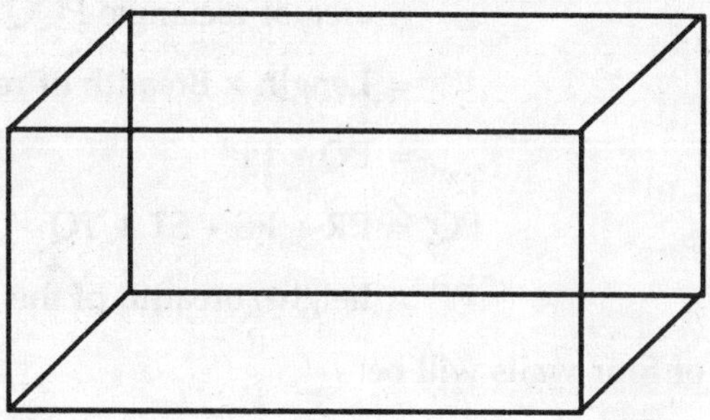

Solution—

(i) Teacher will show a model of the class room made up of card board as a teaching aid and clarify the method to find out the areas of four walls of the room.

(ii) He will cut the walls of the room made of cardboard and will arrange the four walls on the table.

(iii) The teacher will tell that if the four cardboard pieces (walls) are placed in a line then it will form a long wall which is reactangular in shape. Teacher will draw following figure so that students can understand easily—

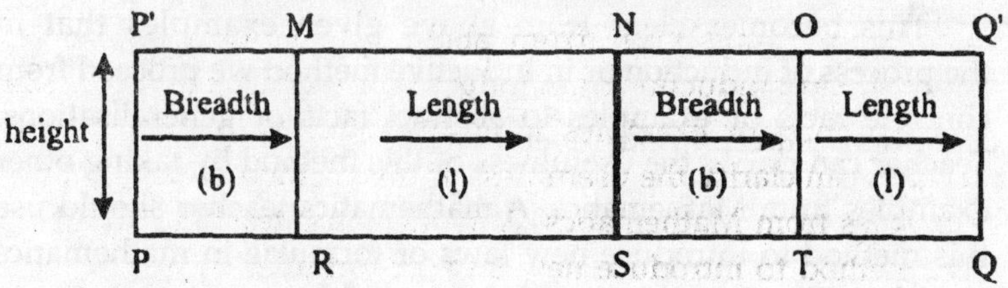

(iv) Now PQQ′ P is a rectangular wall in which there are two sections of length and two sections of breadth because a room has four walls. In this way the length of this wall is PQ or P′Q′ and breadth (height) is PP′ or QQ′.

(v) So the area of the four walls of the room will be equal to area of this rectangular figure.

Area of four walls of room will be

$$= \text{area of rectangle } PQQ'P'$$

$$= \text{Length} \times \text{Breadth of rectangle}$$

$$= PQ \times PP'$$

$\because$ $PQ' = PR + RS + ST + TQ$

and $PP' = \text{height/breadth of the rectangle}$

$\therefore$ area of four walls will be

$$= (PR + RS + ST + TQ) \times PP'$$

Or $= (\text{Breadth} + \text{Length} + \text{Breadth} + \text{Length}) \times \text{Height}$

Or $= (l + b + l + b) \times h$

Or $= (2l + 2b) \times h$

Or $= 2(l + b) \times h$

So area of four walls of room $= 2(l + b) \times h$

Thus the students will be able to generalise the formula of calculation of the area of four walls of a room and they will be able to verify it with the help of other examples.

This becomes clear from above given examples that in the process of induction or in Inductive method we proceed from concrete facts or examples to abstract facts or generalisations. Teacher can clarify the usefulness of this method by taking other examples from Mathematics. A mathematics teacher should use this method to introduce new laws or formulae in mathematics teaching. Because this method has been proved to be very successful in teaching new knowledge, law or formula.

Merits

1. It is a scientific method because knowledge attained by this method is based on real facts.
2. The Child gets the knowledge of the process of deciding and generalising laws, formulas etc.
3. The knowledge gained by the use of this method is more durable because in this method child himself attains the knowledge by examples, observation and testing.
4. The critical observation and logical power of children are developed by inductive method.
5. This is a psychological method because many important principles of psychology are used in this method.
6. This method guides the child to do the work himself. So this develop self-reliance and self-confidence in them.
7. This method helps to ascertain or establish many laws, relations, formulae and new principles of mathematics.
8. This method is very useful and suitable for lower classes.
9. This method develops curiosity and interest in the child to learn mathematics.
10. In this method children themselves attain the knowledge with the help of examples so they don't feel bored (fatigue). They remain active to attain new knowledge.

Demerits. This is certainly true that Inductive method is a very important and useful method of teaching Mathematics. Inspite of having so many merits it has some demerits also which are as follows:

1. This is a very slow process, so gaining knowledge by this method costs more time and labour.
2. It needs sharp mind, proper planning and enough labour. So it is not easy to attain knowledge by this method for students of all levels.

3. This method is useful only for lower classes because syllabus is very wide in higher classes and it is not possible to cover the whole syllabus.

4. Only an experienced and able teacher can use this method successfully.

5. The ability and capacity of problem solving can not be developed by the use of this method.

6. It is neither easy for teacher nor for students to select or present real examples for generalisations.

7. Results drawn by the use of this method are not always true. Their truthfulness depends upon a number of examples on which they are based. Because the truthfulness or reliability of any result is more if it is drawn from more number of specific examples.

Deductive Method

Deductive method is exactly opposite to inductive method. Deductive logic is used in this method. Deductive method is mainly used in Algebra, Geometry and trigonometry because different relations laws and formulae are used in these sub-branches of mathematics. It is impossible to verify each law and formula practically. In this method help is taken from assumptions, postulates and axioms of mathematics. This method is used for teaching mathematics in higher classes. This is based on deduction.

Procedure. In deductive method we proceed from 'abstract to concrete', from 'general to particular' and 'from general rule to example'. In this method principles, laws, formulae, and relations are presented before the students in real form. Children learn the told laws, principles and formulae by heart. Generally teacher give the knowledge of the facts to the students. Such as:

1. Knowledge of formulae as $(a + b)^2 = a^2 + 2ab + b^2$ etc.

2. The sum of three angles of a Triangle is 180°.

3. Knowledge of Geometrical formulae like area of a circle $= \pi r^2$ etc.

4. Formula to calculate S.I. = $\frac{\text{Principal} \times \text{Rate} \times \text{Time}}{100}$

5. Similarly in trigonometry formulae like $\sin\theta = \frac{1}{\operatorname{cosec}\theta}$

and $\tan\theta = \frac{1}{\cot\theta} = \frac{\sin\theta}{\cos\theta}$ etc.

Example 1—If length and breadth of a rectangle is 6 m and 4 m respectively, then find out the area of rectangle.

Solution—Children can solve the problem by using the formula to find out the area of the rectangle.

$\therefore$ Area of rectangle = (Length × Breadth) = 6 m × 4 m

or = 24 m^2

$\therefore$ = 24 square metre.

Example 2—Find out the interest on Rs. 500 at the rate of 5% for 2 years.

Solution—In deductive method students are told the formula of calculation of S.I. So the students find the solution suitably and in less time. While it takes more time to solve the problem by unitary method in Inductive method. According to this method the given example can be solved by proceeding as follows:

1. Formula to find out S.I. = $\frac{\text{Principal} \times \text{Rate} \times \text{Time}}{100}$

2. In the given example

Principal = Rs. 500,

Rate = 5% yearly,

Time = 2 years

3. Simple interest = Rs. $\frac{500 \times 5 \times 2}{100}$

= Rs. 5 × 5 × 2 = Rs. 50.

Example 3—Find out $(4a + 2b)^2$.

Solution—To solve the given problem, students will be told the formula $(a + b)^2 = a^2 + 2\,ab + b^2$ for solving the problem. Students will be able to find the solution of the problem with the help of formula told to them and check the validity of their answer.

Formula— $(a + b)^2 = a^2 + 2\,ab + b^2$

or (First variable + Second variable)^2 = (First variable)^2 + 2 (First variable × second variable) + (second variable)^2

Therefore,

$$(4a + 2b)^2 = (4a)^2 + 2 \times 4a \times 2b + (2b)^2$$

$$= 16\,a^2 + 16ab + 4b^2$$

Similarly while solving linear equations, teacher tell in advance that for solving it we arrange unknown quantities on one side and known quantities on other side and while transposing the quantities the sign of quantities change. With the help of this children check the truthfulness of solutions after solving the questions.

Therefore in deductive method students directly apply the formula for solving the problem and came the formulae and laws to use them in future.

Merits

1. By using this method Mathematics work becomes very easy and comfortable.
2. By deductive method craming power of students increases.
3. By using this method the speed of gaining knowledge increases because students directly use the formula for solving the problem.
4. This method should be used when there is shortage of time.

5. This method is used for teaching theorem and axioms of Geometry, tables in Arithmetics etc.
6. Both the teacher and pupil do not find any difficulty in using this method.
7. More knowledge can be attained in less time by the use of this method.
8. Laws, principles and formulas can easily be checked by using this method.
9. Children can do the exercise quickly and easily by using this method.
10. This method is short as well as practical.

Demerits. Like Inductive method, Deductive method is also an important method of teaching mathematics. It has its own qualities but still it has some demerits and limitations. Following are the main demerits of this method —

1. This method is not in accordance with psychological principles.
2. In this method more emphasis is given on cramming than understanding or discovering.
3. In this method students work like machines without knowing the purpose of proceeding in that particular way.
4. Knowledge gained by this method is unclear and unstable, because it is not gained by their own efforts.
5. In this method there is hot scope of developing powers like logical, thinking and investigation.
6. This method is not suitable for lower classes because it is very difficult for the students of lower classes to understand different formulae laws etc.
7. By using this method the teaching-learning process becomes uninteresting and dull.
8. Children don't get opportunities to gain new knowledge by using this method.

Difference between Inductive and Deductive Methods

We know that Inductive and Deductive methods are complementary to each other. Still they have difference in their working functioning and nature. The difference between these two methods can be explained by following points—

	Inductive Method		Deductive Method
1.	In this method we proceed from 'particular general', from 'example to general rule' and from 'concrete to abstract'.	1.	In this method, we proceed form general to particular, from general rule to example and from abstract to concrete.
2.	In this method child acts as or researcher and draws law or formula by active participation.	2.	In this formulae and laws are already told to the child. He is not able to verify the law or formula.
3.	By this method, a habit of discovery is developed in students.	3.	By this method, a habit of discovery is not developed in students.
4.	This is best method of teaching.	4.	This is best method of learning.
5.	Inductive method is suitable for teaching in lower classes.	5.	This method is suitable for teaching in higher classes.
6.	In this method children them selves decide the law or formula it develops self-relianceand self-confidence in them.	6.	In this method laws and formulas are told in advance so they do not gain any confidence.
7.	This method is helpful in discovering new knowledge.	7.	In this method children use the knowledge gained by others.
8.	This is a scientific method by which scientific attitude is developed in students.	8.	This method does not give any scope for developing scientific attitude in children.
9.	This method is the way of discovery and research.	9.	This method is the way of following because child follow the given laws and principles.
10.	In this method both the teacher and pupilare active. So this is a student-centered method.	10.	In this teacher is more active and pupil is a passive learner. So this is a teacher-centered method.
11.	This method give emphasis on original and creative work.	11.	This method gives emphasis on problem-solving.
12.	Teaching-learning process	12.	Teaching-Learning process becomes

becomes interesting by the use of this method.	dull by the use of this method.
13. In this method every step is important to write so many steps.	13. In this method children do not learn and children learn to write them.
14. This is a slow method so it needs more labour and time.	14. This is a fast method so it needs less labour and times.
15. This is a psychological method which is understanding-centered.	15. This is an unpsychological method and is memory-centered.

The Correlation

Indeed inductive and deductive methods are supplementary to each other. So in the beginning laws and formulae should be proved with the help of examples by the use of inductive method. After that these laws and formulae should be applied and practiced with the help of deductive method. As both feet are essential to walk properly both inductive and deductive methods are necessary to teach effectively. The main basis of inductive method is origin and development of knowledge, while perceptual presentation is the main basis in deductive method. So inductive method is a forerunner and deductive method is its follower or companion. Both the methods remove the demerits of each other.

Hence, the process of establishing the formulae and laws and then proceeding ahead and practicing is known as Inductive-Deductive method. Therefore, the knowledge of new facts, laws, principles and formulae related to mathematics should be given by inductive method but its application and drill should be done with the help of deductive method.

The combined form of both the methods can be made more clear by the following example—

Example—If length, breadth and height of a room is 6m, 4m and 3m respectively. Then find out the area of four walls of a room.

Solution 1. By Inductive Method

This problem has been solved while discribing and explaining inductive method in the previous pages. So here we are solving it by deductive method only.

Solution 2. By Deductive Method

For finding the solution by deductive method students are told the formula of area of four walls of a room. By applying this formula directly they can findout the solution of the problem.

Formula—

Area of four walls of a room	= 2 (length + breadth) × height
Here in this problem, length	= 6m, breadth = 4m, and Height = 3 m.
Area of Four walls of a room	= 2 (6m + 4m) × 3m
	= 2 (10 m) × 3 m = 20 m × 3 m
	= 60 m^2

Hence we can conclude that inductive and deductive methods are supplementary to each other. Both the methods should be used simultaneously in mathematics teaching.

Analytical Method

The original meaning of the world Analysis is to unloose or to separate things that are together. Analysis starts with "what we have to findout, and traces the connection between it and the data. With the help of this method, the difficult parts of any problem can be analysed to findout the solution of the given problem. Thus separation of different parts of a problem is known as analysis. In this method we proceed from 'unknown to known' or from 'conclusion to hypothesis'. In this method we start from 'what is to be determined' or 'what is to be proved'. In this way we reach to the conclusion. This method is used in the following conditions:

* When we have to prove any theorem.
* When construction work is to be done in the geometry.
* When we have to findout the solution of some new arithmetical problems.

In this method every step has its own importance and reason. Therefore analysis of a problem should be done properly. The method of analysis is the method of discovery and it is based on heuristic approach.

Application in Geometry

Example—The line segment joining the middle points of the two sides of a triangle is parallel to the third and half of it.

To prove the above theorem side DE is produced to F such that DE = EF and C is joined to F. This method gives the clarification that why we need above given construction and how it will be helpful to us to prove DE = $\frac{1}{2}$ BC and DC || BC. To prove the theorem the teacher will ask questions to the students. Expected answers given by students are also mentioned in the brackets.

A

1. What is given to us?

   (ABC is a triangle D and E are mid-points of its sides AB and AC respectively)

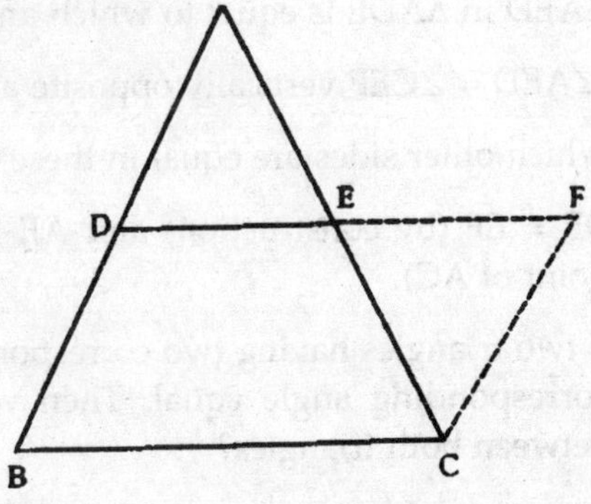

2. What is to be proved?

   (DE || BC and DE = $\frac{1}{2}$ BC)

3. When can line DE be half of line BC?

   (When line DE is doubled (2 DE = BC), so DE is produced to F such that DE = EF)

4. What is the second thing to be proved? (DE is parallel to BC)

5. How can it be proved?

   (If we prove that ΔBCF is a parallelogram)

6. How can ΔBCF be proved to be a parallelogram?

   (If can be proved that DB and CF are parallel and equal)

7. How can we prove that DB = CF?

   (If it can be proved that CF = AD; (... B = AD)

8. How can we prove that DB || CF?

   (If ∠DAE = ∠ ECF alternate angles)

9. How can it be proved that CF = AD and ∠ DAE = ∠ ECF?

   (if we prove that ΔADE and ΔECF are congruent)

10. How these triangles can be proved to be congruent?

    (by comparing both triangles)

11. ∠AED in ΔADE is equal to which angle in ΔECF ?

    (∠AED = ∠CEF vertically opposite angles)

12. Which other sides are equal in these two triangles?

    DE = EF (by construction) and AE = EC; (... E is mid-point of AC).

13. If two triangles having two corresponding sides and one corresponding angle equal. Then what is the relation between both triangles?

(They are congruent triangles. So $\Delta ADE \cong \Delta ECF$)

14. $\angle$ DAE is equal to which angle? When transversal AC cuts AB | | CF. ($\angle$ DAE = $\angle$ CEF; alternate angles)

15. What is the relation between DB and CF when AB | | CF ? (Then DB is parallel and equal to CF)

    $\therefore$ DB | | CF and DB = CF

16. When DB | | CF and DB = CF, what name would you give to figure DBCF? (DBCF is a parallelogram)

17. When DBCF is a parallelogram; how is DF, related to BC.

    (DF will be parallel and equal to BC) $\therefore$ DF | | BC and DF = BC.

18. How are lines DE and DF are related to each other? (DF = 2 DE or DE = $\frac{1}{2}$ DF)

19. 21DE = $\frac{1}{2}$ BC and DE | | BC.

    In this way by disclosing the secrets of what is to be proved we discover the things needed to be proved.

Application in Algebra

Example 2 — If $\frac{a}{b} = \frac{c}{d}$ then prove

$$\frac{ac + 4b^2}{bc} = \frac{c^2 + 4bd}{dc}$$

Analysis — We have to start from equation that is to be proved and proceed towards the known. Thus, we start from

$$\frac{ac + 4b^2}{bc} = \frac{c^2 + 4bd}{dc}$$

1. How to write this identity in easy form? (We cut 'c' in the denominators of both sides and then cross multiply.)

   Thus, $$\frac{ac + 4b^2}{b} = \frac{c^2 + 4bd}{d}$$

or $$9\frac{ac+4b^2}{b} = \frac{c^2+4bd}{d}$$

by cross multiplying

or $$acd + 4\,b^2d = c^2\,b + 4b^2\,d$$

2. How can it be solved further?

(4 b²d can be cut from both sides and 'c' can also be cut.)

$$acd + 4\,b^2d = c^2b + 4\,b^2d$$

or $$acd = c^2b$$

or $$ad = cb$$

3. How can we write it in some other form?

$$ad = cb$$

Or $$\frac{a}{b} = \frac{b}{c}$$ (which is given).

This type of the solution of the problems can be easily obtained by analysis.

Application in Arithmetic

Example 3— If length and breadth of a field are 50m and 20m respectively. There is a 5m wide path enclosing the field. Find out the area of the path.

Answer—Solution by Analytic-method.

1. What is given in question? (Length and breadth of a rectangular field and width of the path)
2. What is the length of field? (Length of field = 50m)
3. What is breadth of field? (Breadth of field = 20 m)
4. What is width of path? (Width of path = 5m)
5. What has to be calculated in the given question? (Area of the shaded portion).

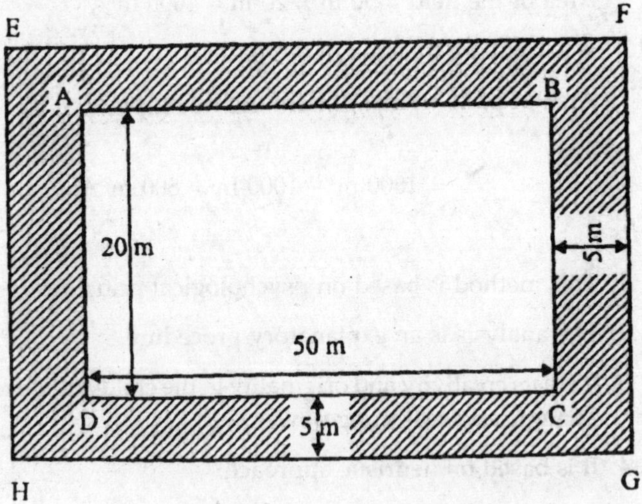

6. How to find out the area of path enclosing the field?

   (If area of the field is subtracted from the area of the field with the area of path.)

7. How do we find out the area of field including path?

   (When length and breadth of paths are known)

8. How do we can findout the length and breadth of the path?

   (By adding twice of the width of path in length and breadth of the

9. Thus what will be the length and breadth of the field with path?

   (Length = 50 + 10 = 60 m)

   (Breadth = 20 + 10 = 30 m)

10. Thus what will be the area including the path.

    Area = Length x Breadth = 60 m × 30 m

    = 1800 m^2

11. What will be the area of the field ?

Area of the field = 50 m × 20 m = 1000 m^2

12. What will be the area of the paths ?

Area of path = Area of field including path – Area of field

= 1800 m^2 – 1000 m^2 = 800 m^2 ***Ans.***

Merits

1. This method is based on psychological principles.
2. The analysis is an explanatory procedure.
3. It creats creativity and originality in the child and develops analytic and reasoning power.
4. It is based on heuristic approach.
5. It develops scientific attitude.
6. It leads to the spirit of enquiry and investigation.
7. Analysis is the process of thinking.
8. This develops self-confidence and logical abilities in the child.
9. Knowledge gained by this method is more solid and durable.
10. The child is always curious for attaining new knowledge.
11. It is a formative method and based on inductive reasoning.

Demerits

Inspite of being so important and useful method of teaching mathematics, it has some limitations. Which are as follows:

1. This is a lengthy method.
2. It is not possible to acquire speed and efficiency.
3. Every teacher cannot use this method successfully.
4. The whole syllabus can not be completed with in the certain period.

5. The use of analytic method is possible only when we have the knowledge of known facts and unknown conclusions.

Synthesis Method

It is reverse of the analytic method. Synthesis means to place together things that are apart or "to join seperate parts". In this method we proceed "from known to unknown", or we start with hypothesis and end with conclusions. Thus synthesis begins from the data and connects them with the conclusion. Synthesis is the method of formulation, recording and presenting concisely the discovered solution omitting the trials and errors. Synthesis leads to rote memory and doing by mere imitation. Thus analysis is the process of discovering the solution and synthesis is the method of setting out the solution in a concise form so as to convince yourself and others. Synthesis without analysis is dogmatic. But synthesis is after analysis has a place in the class-room.

Therefore, mathematics teacher should use both analytic and synthetic method together. In teaching arithmetical problems and geometrical constructions, analysis will only help us to find out a solution.

Application in Algebra

Example 1. If $\frac{a}{b} = \frac{c}{d}$ then prove

$$\frac{ac + 4b^2}{bc} = \frac{c^2 + 4bc}{dc}$$

Solution — We know that $\frac{a}{b} = \frac{c}{d}$. Thus in this method we start from known and proceed to unknown.

Adding $\frac{4b}{c}$ on both sides

$$\frac{a}{b} + \frac{4b}{c} = \frac{c}{d} + \frac{4b}{c}.$$

Or, $$\frac{ac + 4b^2}{bc} = \frac{c^2 + 4bd}{dc}$$

Which was to be proved.

Note: No logic or reason is gives here for why $\frac{4b}{c}$ is added on both sides.

Application in Arithmetic

Example 2—Length and breadth of a field is 50m and 20m respectively. A path enclosing the field has a width of 5m. Find out the area of the path.

Solution— Given—

Length of field = 50 m

Breadth of field = 20 m

Width of path = 5 m

To find—Areas of the Path.

Proof — Length of field with path = (5 + 50 +5) = 60 m.

Breadth of field with path = (5 + 20 + 5) m = 30 m.

∴ Area of field including path =60 × 30 = 1800 m^2.

Area of field = 50 × 20 = 1000 m^2.

∴ Area of path = Area of field including path – area of field

= 1800 m^2 – 1000 m^2 = 800 m^2.

Note: Here no logic or explanation is given for why length and breadth of field will be 60 m and 30 m. respectively and why area of path will be 800 m^2?

Application in Geometry

Example 3 — ΔABC, if ΔD is perpendicular on side BC. Then prove

$$AB^2 + DC^2 = CA^2 + BD^2.$$

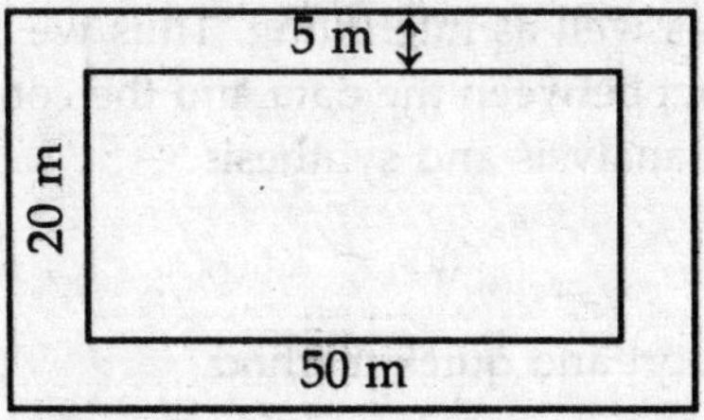

Solution 3— Given—ABC is a triangle. AD is ⊥ to side BC.

To prove— $AB^2 + DC^2 = CA^2 + BD^2$

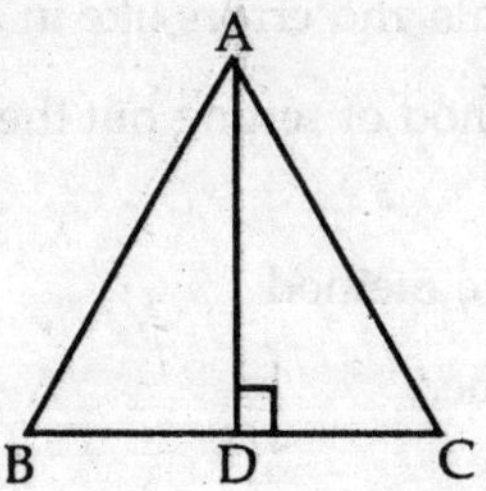

Proof—In ΔABD

$$AB^2 = (AD)^2 + (BD)^2 \quad ...(1)$$

Similarily in Δ ADC

$$AC^2 = (AD)^2 + (DC)^2 \quad ... (2)$$

Now substraction equ. (2) from equ. (1)

$$AB^2 - AC^2 = [(AD)^2 + BD^2] - [(AD)^2 + (DC)^2]$$

$$= AD^2 + BD^2 - AD^2 - DC^2$$

or ∴ $AB^2 - AC^2 = BD^2 - DC^2$

or $AB^2 + DC^2 = BD^2 + AC^2$

Here the fundamental reason behind each and every step has not been explained. Hence in teaching mathematics both the methods should be used together for effective teaching-learning.

Analysis and synthesis refer to the details of development, laboratory and project methods are intended to make teaching more effective as well as interesting. Thus we can more quickly establish contract between the data and the conclusion, which is the objective of analysis and synthesis.

Merits

* It is a short and quick method.
* It glorifies the memory of the child.
* It formulates, records and presents concisely the discovered facts.
* It omits the trials and errors like in analysis
* This is the method of setting out the solution in a concise form.
* It is informative method.
* It takes less time.

Demerits

1. In this method, there is no scope of discovery.
2. It leads to rate memory.
3. It creats many doubts in the mind of the child.
4. It does not give full satisfaction to the child.
5. There is no opportunity for developing thinking, reasoning, and other mental abilities.
6. The recall of each step can not be possible for every child.

Difference Between Analytic and Synthetic Method

Analytic Method	Synthetic Method
1. We proceed from unknown to known or from conclusion to hypothesis.	1. We proceed from known to unknown or hypothesis to conclusion.

2. It is based on inductive reasoning.	2. It is based on deductive reasoning.
3. It is based upon heuristic approach.	3. It is not based on heuristic approach.
4. It is laborious and very lengthy method.	4. It is short and quick method.
5. It helps in the development of self confidence and self reliance.	5. No development of self confidence and self reliance with the help of this method.
6. Helps in the development of Intellectual abilities.	6. It does not help in the developments of intellectual abilities.
7. It is psychological in nature.	7. It is unpsychological in nature.
8. Approach is scientific in nature.	8. Approach is unscientific in nature.
9. It is a formative method.	9. It is an informative method.
10. It develops originality and creativity with reasoning.	10. More stress on memory of the child without reasoning.
11. This method leads in the discovery of something new.	11. This method does not lead on the discovery of something new.
12. Subject matter becomes solid and durable for a longer time.	12. It is time being and the content is not durable for a longer time.
13. Proof can be easily recollected if forgotten.	13. Once forgotten proof can not be recollected.

The Relationship. Analysis is aften identified with induction and synthesis with deduction. Both analysis and synthesis are required in induction as well as in deduction. We analyse in order to see the relation better. Thorndike seems to think that all thought, at any rate, all the highest intellectual performance of the mind is analysis. He remarked, "The mind's most intellectual act to connect one thing with the other, but its highest performance is to think a thing apart into its elements." But most of the philosophers, educationalists and logicians says that the highest form of man's intellectual activity is synthesis. The confusion is due to the mixing up of the original or the root meaning of these words and the meaning given by the various investigators in the different fields of thought. According to N. Kuppuswami:

In logic and mathematics we analyse in order to findout how these things can be combined together to make up the whole?

Synthesis means more or less the same—the putting together of the analysed elements so as to bring about the desired effect. Therefore, in all the cases it is the purpose that governs their meanings. Hence we can say that synthesis is the complement of analysis and in logic and mathematics the two always go together. Moreover Analysis leads to synthesis and synthesize makes clear and complete the purpose of analysis. We cannot synthesis without analysing or analysis without synthesis. Analysis is useless followed by synthesis. Just as we cannot have induction without deduction or deduction without induction. It should be noted that analysis helps the mind to synthesise, but actual synthesis, consists in the mind seeing through the common elements.

Hence analysis is the instrument used, and the final result is the outcome of the process of synthesising the analysed facts. This is the reason why philosophers think that synthesis is the highest form of intellectual activity.

Laboratory Method

To make mathematics more interesting and meaningful, Laboratory method is used in teaching of mathematics. In this method students get the opportunity to acquint themselves with the facts through direct experiences individually. In this method student themselves verify the facts and laws of mathematics with the help of experiments. This method needs a laboratory in which equipments and other useful teaching aids related to mathematics are available. For example—equipments related to geometry, mensuration, mathematical model, chart, balance, various figures and shapes made up of wood or hardboard, graph paper, etc.

Procedure. In this method the pupils carry out experiment themselves in the laboratory and gain knowledge through direct experiences. They themselves find the solution by viewing, observing and calculating They establish and verify a law or principle in their own words. The teacher observes the student's working from time to time and guides them by giving instructions whenever needed. Thus in this method the teacher also has to be active with the students. In this method pupils arrive at some conclusion by active participation so this develops creative and heuristic attitude amongst them. This method is more useful and scientific as compared to other methods. The success and effectiveness of experiments in laboratory depend upon the ability, capacity and intelligence of both teacher and student.

Example—"Sum of three angles of a triangle is 180°." How we can prove this in the laboratory.

Objective—To prove that sum of the three angles of a triangle is equal to two right angles or 180°.

Appratus—Card board sheet, pencil, scale, triangle and other necessary equipments.

Procedure—In the laboratory pupils will be given one cardboard sheet each and then they are told how to draw (make) triangles of different sizes on it. After drawing the triangles they cut this separately with the help of scissors.

Observation—Students will measure the angles of the triangles drawn and write these in a tabular form—

Figure No.	Measure of Different Angles			Total (sum)
	∠A	∠B	∠C	∠A + ∠B + ∠C
1	90°	60°	30°	180°
2	120°	30°	30°	180°
3	60°	60°	60°	180°

Calculation—After measuring the angles of different triangles in the form of cardboard sheet. We calculate their sum.

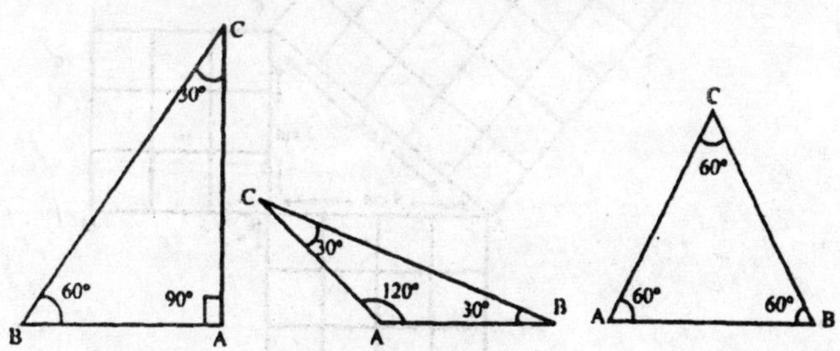

Fig. Triangles of different sized measure

1. In figure 1—

$$\angle A = 90°, \angle B = 60°, \angle C = 30°$$
$$\angle A + \angle B + \angle C = 90° + 60° + 30° = 180°$$

2. In figure 2—

$$\angle A = 120°, \angle B = 30°, \angle C = 30°$$
$$\angle A + \angle B + \angle C = 120° + 30° + 30° = 180°$$

3. In figure 3—

$$\angle A = 60°, \angle B = 60°, \angle C = 60°$$
$$\angle A + \angle B + \angle C = 60° + 60° + 60° = 180°$$

Result—In this way by calculating the three angles of a triangle the students will be able to conclude with inductive reasoning that the sum of three angles of a triangle is 180° or two right angles. The students will generalise the result drawn.

In this way in other triangles by giving the measure of two angles, the third angle can be measured and can be understood by the students.

Example 2—To prove Pythagorous Theorem by Laboratory method

$$(\text{Hypotenuse})^2 = (\text{Perpendicular})^2 + (\text{Base})^2$$

This theorem can be proved by children in the laboratory by following method—

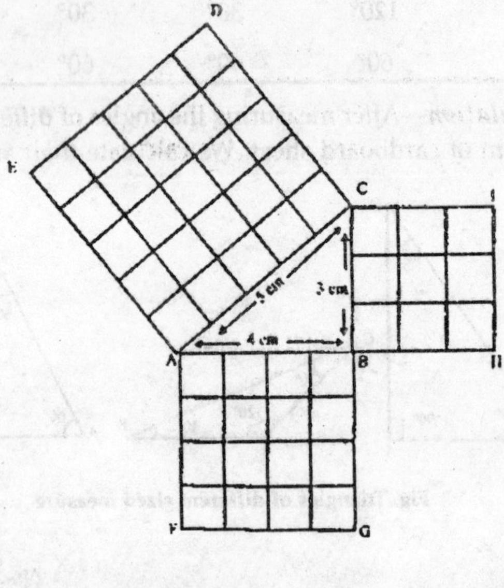

(i) To make the theorem clear the teacher will ask to the students to prepare a hard board or wooden model in which perpendicular = 3 cm, Base = 4 cm, and Hypotenuse = 5 cm.

(ii) Students will make a model related to the theorem according to given measures,

(iii) After making the model, the squares drawn on three sides of the triangle are divided into squares of sides 1 cm as shown in the figure by dotted lines.

(iv) In this way the students will observe the squares drawn on perpendicular, base and hypotenuse.

No. of squares on base ABGF = 16.

No. of squares on perpendicular BCIH = 9.

No. of squares on hypotenuse ACDE = 25.

To make the experiment more interesting, a creative and effective teacher can tell students to cut squares drawn on perpendicular and base and then arrange these on hypotenuse ACDE by cutting them separately.

(v) In this way by observing themselves students can draw this conclusion, that—

(a) No. of squares drawn on hypotenuse = 25.

(b) No. of squares drawn on perpendicular and base = 9 + 16 = 25. On the basis of direct observation and experiences students can draw this conclusion and can understand the theorem with the help of experiment. Thus the conclusion drawn is—

$$(\text{Hypotenuse})^2 = (\text{Perpendicular})^2 + (\text{Base})^2$$

For the success of Laboratory Method the teacher should keep following points in his/her mind. These are—

(a) The objectives of different branches of mathematics as Arithmetic, Algebra, Geometry, Trigonometry, etc., which can be taught with the help of this method should be decided well in advance.

(b) Equipments and other necessary things related to the experiments should be made available in advance.

(c) Teacher should observe the work of students and should guide them properly while experimenting in the laboratory.

(d) Students should be encouraged and assisted in order to make the experiment successful so that they can get best possible practical knowledge.

(e) Theoretical knowledge related to the topic or objective should be given before experimenting.

(f) The steps and procedure of experiment should be made clear so that students do not face any problem while experimenting.

(g) In case of large number of students in a class they can be divided into groups.

Merits

* This method is based on psychological principle, "learning by doing" so that students take interest in their work.
* The knowledge acquired by this method is more solid and durable.
* This method presents mathematics as a practical subject.
* It helps in developing the habit of discovery and self-study.
* The knowledge acquired by this method is more meaningful.
* This method helps in the development of observation and logical power amongst the students.
* It develops scientific attitude in the students.
* It helps to develop positive attitude towards mathematics.
* This method helps in developing problem-solving ability.

* The problems of Algebra and geometry can be solved easily by the use of this method.
* The children get the opportunity of creative and practical work.
* This method helps in developing self-confidence amongst students.
* The children enjoy as they remain active in the laboratory.
* The children learn the use of different equipments which are used in laboratroy.

Demerits

* It is an expensive method so due to financial constraints, all schools are not able to adopt this method.
* This method can be used for a small class only.
* It takes more time to teach so vast syllabus can not be completed with in the time.
* This method requires laboratroy equipped with different apparatus.
* Individual attention cannot be paid to classes with large number of students.
* This is not fit for students of lower classes because they cannot perform experiments in the laboratory.
* Only some topics of mathematics can be taught by the use of this method.
* All mathematics teachers cannot use this method effectively.
* It is not an easy job to prove all mathematical principles, laws and formulae in the laboratory.
* It is exceedingly laborious and slow method.

In this way a teacher can use this method effectively in Mathematics teaching by keeping its merits and demerits in mind, and he/his can make his/her teaching more effective. Different mathematical laws, formulae principles etc. can be proved in the laboratory. Some experiments related to Mathematics which a student can easily verify in the laboratory are as follows—

(i) Experiments related to weight and measurement.

(ii) Experiments related to speed, time, distance, work and average.

(iii) To prepare a table of square roots and cube roots of numbers and to calculate their values.

(iv) To calculate area, volume and surface area of different geometrical figures or shapes and prepare their models.

(v) To represent different mathematical numbers in figures.

(vi) To prove different theorems of conic section and to make models related to them.

(vii) To collect Mathematical facts, laws, formulae etc. and to prepare their table or chart.

Difference between Laboratory and Demonstration Method

The difference between laboratory and demonstration method can be explained by following points—

Laboratory Method	Demonstration Method
1. This is a psychological method and it is based upon the principle of "Learning by doing".	1. This method is not appropriate form the psychological point of view. It is based upon the principle of "see , hear and understand."
2. By this method creative and searching habits can developed in students.	2. In this method students do not get opportunity to develop their creative and investigation powers.
3. In this method students get direct experiences by experimenting individually in the laboratory.	3. In this method teacher himself demonstrates the related experiment while teaching in the class-room.
4. In this students use different type of experiments and do different activities in the laboratory.	4. In this students see different equipments, experiments and processes in class room only.

5. Students are more active in this method in comparison to teacher.	5. In this teacher is more active than students.
6. This is an expensive method.	6. This is not an expensive method.
7. New facts can be discovered by this method. And formulae and principles can used by learning these practically.	7. New facts can not be discovered by Demonstration method.
8. This method has very slow speed so it takes more time.	8. This has fast speed in comparison so it takes less time.
9. Scientific attitude developed in students by this method.	9. It provides very less opportunities for the development of scientific attitude.

Heuristic Method

Like other method Heuristic method also has a special place in mathematics teaching. The word heuristic is believed to be originated from Greek word "Heurisco" which means "I find out". The profounder of this method was Proff. Henery Edward Armstrong.

This method is more important from educational point of view because in this method students work like a researcher and solve the problems.

By the use of this method scientific and mathematical attitude can be developed in students. Herbert Spencer has thrown light on this method and stated that—"Students should be told minimum and as much as possible they should be encouraged to discover."

Definition : According to Prof. H.E. Armstrong—"This is the method of teaching which places the pupils as far as possible in the attitude of a discover."

According to Westaway—The Heuristic method is intended to provide a training in method. Knowledge is a secondary consideration all together.

Therefore, the main aim of this method is to make the student a researcher or discoverer.

In this method more emphasis is given on 'How the

knowledge can be obtained rather than the teaching of facts, principles etc?"

Example—The population of a city is 50,000. If percentage increase in population is 4% per year then find out the population of the city after 2 years.

Solution—Teacher will tell the students to repeat this question many times and will tell them to find the solution with the help of suitable rearching questions and he will encourage them for finding correct solution. We can understand the solution of the problem with the help of questions asked by the teacher.

The question asked by the teacher and expected answers given by the students are listed in the following table—

Question asked by Teacher	Expected answer given by students
1. What has to be calculated in the given question?	1. Population of city after 2 years.
2. How can we find out this?	2. First we find population after one year.
3. What is percentage increase in population every year?	3. 4% increase per year.
4. How can we find population at the end of first year ?	4. Students can find that increase in population at the end of first year = 50,000 × 4/100 = 2000
5. In this way what will be the total population at at the end of first year?	5. Students can tell after solving that— Population at the end of first year = 50,000 + 2000 = 52,000.
6. Population increase for second year can be calculated on which figure?	6. Students tell that population increase for second year can be calculated on 52000.
7. How can we calculate this increase.	7. Students can solve by their efforts. Population increases at the end of second year— = 52000 × 4/100 = 2080

8. Now how to calculate the population at the end of second year?	8. Students will be able to understand that population of the two years will be = 52000 + 2080 = 54080.

In this way solution to the given problem can be found by Heuristic method. Similarly other problems can also be solved. The books should be written on heuristic lines.

So that it will be easy for the students to work. Inspire of so many merits this method has some demerits. This method is not very useful practically because knowledge gained by this method is not sufficient. This method can prove to be more useful if teacher teaches keeping in mind the discovery attitude curiosity and other needs of students. This method should be used for certain objectives only when pupils will have sufficient knowledge of mathematics. If the attitude of students is kept explorative or heuristic in Inductive, Deductive, Analystic, Synthetic and laboratory methods etc., then these methods can also take the form of heuristic method.

N. Kuppuswami Aiyanger have pointed out that the heuristic method is intended to change the passive recipient of knowledge into an active independent enquirer and discoverer of knowledge. The maxims, 'Practice makes a man perfect' and 'Learning by doing' are applicable not only to physical activities but to intellectual activities also. The main purpose of this method is to train the pupil to think. This is very important method from educational point of view because scientific and mathematical attitude is developed in the minds of students. The success of this method depends upon the teacher. As a general rule it can be said, 'Give the minimum amount of help, donot tell anything which the child can find out for him self. Avoid leading questions, let the questions be such as require real thinking on the part of the pupil to find solutions for'. Too much help is of course against the spirit of this method.

Moreover, it is the essance of all the methods. Any method of teaching mathematics that develops in the pupils the attitude of doing thinking and discovering by themselves is heuristic. Infact, the heuristic method, in a sense, in not a method of teaching but an attitude.

Merits

(i) This is a psychological method.

(ii) It develops self-confidence, self-reliance and scientific attitude.

(iii) It develops ability of observation and spirit of enquiry to solve the problems.

(iv) This method makes them exact and brings them closer to truth.

(v) Contemplation and awakening increases in the children.

(vi) The knowledge obtained by this method is more stable.

(vii) Pupil gets the opportunity to develop the mental and thinking powers.

(viii) This method is based on the psychological principles. Learning by doing takes place in this method.

(ix) This method is based on the principle of activity.

(x) Individual attention of the teacher is possible and the relation between the teacher and learner becomes more intimate.

Demerits

1. It is not suitable for lower classes.
2. It is a very slow method.
3. It is very lengthy method. Whole syllabus cannot be finished in the limited time.
4. It is very expensive method.
5. There is lack of text-books written on heuristic approach.
6. This is formational method rather than informational.

7. It presupposes a very small class. Which is not possible in Indian conditions.

Project Method

Project method was advocated by Kilpatrick, an American educationist. This method is based on pragmatic philosophy. This method consists chiefly of building a comprehensive unit around an activity which may be carried on in the school or outside. It involves a variety of activities. In this method all the students work co-operatively.

Definitions of Project

According to Kilpatrick—"A project is a whole-hearted purposeful activity proceeding in a social environment."

According to Stevenson—"A project is a problematic act carried to completion in its natural setting."

According to Ballard—"A project is a bit of real life that has been imported into school."

It is clear from the above definition that a project is a purposeful and problematic activity which is achieved in natural, real and social environment. In this method the problem is presented in a practical and real sense.

Types of Project. Generally projects are of the two type.

1. Individual Projects, and
2. Group Projects

According to Kilpatrick, there are four types of projects—

1. Creative or constructive Projects.
2. Artistic Projects.
3. Problematic Projects.
4. Drill Projects

Steps

Following steps are involved in project method—

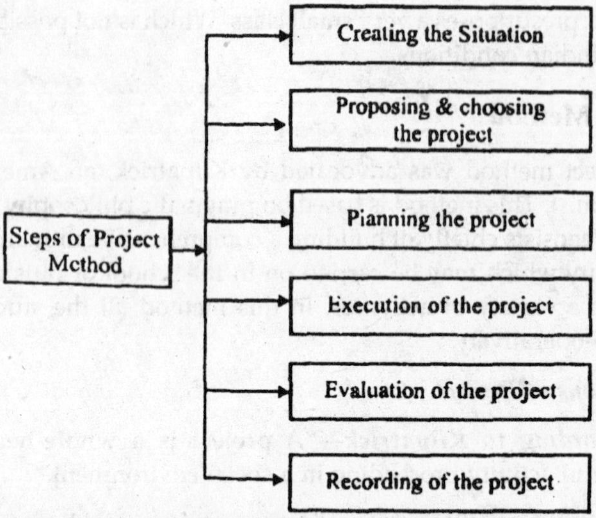

Creating the Situation. The teacher creates problematic situation in front of students while creating the appropriate situation student's interest and abilities should be given due importance.

Proposing and choosing the project. While choosing a problem teacher should stimulate discussions by making suggestions. The proposed project should be according to the real need of students. The purpose of the projects should be well defined and understood by the children.

Planning the Project. For the success of the project, planning of project is very import. The children should plan out the whole project under the guidance of their teacher. It should be kept in mind that every child should be encouraged and motivated to participate in the discussion. All the children should be asked to write the plan in a proper manner. The teacher should also assign duties and distribute the work among the children according to their interests.

Execution of the Project. Every child should contribute actively in the execution of the project. It is the longest step in the project. While distributing the work during execution of the problem interest of children must be considered. For example a child interested in reading should be assigned the task of reference books and literature. One interested in physical work should be given the similar work. The teacher should guide and observe the progress of the projects.

Evaluation of the Project. When the project is completed the teacher and the children should evaluate it jointly discussed whether the objectives of the project have been achieved or not. The children discuss their work and rectify their doubts and mistakes. Thus the whole project is reviewed by the children under the guidance of teacher.

Recording of the Project. This is also an important step of the project method because the work done should be recorded also. The children maintain a complete record of the project work. While recording the project some points like-how the project was planned, what discussions were made, how duties were assigned, how it was evaluated etc. should be kept in mind.

Merits

* This is based on various psychological laws and principles.
* The children remain active throughout the execution of the project.
* It develops the value of dignity of labour because children perform physical as well mental work.
* This is based on principle of activity, reality, effect, and learning by doing etc.
* It develops co-operative feeling and group-interaction.
* The gained knowledge becomes solid and durable.
* The child realizes his responsibilities and duties.
* It is democratic and scientific in nature.
* It is based on the principle of individual differences.
* It develops discovery attitude in the child.
* It develops self confidence and self discipline.

Demerit

* It takes more time.
* The knowledge is not acquired in a sequentials and systematic manner.
* It is very difficult to complete the whole syllabus by the use of this method.
* It is not economical.
* In this method it is assumed that the teacher has an, all-round knowledge of every subject which is practically not possible.
* Text books and written learning material on project method are not available.
* There is no provision for drill and practice for skills required in mathematics.
* In this method the teaching and learning become disorganised, irregular and discontinuous.
* In this method the teacher has to work as a careful guide during the planning, executing, evaluating and recording the project.

Role of the Teacher

* The teacher should provide democratic atmosphere in the classroom.
* The teacher should be active and careful all the time to observe the progress of the project.
* The teacher should work as a friend, guide and working partner.
* He should give chance to shy and introvert pupils to come forward and participate actively.
* The teacher should have thorough knowledge and experiences.

Some More Projects

* Execution of school bank.
* Study of school budget.
* Running of Book-Bank.
* Execution of Hostel mess.
* Collection and study of the currency of different countries.
* Study of the working of Bank and post office.
* Uses of mathematics in large and small business.
* Collection of data about National and provincial budgets.
* Executing the activities of mathematics club.
* Bus and train fares.
* Collection of data regarding population, death rate, birth rate etc.

Problem Solving Method

The child is curious by nature. He wants to findout solutions of many problems which sometimes are puzzling even to the adults. Nevertheless, he must be helped to satisfy his curiosity, whenever possible, by solving various problems. We must teach the pupils how to think so that they are able to transfer these techniques to a vast number of varied problematic situations. Life is full of problems and the successful man in life is he, who is fully equipped with adequate knowledge and reasoning power to tackle these problems. The solution of these problems enables him to have a mastery over his environment. Whenever there is some obstruction in the teaching-learning situation, we say that there is some problems. It is a difficulty that is clearly present and recognized by the learner. It may be a purely mental difficulty or it may be physical and involve the manipulation of data. The children recognise it as a challenge.

Definitions

1. "Problem solving is a set of events in which human being was rules to achieve some goals." — *Gagne*

2. "Problem solving may be defined as a process of raising a problem in the minds of students in such a way as to stimulate purposeful reflective thinking in arriving at a rational solution." —*Risk.*

3. "Problem solving involves concept formation and discovery learning." —*Ausubel.*

Characteristics

A problem should have following characteristics :

* The problem should be meaningful, interesting and practical.
* It should be well defined.
* It should have some educational value.
* As much as possible the problem should be related with the daily life of the child.
* It should be challenging so that the powers of thinking and reasoning can be developed.
* It should have correlation with other study subjects also.
* It should be related with the previous knowledge of the child.
* It should be according to the mental and physical level of the child.
* It should develop imagination and critical powers.
* It should develop mathematical skills.
* It should develop scientific attitude amongst the children.

Steps

1. Selection and formation of Problem.
2. Presentation of the Problem.
3. Formulation of hypothesis.
4. Collection of relevant data and informations.

5. Analysis and organisation of data.
6. Drawing conclusions.
7. Testing of conclusions.

Selection and Formulation of Problem—The nature of problem should be made very clear to the pupils. The pupil should feel the necessity of finding out the solution of the problem which is selected and formulated. The selection of the problem should be done by the teacher and child both.

Presentation of the Problem—After selecting and formulating a problem, teacher should present the problem well before the students. The teacher should also make it clear that how this problem can be solved and how the related data and informations can be collected to get the solution of the Problem.

Formulation of Hypothesis—Formulation of hypothesis means; preparation of a list of possible reasons of the occurrence of the problem. Formulation of hypothesis develops thinking and reasoning powers of the child. It should be kept in mind that formulated hypothesis must be testable.

Collection of Relevant Data and Information—The child should be stimulated to collect data and information in a systematic and scientific manner. The teacher can suggest many points regarding collection of data to the students. He can ask them to refer extra books and literature.

Analysis and Organisation of Data—On the basis of collected data and information, the formulated hypothesis are tested. Various statistical techniques are used to analyse and organize the data.

Drawing conclusions—After analysising and organising the data, conclusions are drawn. The selection and rejection of hypothesis is made on the basis of data. Care should be taken that judgements are made only when sufficient data is collected. Discussions and conclusions should be arranged collectively or individually with each child.

Testing of Conclusions—No conclusions should be accepted without being properly verified. The students must be asked to be critical while testing conclusions. Thus the correctness of the conclusions is proved by applying them in new or different situations.

Example: Define union of two sets. If $A = \{2, 3, 5\}$, $B = \{3, 5, 6\}$ and $C = \{4, 6, 8, 9\}$. Prove that $A \cup (B \cup C) = (A \cup B) \cup C$.

Solution—

Step. l. After selecting and understanding the problem the child will be able to define the problem in his own words that the union of two sets A and B is the set which contains all the members of set A and all the members of set B. The union of two sets A and B is expressed as '$A \cup B$' and symbolically represented as—

$$A \cup B = \{x : x \in A \text{ or } x \Leftarrow B\}$$

or $$x \in (A \cup B) \Rightarrow x \in A \text{ or } x \in B.$$

The common elements are taken only once in the union of two sets.

Step. 2 — After defining the problem in his own words, the child will analyse the given problem that how the problem can be solved?

Step. 3 — After analysing the various aspects of the problem he will be able to make hypothesis that first of all he should calculate the union of sets B and C i.e. $B \cup C$. Then the Union of set A and, $B \cup C$. Thus he can get the value of $A \cup (B \cup C)$. Similarly he can solve $(A \cup B) \cup C$.

Step. 4 — Then on the basis of given data, the child will be able to solve the problem in the following manner :

In the example it is given that

$$A = \{2, 3, 5\},$$

$$B = \{3, 5, 6\} \text{ and}$$

$$C = \{4, 6, 8, 9\}$$

$$\therefore \quad B \cup C = \{3, 5, 6\} \cup \{4, 6, 8, 9\}$$

$$= \{3, 4, 5, 6, 8, 9\}$$

$$\therefore \quad A \cup (B \cup C) = \{2, 3, 5\} \cup \{3, 4, 5, 6, 8, 9\}$$

$$= \{2, 3, 4, 5, 6, 8, 9\}$$

Similarly,

$$A \cup B = \{2, 3, 5\} \cup \{3, 5, 6\}$$

$$= \{2, 3, 5, 6\}$$

$$\therefore \quad (A \cup B) \cup C = \{2, 3, 5, 6\} \cup \{4, 6, 8, 9\}$$

$$= \{2, 3, 4, 5, 6, 8, 9\}$$

Step. 5—After solving the problem the child will analyse the result on the basis of given data and verify his hypothesis whether $A \cup (B \cup C)$ is equals to $(A \cup B) \cup C$ or not.

Step. 6—After testing and verifying his hypothesis the child will be able to conclude that

$$A \cup (B \cup C) = (A \cup B) \cup C$$

Thus the child generalises the results and apply his knowledge in new situations.

Merits

* This method is psychological and scientific in nature.
* It helps in developing good study habits and reasoning powers.
* It helps to improve and apply knowledge and experiences.
* This method stimulates thinking of the child.
* It helps to develop the power of expression of the child.
* The child learns how to act in new situation.
* It develops group feeling while working together.
* It helps to verify an opinion and satisfies curiosity.
* Learning becomes more interesting and is easily assimilated as it is the result of a purposeful activity.

* This method helps in maintaining discipline in the class.
* Teachers becomes familiar with his pupils.
* It develops analytical, critical and generalization abilities of the child.

Demerits

* This is not suitable for lower classes.
* There is lack of suitable books and references for children.
* It is not economical. It is wastage of time and energy.
* Teachers find it difficult to cover the prescribed syllabus.
* Mental activities are more emphasized as compared to physical activities.
* To follow this method talented teachers are required.
* There is always doubt of drawing wrong conclusions.

Teaching Factors

In general the factors affecting the methods of teaching can be classified as fellows—

Factors Related with Instructional Objectives—The usefulness and practicability of instructional objectives affects the selection of teaching method. So before selecting the method of teaching the teacher should decide the instructional objectives. Keeping in mind, the mental level, interest and attitude of children, he should use that method in an effective manner.

Factors Related with Content—Content is that matter whose communication is the main basis of teaching. Therefore, the nature and standard of content affects the selection of teaching methods in real sense. That is why the school curriculum should be based on the principles of "Activity centered" or "Learning by doing" and "Learning through Experiences" so that learning of children become more effective.

Factors Related to Teacher—The teacher has most active role in teaching process. The teaching process can be made more powerful and effective by using teaching methods. The power of communication of the teacher, this facilities available to him and time can affect the selection of any teaching method. Apart from this the law capability of the teacher, less knowledge of the subject and dissatisfactory professional training also affects his work.

Factors Related to Students—From psychological point of view, the child is centre of all teaching Methods. So his mentality, ability, interest, will to learn and attitude affects the selection of teaching method. Therefore, the teacher should keep all these things in his mind before selecting any specific method.

Precautions While Selecting Methods of Teaching—A successful mathematics teacher should has some precautions before selecting a method of teaching, so that the method selected by him be effective and useful to the students. The secondary education commission/Mudaliar Commission (1952-1953)has thrown light on the following points regarding the selection of teaching methods—

1. The aim of teaching methods should not only be to provide maximum knowledge to the students but the education should be provided in such a way that they themselves gain knowledge by their efforts.
2. The teacher should select such a method by which children can develop desirable values, good attitude and habit to work hard.
3. The teaching method should develop different skills, honesty, self dependence and self-reliance amongst the children.
4. The teacher should keep in mind the individual differences of the children while selecting a specific method, so that the children of all levels; average, below average and sharp mind can get opportunity to learn according to their abilities, mental power and speed.
5. The children should be given opportunity to work together in groups.

6. In mathematics emphasis should not be given on verbalism and memorization.
7. Such a teaching method should be selecting by which the knowledge given be purposeful, concrete and real.
8. Such method should be selected by which the children get proper opportunities to apply or use the acquired knowledge.

Like in other subjects. Many methods are common in mathematics teaching. But now the question is that which method is more useful? It is better to leave this decision to the teacher because he has the closest relationship with teaching learning process.

A successful, intelligent and experienced teacher should keep in mind, the mental level, interest, habits and attitude of children before selecting a method. Along with this the teacher should also keep in mind the individual differences, because by using proper and effective method, the children take interest in mathematics.

Conclusions. Methods of teaching have an intimate relationship with teaching and instructional objectives. Methods are the way or mode to understand and practice the art of teaching. The word method has been drived from Latin word which means 'Mode' or 'Way'. Therefore the process of imparting the world of knowledge to pupil's mind is called the method of teaching. It is just a way to teach. Generally, children like that method which makes the subject matter more clear and easily understandable.

The Philosophy

Idealists—Not adopted any scientific and definite method of teaching like—lecture, discussion, etc.

Realists—emphasized scientific and objective method like—heuristic, experimental etc.

Naturalists—emphasized learning by doing, learning by experiences, montessori, Dalton etc.

Pragmatists—also emphasized the principles of learning by doing, learning by experiences etc. On the basis of these principles kilpatric advocated project method.

Herbart Spancer emphasized that methods of teaching should be based on some principles like—from simple to complex, contrele to abstract, known to unknown, direct to indirect etc.

Methods and Techinques

I.K. Davis remarked that strategies are broad methods of teaching and instruction. The main objective of methods is the impressive presentation while main objective of techniques is to create complete learning situations.

The Categorisation

Child-centred Methods—The child occupies a central position in the classroom, e.g. Project, laboratory etc.

Teacher-Centred Methods—The teacher occupies a central position in the classroom, e.g. Lecture, Demonstration, Historical etc.

Various Methods

Procedure, Merits, and Demerits

1. Lecture
2. Demonstration
3. Lecture-cum-demonstration
4. Inductive-deductive.
5. Analytic-synthetic
6. Laboratory
7. Heuristic
8. Project
9. Problem-solving.

There are many factors which affect the methods of teaching

such as factors related with instructional objectives, content teaches and students.

The method should develop desirable values, attitude, habit of work hard, various skills, self dependence, co-operative feeling, confidence, etc.

QUESTIONS

(A) Essay type Questions

1. What is the difference between laboratory and demonstration method of mathematics teaching? Giving an example from mathematics clarify the application of Laboratory method.
2. What do you understand by inductive method in mathematics teaching? By taking a situation, explain how this method can be applied.
3. What is the utility of inductive-deductive method in mathematics teaching? Clarify with suitable examples.
4. What is analytic method of teaching mathematics. Give a comparative study of analytic and synthetic method.
5. What do you mean by project method of teaching mathematics? Discuss its merits and demerits.
6. Clarify the Heuristic method of teaching mathematics and explain its merits and demerits.
7. "No induction is complete without deduction." Explain this statement and mention the merits and demerits of inductive method.
8. In which situation Lecture and Discussion method can be applied in mathematics? Discuss.
9. What is problem solving method? Explain with suitable example. Discuss its importance in mathematics teaching.
10. What do you mean by Demonstration method? Explain with an example.

11. Write notes on following—
    (a) Difference between deductive and inductive method.
    (b) Advantages and disadvantages of Lecture method.
    (c) Factors which affect the teaching methods.
    (d) Precautions in the selection of suitable method.
    (e) Difference between Laboratory and Demonstration method.
12. Discuss the lecture method in teaching of mathematics. How a mathematics teacher can improve his lecture?

(B) Objective Type Questions

Write answer selecting the right choice—

1. Appropriate method for the establishment of the formulae in mathematics is—

   (a) Induction (c) Planning
   (b) Synthesis (d) None of these

2. The method based upon real thinking, experiments and inspection—

   (a) Analysis (c) Synthesis
   (b) Deduction (d) Laboratory

3. 'Unknown to known' is advanced in which method—

   (a) Synthesis (c) Deduction
   (b) Analysis (d) Induction

4. Project method was advocated by —

   (a) Kilpatrick (c) Gagne
   (b) Ballard (d) None of these

5. Meaning of the word 'Heurisco' is—

   (a) To know (c) To learn
   (b) To think (d) To discover

6. The method based on scientific method is—

   (a) Induction (c) Project
   (b) Speech (d) None of these

True/False Statement

Write 'True' for right statement and 'False' for wrong statement—

1. The Heuristic method is the method which can be applied any number of the student.
2. The inspection and experiment remain absent in speech method.
3. The laboratory method is helpful in the achievement of high levelled cognitive objectives.
4. The lecture method is suitable for the students of all levels.
5. Time can be saved in Induction method.
6. Synthetic method is psychological.
7. In analytic method, there is analysis of facts as well as their logics are also presented.
8. The demonstration method is based on the principle of induction.
9. In Discussion method, importance is not given to the social and psychological principles.
10. Concept formation and invention of learning are included in Problem-solving method.
11. Lecture cum demonstration method is the modified form of lecture and demonstration method.

7
Teaching Aims

Education is a process of bringing about changes in the individual in desired directions, such as the development of interests, attitudes and skills, to carry out the certain activities. This help the child to lead a happy, productive and socially acceptable life. An objective presents the end point towards which action is directed and therefore it reflects the purposefulness of the educational process. It represents the first step in the teaching-learning process because it is the starting point of activities planning and instruction. It also provides basis for selection of evaluation procedures and curriculum development. Thus objectives validate whole teaching-learning process. objectives

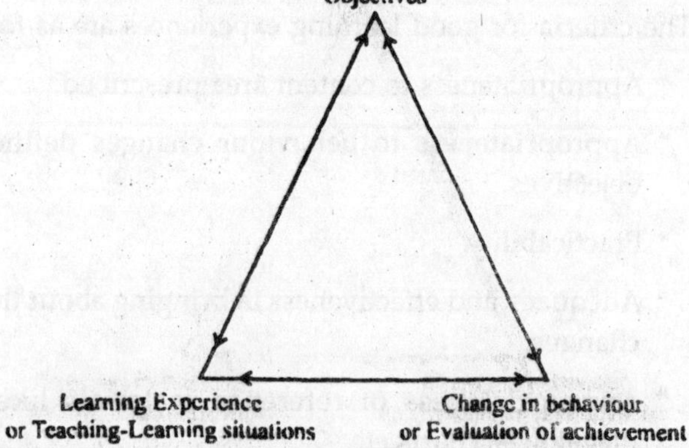

Dr. B.S. Bloom accepted education as a triangular process. The poles are objectives, learning experiences (Means) and change in behaviours (evidences). The relationships between these poles can be shown as follows—

It is clear from the above diagram that objectives are the basis for teaching activities and evaluation techniques. The learning experiences are provided by teaching activities in order to achieve objectives and change in behaviour is evaluated in terms of objectives.

Learning—Learning is change in behaviour of the child.

Behaviour—Behaviour refers to any visible activity displayed by the learner.

Terminal Behaviour—This refers to behaviour or performance demonstrated by the learner at the end of the lesson.

Criterion—Criterion refers to standards or test by which terminal behaviour is evaluated.

Learning Experiences—Learning experiences may be defined as-learning experiences are pupil activities planned with the specific purpose of producing the desired behavioural changes in them. In providing learning experiences in mathematics we should formulate appropriate learning situations and activities for the people. Also, we should start with the objectives and their clarification in terms of pupil behaviours.

Process of Learning

The criteria for good learning experiences are as follows—

* Appropriateness to content area prescribed.
* Appropriateness to behaviour changes defined under objectives.
* Practicability.
* Adequacy and effectiveness in bringing about the desired changes.
* Appropriateness of reference materials like—books, magazines, charts etc.

Motives and Purposes

Aims of Teaching **:** Before we proceed further, we must briefly differentiate objectives from aims in order to avoid confusions. Aims are general and long term goals and may be common to more than one subject. Long term goals refer to high level aims and tend to be related to broad reasons, why a particular subject or activities are being organised or why a particular course is being done. Thus aims or long term goals can be regarded as expressions of strategy. While objectives are specific, immediate and attainable goals, specific to one subject, precise and clearly defined, objectives are more directly concerned with what specifically is being attempted over a relatively short period.

General Aims. The general aims of teaching mathematics are as follows—

1. To enable the child to understand the use of numbers and quantities related to their daily life.
2. To enable the child to solve mathematical problems of his daily life.
3. To create a suitable type of discipline in the mind of the child.
4. To familiarise the child with the latest mathematical knowledge to fulfil the existing needs of the society.
5. To give knowledge about the broad objectives of teaching mathematics such as—knowledge, understanding, application etc.
6. To develop in the child fundamental skills and process of mathematics.
7. To develop in the child a sense of appreciation of cultural arts.
8. To prepare the child for elementary as well as higher education in science, engineering etc.
9. To develop the habit of concentration, self-confidence, self-reliance and discovery.
10. To develop in the child the mental powers like thinking, reasoning etc.

11. To develop scientific and realistic attitude towards life.
12. To give practical knowledge of mathematics to face the day-to-day problems.
13. To prepare the child for technical professions such as those of accounts, audits, bankers, surveyors, cashiers, scientists, architects and mathematics teachers.
14. To bring an all-round and harmonous development of the personality of the child.
15. To develop the sense of appreciation of mathematical knowledge and contribution of mathematicians.
16. To develop the skills to use the modern mathematical devices like computers etc.
17. To develop the abilities of analysis, synthesis, reasoning, computation etc.
18. To develop interest in mathematics.

On the basis of values of teaching mathematics, the aims of teaching mathematics have been classified as follows—

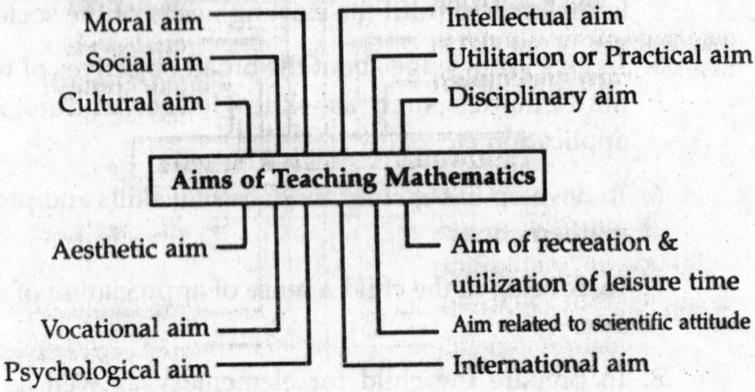

The detail explanation of above aims of teaching mathematics is not given here. They have been discussed in the previous chapter in the form of values of teaching mathematics. Other eminent educationist and writers have categorised the aims of teaching mathematics as follows—

Aims of teaching Mathematics
- Disciplinary aim
- Cultural aim
- Utilitarian or Practical aim

Objectives of Teaching. The objectives imply the changes that we try to bring about in the children. According to NCERT's Evaluation and Examination issue. "An objective is a point or end in view of some thing towards which action is directed, a planned change sought through any activity what we set out to do."

In other words we can say that the objective is a statement or a form of category which suggests any kind of change. It indicates the direction of pupil's growth and provides basis for selection of evaluation procedures. Objectives provide link between teachers, pupils, testers and parents by focussing their attention with intended outcomes of learning. Thus objectives validate the process of education. Hence objectives have the following characteristics—

* They provide direction to the activities.
* They help for the planned change.
* They provide basis for organising teaching-learning activities.

An objective obviously has to serve as guideposts in learning or rather, the foundation of an educational programme. A well defined educational objectives provide the basis for systematisation, articulation, unity, balance and for determining priorities in an educational effort. An objective provides basis for planning and organization of learning experiences. The objectives are classified in two categories—

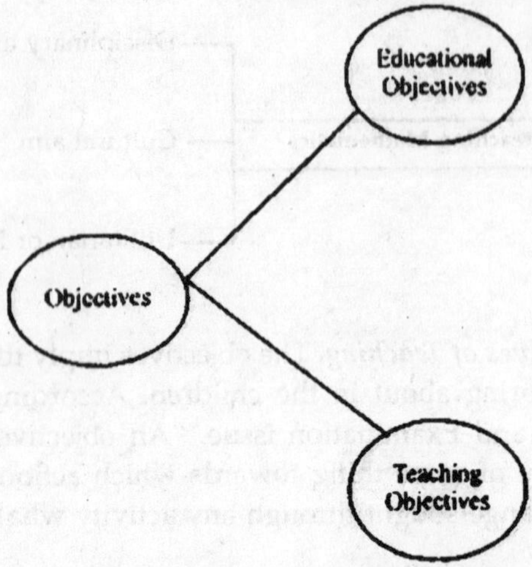

Educational Objectives. Educational objectives are broad and philosophical in nature. They are related to the schools and educational system. E.J. Furst has well defined, "educational objective as a desired change in behaviour of a person that we try to bring about through education." According to B.S. Bloom. "Educational objectives are not only the goals towards which the curriculum is shaped and towards which instruction is guided, but they are also the goals that provide the detailed specification for the curriculum and use of evaluation techniques."

The educational objectives are achieved with the help of teaching or instructional objectives. These include several teaching or instructional objectives.

Teaching objectives are narrow and psychological in nature. Teaching objectives may be achieved in a certain period in the classroom, for example a period of 30 or 35 minutes duration. These are related with the expected change in behaviour of the child. So they are also called behavioural objectives. Teaching objectives are directly related with the learning process and they are well defined, definite, clear, specific and measurable. These give direction to the learning process, learning-experiences and teaching. They provide the foundation of the entire educational structure. Therefore, teaching objectives are also called

Instructional objectives. The teaching strategies methods and techniques are selected on the basis of teaching or instructional objectives.

Difference between Aims and Objectives. Aims and objectives may be compare on the basis of following points—

Aims	Objectives
1. Aims are very broad and comprehensive.	1. Objectives are narrower and specific
2. Philosophy, sociology is main source of aims.	2. Psychology is the main source of objectives.
3. They are not definite and clear.	3. They are definit and clear.
4. They are difficult to achieve.	4. They can be achieved conveniently.
5. Long time duration is needed in order to achieve aims.	5. They need short duration i.e. in the period of class-room teaching.
6. They are subjective.	6. They are objective.
7. These can not be evaluated	7. These can be evaluated.
8. These include objectives	8. Objectives are a part of aims.
9. They are related with the whole education system and whole curriculum.	9. These are related with the teaching and any specific topic.
10. It is the responsibility of school, society and nation to achieve them.	10. Generally teacher is only responsible.
11. These are theoretical and indirect.	11. Objectives are direct and concerned with the teaching learning process.
12. Aims are formal.	12. These are functional and informative.

Various Categories

Dr. Benjamin S. Bloom (1956) has classified the changes of behaviour in three categories or Domains;

1. Cognitive Domain
2. Affective Domain
3. Psychomotor Domain.

All these three domains are interrelated as shown in figure below—

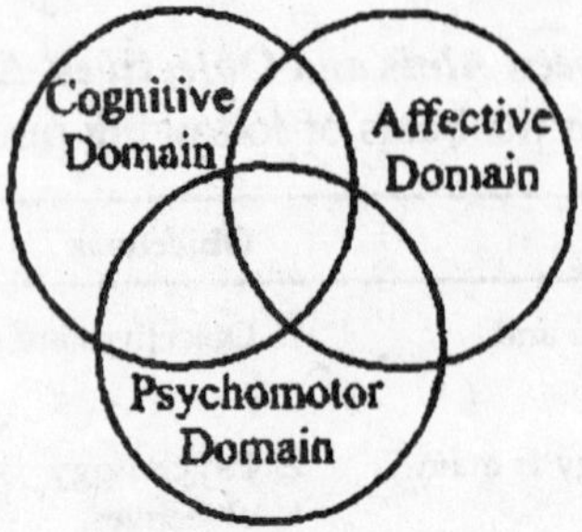

Dr. B.S. Bloom and his associates in the university of Chicago, gave the classification of objectives of all the three domains.

1. Classification of cognitive domain or objectives by Bloom (1956).
2. Affective domain by Krathwohl (1964), and
3. Psychomotor domain by Simpson (1969).

Dr. Bloom concentrated on the study of cognitive Domain. He assumed that in thinking about a problem a hierarchy of cognitive process is involved. While teaching, a teacher follows this hierchical order. This classification of objectives is known as "Taxonomy of educational objectives" or "Bloom's Taxonomy" of objectives.

Taxonomy of Teaching Objectives

S. No.	*Cognitive Domain Category*	*Affective Domain Category*	*Psychomotor Domain Category*
	Dr. B.S. Bloom (1956)	*Krathwohl (1964)*	*Simpson (1969)*
1.	Knowledge	Receiving	Impulsion
2.	Comprehension	Responding	Manipulation
3.	Application	Valuing	Control
4.	Analysis	Conceptualisation	Co-ordination
5.	Synthesis	Organisation	Naturalisation
6.	Evaluation	Characterisation	Habit formation

Cognitive Objective—Cognitive objective stress that the pupils should acquire more and more knowledge. It was defined to include all those activities which deal with the recall or recognition of knowledge and the development of intellectual abilities and skills.

Affective Objective—Affective objective is concerned with the attitude, interest, emotions, values and mental tendencies of the pupils. This part of the taxonomy also includes appreciations and social adjustment of the child.

Psychomotor Objective—This is the third part of taxonomy and includes the manipulative and moto-skill areas. The physical actions involved in handwriting, playing, using equipments, making outline, drawing figures and many others are in the psycho-motor domain.

Bloom defined six main categories in the hierarchy, each higher step encompassing those below. These were in an ascending order of difficulty. The hierarchy of cognitive objective is shown on next page.

Behaviour of Students

After selection and formulation of objectives the next step is to define or write them to specific terms in relation to what the children can do? We should bring about some specific change in what the children act, feel and think? These are the changes that indicate how far that objective has been achieved. Such changes are known as "behaviour or action patterns" or "Pupil's behavioural changes".

It must be noted that the identification and determination of objectives is not an end. It is also essential to define them in terms of pupil's behaviour. Defining objectives means, "making the specifications of objectives in simple language." Therefore the teacher should make it clear in simple language that 'What changes?' and 'What aspects'? are to be brought in order to achieve the objectives. Thus without defining the objectives in behavioural terms, it would not be clear that what changes are to be brought by pre-determined objectives and "in which areas these changes

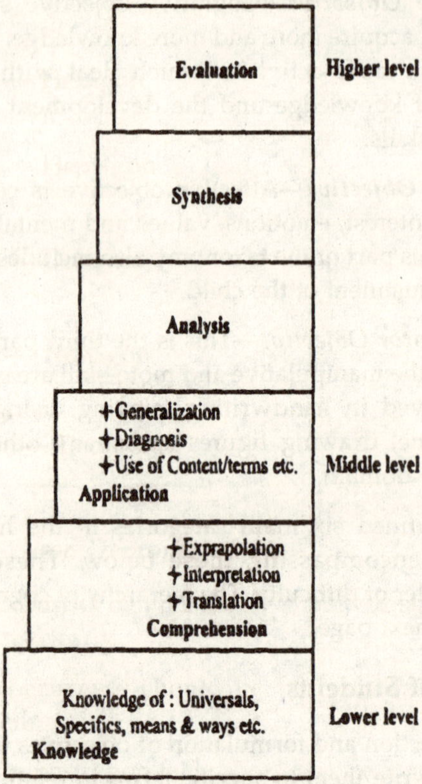

Hierarchy of Cognitive Objectives

are to brought?" Hence it is necessary to define objectives in terms of behavioural changes. The objectives in terms of pupil's behavioural changes reveal the learning activities.

While writing objectives in behavioural terms following point should be kept in mind—

* Nature of the objectives: knowledge, comprehension, application etc.
* Area or domain of the behaviour: cognitive, affective and psychomotor.
* Specific content areas in which behavioural changes are planned to be brought about related with the topic.

We can say that behaviour is a specification of objective expressed in terms of what the child does. The criteria for judging the validity of a behaviour are as follows—

* It should flow from the objective.
* It should be expressed in terms of what the child can do after the objective has been attained by him.
* It should be realistic from the point of view of the child's mental abilities at that stage.
* It should make explicit and idea which is implicit in the objective.

Need and Importance of Writing Objectives in Behavioural Terms. The need and importance for writing objectives in behavioural terms is given below—

* The teacher gets help in selecting teaching strategies.
* It helps in making certain and specific teaching activities.
* Teacher gets help in selecting questions for evaluation.
* It helps in selecting Audio-Visual Aids for effective teaching.
* With the help of writing objectives in behavioural terms learning-experiences can be determined and measured.
* A balance between teaching and learning can be maintained.
* It helps in advance study.
* It indicates the desired/expected behaviour of the child.
* It helps in managing examination for the achievement of objectives.
* It helps in the measurement of performance and other activities of the child.
* The teaching and learning process can be made objective centred.

* It helps teacher and children both in differentiating amongst various behaviours.
* The specification of objectives present the complete level of curriculum.
* Writing objectives in behavioural terms helps in making the learning objectives definite.

According to Scafold, there are following advantages of writing objectives in behavioural terms; It helps in—

* Specification of objectives
* Selection of appropriate teaching strategies, tactics and teaching aids/audio-visual aids.
* Teaching can be related to learning effectively
* Integration between change in behaviour and learning-experiences.
* Selection of items/questions for preparing a test.

Behavioural Terms

There are various methods of writing objectives in behavioural terms. Some of them are as follows—

Dr. B.S. Bloom (1956) has suggested the reformation in examination system. He emphasised that achievement tests should be objective-centred rather than content-centred. Each item or question should evaluate one specific objective.

Robert Mager's Approach (1962). This method was practiced and advocated by Robert Mager. He concentrated on the objective of cognitive and affective domain. Mager specified three criteria which every terminal behaviour must satisfy. They are—

* The specific performance of the child.
* The conditions under which this performance is expected.
* The minimum acceptable level of performance.

In these three criterion, the performance of the child

is must. Some times the other two criterion will be implied or be precise and concise and not over worded. Mager suggested that the instructional objectives are best described in terms of 'Terminal performance' or 'Terminal behaviour objectives'.

While writing objectives in behavioural terms, a list of specific performances or behaviour is prepared. Terminal behaviour means that behaviour which the pupils are to exhibit at the end of the instructional period. According to Mager's approach 'action verbs' are used to write objectives in behavioural terms. First of all the teacher selects an action verb and then writes objectives in behavioural terms. For example—

1. The pupil/child will be able to state Pythagoras theorem in his own words/language.
2. The pupil will be able to define Pythagoras theorem in his own words.
3. The child will be able to verify the theorem geomet-rically.
4. The child will be able to calculate the problems applying Pythagoras theorem.

A list of 'Action Verbs' was prepared for each category of cognitive objective suggested by Bloom. The list of Action Verbs is as follows—

Lists of Action-Verbs (Cognitive Domain)

Objectives	**Action-verbs**	
Knowledge	Define	Recall
	Select	Recognition
	State	
	Measure	Write
	List	
Comprehension	Explain	Indicate
	Interpret	Judge
	Translate	Select
	Formulate	Present
	Classify	

Application	Compute Predict Assess Demonstrate	Use Construct Find
Analysis	Analyse Divide Compare Criticize	Discriminate Seperate Conclude Justify
Synthesis	Discuss Conclude Organise Generalise	Summerise Select
Evaluation	Judge Avoid Criticize	Defend Identify Evaluate

Gronlund's Approach. This method was advocated by N.E.Gronlund. This method is more suitable for teaching at degree and diploma levels. This method has a greater acceptance and usage. This method consists of two steps. These are as follows—

a. Write a general objectives; this is also known as educational objectives.

b. Then clarify each general objective by writing a sample of specific objective. These objectives are accepted as evidence for attainment of general objectives.

For example:

General Objective—

The construction of an angle or a triangle.

Specific Objectives

1. The child will be able to identify the factors governing in the constructions of an angle/triangle.

2. The child will be able to select the types of angles/triangles.

3. The child will be able to calculate the degree of the angle or measure the size of the triangle.

4. The child will be able to prepare a detail drawing of an angle or triangle.

5. The child will be able to estimate the size of triangle/ angle.

6. The child will be able to prepare a process chart for drawing/ constructing an angle/triangles.

The Process of Gronlund can be summarised as follows—

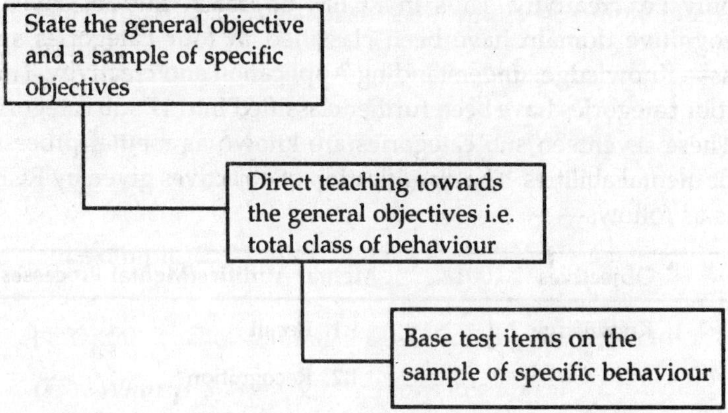

This method of writing objectives in behavioural terms is prefered because the objectives provide direction to teacher and pupil both with regards to the type of teaching and learning.

Robert Miller's Approach (1962). Miller's method is used for writing objectives of Psychomotor domain in behavioural terms. While in Mager's approach Cognative or psychomotor domain of pupil's behaviour was neglected in this approach Miller has emphasised skill-analysis. The origin of this method is from the military science. Therefore, the training objectives can be best written by Miller's approach. This approach can be used as a procedure manual for doing the job.

RCEM Approach (1972). Regional college of Education, Mysore developed a new approach for writing objectives in behavioural terms to remove the limitations of Mager's approach. This approach is known as RCEM approach or system. This approach gives emphasis on "Mental abilities" or "mental process" rather than "terminal behaviour."

While writing objectives in behavioural terms Mager has given emphasis on Learning out comes. In RCEM approach emphasis is given on learning processes. While writing objectives in behavioural terms, the word 'mental processes' or 'mental abilities' is used rather than action verbs. In this approach Bloom's Taxonomy of objectives is used with some modifications. Bloom's Taxonomy's last three categories are denoted by one category only i.e. creativity. Thus in RCEM approach the objectives of cognitive domain have been classified in four categories such as— Knowledge, understanding Application and creativity. These four categories have been further classified into 17 sub categories. These seventeen sub categories are known as mental processes or mental abilities. The classification of objectives given by RCEM is as follows—

Objectives	Mental Abilities/Mental Processes
1. Knowledge	1.1. Recall
	1.2. Recognition
2. Understanding	2.1. Cite example
	2.2. See relationship
	2.3. Classify
	2.4. Generalise
	2.5. Interpret
	2.6. Discriminate
	2.7. Verify
3. Application	3.1. Establish Hypothesis.
	3.2. Predict
	3.3. Infer
	3.4. Reasoning
	3.5. Formulate Hypothesis

4. Creativity	4.1. Analyse
	4.2. Synthesis
	4.3. Evaluate

Characteristics of RCEM Approach

* RCEM approach is very useful and easy.
* It is definite and more specific.
* It is applicable for writing objectives of Cognitive, Affective and Psychomotor domain.
* It explains the human-learning in terms of mental abilities or mental processes.
* In this method emphasis is given on learning process rather than product or outcomes.

Limitations of RCEM

* In this method there is no balance between the various mental abilities in different categories.
* It is difficult to select appropriate mental activities for various elements of content.
* All behavioural objectives cannot be written in 17 mental abilities only.
* More useful for writing Cognitive objectives only.

Mathematics at Different Levels

The major objectives related to various aims of teaching mathematics at different stages are as follows—

At Primary Stage. Objectives related to knowledge and understanding—

* To develop the sense of counting and place values of numbers.
* To teach the concept of size and shape of an article or object.

* To give the knowledge of measurement.
* To teach four fundamental rules of mathematics.
* To give the knowledge of whole numbers, prime numbers, frictions etc.
* To teach tables.
* To give the idea of various concepts like L.C.M., H.C.F., Percentage, Unitary method, Simple interest, Profit and loss, area etc.

Objectives related to Skills and abilities—

* To develop the skills of reading, writing, and counting.
* To develop skills to apply fundamental rules of mathematics.
* Development of skill to use the tables.
* To develop the skills to draw different geometrical figures and shapes.
* To develop the skills of measurement and construction
* To develop the skills of Problem-solving.

Objectives related to personal qualities: To develop;

* Interest in learning mathematics
* Confidence to solve problems
* Sense of logical reasoning, critical reasoning and thinking.
* Concentration and regularity
* Sense of truthfulness and exactness.
* Sense to use mathematical knowledge in their day-to-day life.

At Middle and Secondary (High School) Stage

* To develop thinking and reasoning power of the child.
* To develop problem-solving attitude of the children.

* To develop the sense of accuracy and consistency.
* To enable the child to understand the concepts and various problems of mathematics.
* To enable the child to understand the applications of different branches of mathematics.
* To make the child logical and critical thinker.
* To develop interest in mathematics.
* To enable the child to correlate the knowledge of mathematics with other school subjects.
* To develop the power of concentration and decision making.
* To enable the child to understand the symbolic language of mathematics.
* To help the child to understand the different units of measurement and their application.
* To make the child creative, constructive and research minded.
* To create awareness regarding day-to-day development in the field of mathematics.

Aims and Objectives According to NPE (1986). It is also emphasised in National Policy on Education (1986) that at the end of high school stage, a child should achieve the following objectives—

The child should be able to—

* Acquire knowledge and understanding of the terms, concepts, laws, formulae, principles, symbols, mastery of computation etc.
* Acquire other fundamental knowledge that is required in day-today life and for higher education.
* Develop the skills of measuring, drawing, demons-trating, estimating and decision making.

* Develop the ability to think, analyse, synthesis, reason, criticise, sumrize logically.
* Appreciate the contribution of mathematicians, particularly great Indian mathematicians.
* Appreciate the beauty of mathematics.
* Apply the mathematical knowledge in their daily life.
* Develop necessary skill to work with recent technological devices like calculators, computers, internet etc.
* Develop interest in learning mathematics.

Instructional Objectives

Knowledge—The pupil acquires knowledge of terms, concepts, symbols, definitions, principles, processes and formulae of mathematics at the secondary stage.

Specification—To demonstrate the achievement of above objectives, the pupil; (i) Recalls or reproduces. (ii) Recognises.

Understanding—The pupil develops understanding of terms, concepts, symbols, definitions, principles, processes, and formulae of mathematics at the secondary stage.

Specification

The pupil—

(i) Give illustrations.

(ii) Detects errors and correct them.

(iii) Compares.

(iv) Discriminates between closely related concepts.

(v) Classifies as per criteria.

(vi) Identifies relationship among the given data.

(vii) Translates verbal statements in to symbolical statements and vice versa.

(viii) Estimates the results.

(xi) Interprets.

(x) Verifies.

Application—The pupil applies his knowledge and understanding of mathematics to unfamiliar situations (or new problems).

Specifications

The pupil:

(i) Analyses and finds out what is required.

(ii) Finds out the adequacy, superfluity or relevancy of data.

(iii) Establishes relationship among the data.

(iv) Select the appropriate method for solving the problem.

(v) Suggests alternative methods.

(vi) Generalises (i.e., reasons inductively)

(vii) Infers (i.e. reasons deductively)

Skill—To acquire skills of computation, drawing geometrical figures and grapes reaching tables, charts, graphs etc.

The pupil acquires skill in

(a) Computation

(b) Drawing geometrical figures and graphs

(c) Reading tables, charts, graphs etc.

Computations

Specifications

The pupil:

(i) Carries out oral calculations with ease and speed.

(ii) Carries out written calculations with ease and speed.

Drawing of Geometrical Figures and Graphs

Specifications

The pupil:

(i) Handles geometrical instruments with ease and proficiency.

(ii) Measures accurately.

(iii) Draws free hand figures with ease.

(iv) Draws figures to specifications or to scale.

(v) Draws figures accurately.

Reading Tables Charts, Graphs etc.

Specifications

The pupil:

(i) Reads tables with speed and accuracy.

(ii) Interprets graphs.

Appreciation Objective—The pupil appreciates the role of mathematics in day to day life.

Specifications

The pupil:

(i) Appreciates the role of mathematics in solving problems of other branches of science.

(ii) Appreciates the symmetry of the figures and designs.

(iii) Appreciates the development of qualities like brevity and exactness through the study of mathematics.

Interest Objective—The pupil develops interests in mathematics.

Specifications

The pupil:

(i) Reads literature on mathematics.

(ii) Writes popular articles on mathematical topics for the school journal.

(iii) Solves mathematical puzzles.

(iv) Participates in the activities of maths club.

(v) Give short cuts for solving problems.

(vi) Does additional study in mathematics.

(vii) Brings to the teacher additional problems not related to syllabus.

Attitude Objective—The pupil acquires the positive attitudes towards mathematics.

Specifications

The pupil:

(i) Likes his teacher of mathematics.

(ii) Like to take tests in mathematics.

(iii) Promotes the activities of mathematics clubs in the school.

(iv) Like to be in the company of other student of mathematics.

(v) Helps students who are weak in mathematics.

Objective related to Scientific Attitude—The pupil develops scientific attitudes through the study of mathematics.

Specifications

The pupil:

(i) Accepts a proposition only when logically proved.

(ii) Examines all the aspects of a problem.

(iii) Points out errors boldly if convinced.

(iv) Accepts errors boldly.

(v) Respects opinions of others.

(vi) Keeps an open mind and does not regard any argument as final.

(vii) Develops habit of logical thinking.

Objectives Related to Personality Traits—The pupil develops traits like:

(i) Punctuality
(ii) Regularity.
(iii) Concentration
(iv) Accuracy.
(v) Neatness.

Here some examples are given to write objectives in behavioural terms.

Example: 1—Solution of linear equation with the help of graphical method.

Objectives	Expected Change in Behaviour
Knowledge:	1. The pupil will be able to recall the linear equations.
	2. The pupil will be able to recognize the definition of linear equation.
Comprehension:	1. The pupil will be able to illustrate linear equation.
	2. The pupil will be able to present linear equation on graph.
	3. The pupil will be able to explain the graphical method.
Application:	1. The pupil will be able to demonstrate linear equations on graph.
	2. The pupil will be able to solve linear equation through graphical method.
Skills :	The pupil will be able to develop skills to solve the problems by the use of graphical methods.

Example:2—Suppose teacher has to teach permutation. Then the objectives and expected change in behaviour may be as follows—

Objectives	Expected Change in Behaviour
Knowledge	1. The pupil will be able to recall the order of various objects.
	2. The pupil will be able to recognise the term permutation.
Comprehension	1. The pupil will be able to cite examples of permutations.
	2. The pupils will be able to define permutation in their own language.
	3. The pupil will be able to explain formula of permutation.
	4. The pupil will be able to differentiate between permutation and combination.
Application	1. The pupil will be able to apply the knowledge of permutation in their daily life.
	2. The pupil will be able to generalize the permutation.
	3. The pupil will be able to solve the problems of permutation.
Skills	The pupil will be able to develop skills in solving the problems of permutation.

Conclusion. Education is a process of bringing about changes in the individuals in desired directions. An objectives present the end point towards which action is directed and it reflects the purposefulness of the educational process. Objectives validate whole teaching-learning process.

Aims—Aims are general and long term goals and can be regarded as an expression of strategy.

General Aims of Teaching Mathematics

* To enable the child to understand the use of numbers, quantities, solve the problems of daily life, etc.

* To develop in the child a sense of appreciation, fundamental skills, habit of concentration, confidence, discovery, thinking, reasoning, scientific and realistic attitude, interest, abilities of analysis, synthesis, computation, and to bring an all round developments of the personality of the child etc. Aims of mathematics teaching are as follows:

Intellectual aim, Disciplinary aim, Utilitarian aim, Moral aim, social aim, cultural aim, Aesthetic aim, vocational aim, psychological aim, Aim of recreation and utilization of leisure time, Aim related to scientific attitude and international aim.

Objectives of Teaching Mathematics. The objectives are specific, immediate and attainable goals. Objective is a statements or a form of change and indicates the direction of pupil's growth. An objective provides basis for planning and organisation of learning experiences. Objectives are classified in two categories:

* Educational objectives.

* Teaching objectives.

Difference between Aims and Objectives

Dr. B.S. Bloom and his associates in the university of Chicago, gave the classification of objectives of all the three domains. This classification is known as Taxonomy of educational objectives, classification of cognitive domain or objectives by Bloom (1956), Affective objectives by Krathwohl (1964) and Psychomotor/ conative by Simpson (1969).

Classification of Objectives

Cognitive Objective—knowledge, comprehension, application, analysis, synthesis and evaluation.

Affective Objective—receiving, responding, valuing, conceptualisation, organisation and characterisation.

Psychomotor Objective—impulsion, manipulation, control, coordination, naturalisation and habit formation.

Writing Objectives in Behaviour Terms—The changes that indicate how far that objective has been achieved are known as behaviour or action patterns or pupils behavioural changes. Defining objectives means, making the specifications of objectives in simple language.

Validity of Behaviour

* It should flow form the objective.
* It should be expressed in terms of child's behaviour, realistic etc.

Significance and Importance

It helps in selecting teaching strategies, specific teaching activities, evaluation, Audio-Visual aids, advance study, measurement of performance and other activities etc.

Methods of Writing Objectives in Behavioural Terms—There are various method of writing objectives in behavioural terms:

Blooms Approach—Given by Dr. B.S. Bloom in 1956.

Mager's Approach—Advocated and Practised by Robert Mager in 1962. A list of action verbs was prepared for each category of cognitive objective.

List of Action Verbs (Cognitive domain)

Gronlund's Approach—This was advocated by N.E. Groulund. It is more suitable for degree and diploma levels.

Miller's Approach—Given by Robert Miller in 1962. In this method Miller has emphasised skill-analysis.

RCEM Approach—This was developed by Regional College of Education, Mysore (RCEM) in 1972 for writing objectives in behavioural terms. The word 'mental abilities' or 'mental process' is used rather than 'Action Verbs'. The objectives of cognitive domain was classified in four categories. These four categories have been classified into 17 sub categories i.e. mental abilities.

* Characteristics of RCEM Approach.
* Limitations of RCEM Approach.

Aims and Objectives of Teaching Mathematics at different Stages

— At primary stage.

— At middle and secondary stage.

* Aims and objectives of teaching mathematics according to NPE (1986),

Instructional Objectives of Mathematics Teaching

— Knowledge, understanding, Application, Skill, Appreciation, Interest, Attitude, Objective related to scientific attitude objective related to the personality traits.

— Examples of writing objectives in behaviour terms.

QUESTIONS

1. Write an essay on aims of Teaching mathematics.
2. What is the difference between aims and objectives? List out the major objectives of teaching mathematics on the basis of Bloom's Taxonomy.
3. Explain instructional objectives of teaching mathematics with suitable examples.
4. Differentiate between aims and objectives of teaching mathematics. What is the utility of knowledge of objectives to a mathematics teacher?
5. Enlist the aims of teaching mathematics what is the role of mathematics teacher in achieving the aims?
6. What is meant by 'desirable behavioural change'? Why is it necessary to write objectives in terms of behavioural changes? Illustrate with suitable examples.

7. What do you understand by objectives? Give any three objectives related to any topic of mathematics of your own choice and also express them in terms of behavioural changes.

8. Explain the utilitarian, disciplinary and cultural aims of teaching mathematics.

9. What is the need of writing objectives in behavioural terms? Enlist the methods of writing in behavioural terms.

10. Explain with examples RCEM approach for writing objectives in behavioural terms.

Objective Type Items

1. Who is the pioneer in the field of Taxonomy of Educational objectives—

   (a) A.J.Harrow (b) Krathwohl
   (c) Bloom (d) Simpson.

2. RCEM approach is used to write the objectives of—

   (a) Cognitive domain (b) Conative domain
   (c) Affective domain (d) None of these.

3. A good objective should be—

   (a) Related to teacher (b) Testable
   (c) Small (d) Attractive

4. Which of the following is not a action verb—

   (a) Knowledge (b) Understanding
   (c) Application (d) All the above

5. Any visible activity displayed by the learner is—

   (a) Learning (b) Behaviour
   (c) Terminal behaviour (d) Criterion

Match the Following

Action verb	***Objectives***
1. to define	a. Comprehension

2. to combine	b. evaluation
3. to criticise	c. synthesis
4. to illustrate	d. Analysis
5. to summarise	e. application
6. to predict	f. knowledge

Fill in the Blank

1. The objectives validiate whole.........................process.
2. According to..........................education is a triangular process.
3. Aims are.........................term goals.
4. Highest level of cognitive domain is.........................
5. To predict is an action verb of.........................objective.

8
Teaching Techniques

In mathematics teaching, teaching techniques are such aids which are used to make the lesson interesting, to explain the content and to remember it by heart during teaching-learning process. Techniques are not directly linked with the teaching objectives, but they are linked with teaching methods. While methods are directly linked with teaching objectives. On the other hand, teaching strategies are a purposefully conceived and determined plan of action. Thus teaching or instructional strategies refer to a pattern of teaching acts that serve to attain certain outcomes and to guard against others.

Method is a wider term. It includes techniques and strategies of teaching. Different strategies may be adopted in following a method. Teaching strategies may include different techniques of teaching. Various techniques may be used within the same strategy and method. A teaching strategy assumes that teaching is a science while method assumes that teaching is an art. The term teaching strategy owes its origin to military science where as method is a term of Pedagogy. Hence teaching strategies and techniques are used in order to make the teaching effective, successful and interesting.

Techniques and Strategies

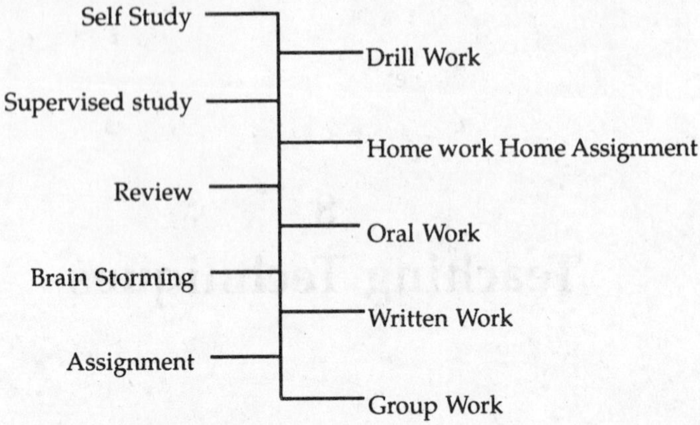

Mathematics Drill

Drill and exercises occupy an important place in Mathematics teaching and learning. Drill work is based on the psychological principles such as learning by doing and Law of exercise. Drill plays a prominent role in learning because it affords a convenient and fairly efficient medium for the rapid memorization of details and the automatization of processes. Drill must be recognized as an essential means of attaining some of the desired controls, just as a strong emphasis upon concepts and meanings must be regarded as essential for understanding. Both are necessary and neither alone is sufficient.

Drill provides an opportunity of self learning and improvement. The speed and accuracy in mathematics can not be possible without drill work. Be certain that understanding precedes the drill. Otherwise, the practice becomes an exercise in academic futility and no one benefits.

How to Make Drill Effective ?—Following points should be consider—

* Drill must be most effective and well motivated.
* Drill exercises should be conducted in such a manner that pupils can work at different rates and at different levels according to their abilities.

* Drill exercises should be brief and distributed over a period of time.
* Drill should consists of several distinct activities involving different strategies of learning.
* Variety of problems will make the drill interesting.
* The drill work should be progressively more challenging.
* Drill should follow developmental & discovery stages of learning and be used to reinforce and extend basic learning.
* Drill exercises should contain enough material to keep all the students profitably occupied throughout the drill period.
* Sufficiently diversified material to provide worthwhile and stimulating practice for students of different attainments and capacities.
* In order to be most effective, drill exercise must be specific.
* Drill should be concentrated upon particular skills or even on particular details of operation.
* Efforts should be made to detect mistakes in children's work and eliminate them at the outset.
* The students should be enabled to take pleasure in drill work.
* To insist upon right practice from the beginning which cannot be too greatly emphasized.
* It is of extreme importance to supervise closely the initial work of the students on any new process.
* After the children have done some practice, the teacher should try to elicit a summary of what has been learned in the classroom.
* The summary can also be developed by asking questions related to the concept developed in the classroom.
* The children could be instructed to carryout some of the

operations in each of the preceding problems as evidence of the level of achievement that has been attained by the class.

Importance/Advantages of Drill Work

1. Learnt material can be retained for a longer time.
2. It is a good technique of learning for beginners.
3. Speed of the learning material can be adjusted according to need.
4. Accuracy of learnt material can be improved.
5. Memory of the child can be checked.
6. Pronounciation of the child can be corrected.
7. It is very economical device of learning and teaching.
8. It is a less time consuming technique of learning.
9. Immediate reinforcement through practice and application is desirable.

Disadvantages of Drill Work

1. It is not suitable for all topics.
2. Drill work creates disturbance in the other classes.
3. It is not effective without good and clear voice.
4. Sometimes drill becomes an exercise in academic futility and no one benefits.
5. Careful questioning by the teacher is usually needed in drill work.

Saxena and Oberai have also remarked that the meaning of drill work is to apply the learnt task or skills or reading material in novel situations. Drill work tells the teacher whether the teaching objectives have been achieved or not. In other words, the knowledge gained by drill work gets consolidated.

Home Task

In modern days the curriculum in secondary schools is so

vast, that school time is not sufficient to enhast everything provided in the curriculum. So, if the teachers want to do justice with the curriculum they have to counter part with home work. It has to be given regularly. Home work plays a vital role, as the teachers get very short time to cover the heavy load of the curriculum. So under the circumstances, it is not only important but also essential to give homework to the students. The home work in mathematics may consist of some problems based on facts taught in the classroom. Student may be asked to learn certain principles definitions, facts, draw graphs, charts, tables etc. By giving home work means creating in the children a study environment at home. The nature and amount of home work should be given according to the capacities of the children. Home work should be assessed as a part of internal assessment and proper weightage should be given.

Moreover, make sure each exercise serves a definite purpose. Do not assign only problems on the newly developed topic of the day. Such type of work could result in the children trying to work on a skill or concept that they do not thoroughly understand. They may even develop some misconceptions, and too much practice in the assigned subjects could result in their fixing these misconceptions in their own mind. It should be remember to keep homework brief. Most of the children are given some homework in every class they have; if each teacher gives one hour of home work, this can result in many hours of work at home.

The Objectives. The objectives of giving home work may be summarised as under—

* It utilizes the leisure time of the child, otherwise the child will waste it in gossipping.
* It cultivates the habit of regularity and hardwork among the children.
* It provides the opportunity of independent work.
* It provides opportunity for the application and practice of the gained knowledge.

* It supplements the classroom teaching.
* It acts as a link between parents and teachers.
* It creates an environment of school feeling at home among the children.

The Principles

* Principle of Accuracy.
* Principle of Interest.
* Principle of Clearness.
* Principle of Relevance.
* Principle of Economy.
* Principle of Sequence.

The Importance

* Home work is essential because the school hours are not enough for the necessary work.
* It brings about closer relationships among the parents and the school.
* It promotes the habit of self study in children.
* It develops a sense of responsibility among the children.
* The constant anxiety of doing Home work promotes the progress of the children.
* It provides opportunity to utilize the leisure time of the students.
* It develops self-confidence and self-reliance amongst the children.

The Disadvantages

* It takes too much time of the children after the school.
* Home donot provide suitable conditions for work.
* Many people involve their parents or others to complete their home work.

* Some children develop emotional tensions because of home work.
* Home work assignments are sometimes misused as punishments.
* It also deprives the children of their leisure time.
* Home work may adversly affect the health of the children.
* Load of home work in one subject may effect the achievement in another subject.

Correction. The correction of home work in mathematics is very important. If it remains unchecked, it does not fulfill its purposes. However, regular correction of home work in mathematics is also a very difficult task for a teacher. In order to do some justice to this task, teacher may have sample checking every day. The teacher may indicate the correct answer and solution on the black board. The teacher may also introduce surprise checking and cross checking or mutual checking by exchange of note books.

The following points should be kept in mind while correcting home work in mathematics—

* Stress should be given upon neat & clean work.
* Transcription should be reduced to a minimum.
* Gradation is very necessary.
* If possible remarks may be written and suggestions should be given to the student.
* The teacher should indicate the mistakes by suitable remarks in ink or pencil of different colour.
* The corrections made by the teacher ought to be written by the children. This may better by checked by the teacher.
* The teacher may make a list of common errors and discuss them in the class.
* The procedure should be to move step by step. No step should be omitted.

The above points should also be considered while correcting the written work of the students.

Precautions. While assigning home work to the children the teacher should keep the following points in his/her mind, so that the purpose of homework may be fulfilled:

* Donot assign the problems to the children discriminately.
* Donot assign too many problems at a time.
* Home work should be given in brief, so that the pupils will be more willing to try to complete it.
* Only the problems on the newely developed topic of the day should not be given in home work.
* Home work should not be use as a punitive device.
* Clear directions should be given to the students.

In mathematics oral work is not only interesting but may be effective especially in the initial stages. An appeal to the eye and ear is more effective than written work alone. Students generally love to listen to talks and talk themselves. Thus the value of oral work in mathematics is immeasurably great. Oral work results in the saving of time and efforts through omission of certain steps. Oral work helps us in mental calculations. It gives a quick and easy start to the process of learning. The lesson can be introduced through short, easy and appropriate oral questions. Oral questions make the lesson easily comprehensible and clears the process of learning. Oral questions can be graded according to difficulty in a better manner. This demands power of careful listening, visualisation, quick thinking and decision making. It is very easy to discover the weakness of the child through oral work in mathematics and his mistakes can be rectified. Hence, all new processes and methods should be introduced initially in the pupils' mind orally. Thus they will develop interest for the new material. When oral work has been done, written work may follow it, because it is an admitted fact that, "Reading maketh a full man, conference a ready man and writing an exact man." Therefore oral work must be supplemented by written work.

Importance

1. With this techinque memory of the child can be tested.
2. Confidence in the process of learning can be developed.
3. Thinking, understanding and imagination power of the child can be developed.
4. Revision of the subject matter taught can be done quickly.
5. Previous knowledge of the student can be checked properly before teaching the new topic.
6. Student become more attentive in the class because at any moment any student can be asked to answer the oral questions.
7. Process of quick questioning makes the students mentally alert.
8. Auditory sense of the child can be developed.
9. This technique can be used for teaching many topics.

Disadvantages

1. Record of the learnt material can not be kept for reference if the work is only carried out orally.
2. It is a very quick device and is not suitable for all the students.
3. All the problems can not be solved verbally.
4. Expression and writing power of the students can not be checked properly.
5. Learning material cannot be retained for a longer time.

Work of Writing

In order to attain precision and accuracy, written work is essential in mathematics. Simple oral discussions are not enough. Moreover, on the basis of the psychology of the visual and auditory types it is evident that all children cannot benefit from oral work alone. Therefore, oral work must be supplemented by the written work. It is better to join both of these techniques together; one without the other is vague and purposeless. They both combine to make the process of instruction complete and an attempt to associate them would be ludicrous. Hence, mental work has to be combined with written work and both oral and written work must be included in the teaching and learning.

Written work enables the teacher to know the amount of work done by his pupils. It helps in testing the knowledge imparted orally. Moreover, in written work we can make the students work in accordance with proper rules, processes and principles.

Importance

1. Learning by this technique is retainable for a longer time.
2. Memory of the child can be tested.
3. Expression and writting power of the student can be checked properly.
4. In case of need suggestion to improve handwriting can be given to the students.
5. Confidence in the process of learning can be developed.
6. Mistakes can be checked properly.
7. Practice of the learnt material can be carried out easily.
8. Verbalism can be reduced in the process of learning and teaching.
9. Speed of writing can be improved.
10. Record of the learnt material can be kept for the purpose of reference.

Disadvantage

1. It is a time consuming device
2. It is very laborious technique.
3. It is not suitable for beginners because learning of tables

and counting can be done more effectively by proper 'Drill work'.

4. Learning by this technique can not be carried out independently. Before writing oral instructions are a must.
5. It is not suitable for physically handicapped children.

Collective Work

It was widely used at Nalanda University. She Greek scholars used to discuss various problems and issues with their disciples. In mathematics there is ample scope of group work. In case the teacher teaches by activities, projects, assignments or practical work. The pupils find many opportunities of group work. In earlier strategies oral and drill were conducted generally in groups. The principles vowels under lie in group work are:

* Principle of active participation
* Principle of freedom for work
* Principle of equal opportunities

The Need

* To consider, examine and investigate the various aspects of a question, topic or the problem.
* Group work for doing home work.
* Thoughtful consideration of the relationships in topic or problem under group study.
* The relationships are analysed, compared and evaluated and conclusion may be drawn.
* Table recitation.
* Collection of mathematical data from the field.
* Prepration of mathematical models or some mathematical material.
* To exchange the ideas, opinions and experiences of the children.

The Characteristics

* Group should be homogeneous in matter of intelligence and levels of achievement.
* Two heads are better than one. Exchange of ideas and opinions.
* It makes competitive co-operation among group members.
* Utilization of experience and learning from one another.
* The best age in which group may be most profitable is the age from eight to twelve years.
* The purpose of group work must be adequately clear.

Essential Constituents

* The teacher
* The problem
* The contents
* The group
* Evaluation

Self-study

Self study means individual's own independents study. The individual learns and studies himself. An individual attempts and solves the problems himself without any out side help. So it is a habit of independent study by which the children are able to solve the mathematical problems with their own effort. Self study can be made more effective and systematic by giving regular home work or assignments. Preparation of project, debates, discussions, seminars and other competitions are also require self study. It is essential to ensure regular progress in mathematics. In this technique the children learn to make use of their own knowledge and experiences in tackling various problems. It also develops self confidence and self independence in the children so that they donot hesitate in tackling problems.

Importance

* It develops the sense of responsibility and regularity,
* The child works/studies independently.
* The child gets the opportunity to use his own knowledge and experiences.
* Self study discourage habit of cramming.
* It helps in proper utilization of leisure time.
* It develops heuristic and problem solving attitude in the children.
* It is the best way to supplement the class work.
* It develops the habit of practice/drill.
* Self study develops initiative and independent thinking in the children.
* The child is his own guide and supervisor.
* It is required for preparation of debates, discussions, seminars, examinations and other competitions.
* It is essential for the regular progress of the child.
* It is also essential to complete the other assignments in mathematics.

How to Make Self Study More Effective

* The habit of self study should be developed as early as possible.
* The teacher should encourage the independent work in the classroom.
* The teacher should encourage the child to make proper use of library, he can suggest them certain reference and text-books.
* The children should be guided to develop the habit to make the notes of their self study and difficulties.

* The independent work of the child should be checked and evaluated by the teacher.

The children who study independently should be praised and recognized in the classroom or school.

Study under Supervision

Nowaday it is an important technique of teaching mathematics. Marrison has presented it for the teaching of understanding level. This technique is based on the principle of activity and individual differences. Dr. N.R. Swarup Saxena and Dr. S.C. Oberoi have remarked that in this technique, keeping in view the individual differences, every child is provided with an opportunity to do his respective takes and study. The teacher solves his individual problems by supervising his task as a friend, helper and a guide. Therefore, in this technique, both the teacher and child remain active.

Supervised study introduces the regularity in work and ensures sustained progress. The mistakes and difficulties of the children can be removed on the spot. This technique develops the habit of self study in students. In supervised study every child has to devote his prescribed time compulsarily for self-study. This technique removes the demerits of the traditional techniques of teaching mathematics such as: illustration, explanation etc. It creates a formal atmosphere for the self-study. This is a well known feature of public schools where the resident children are to assemble or one place at night to study under the guidance of their teachers. In this technique, the child learns according to his abilities and capacities. This technique may be used in two situations:

Keeping in view all the pupils of the class.

Keeping in view especially those pupils who are backward in mathematics.

Forms of Supervised Study. It may be in the following Forms:

Supervisedshidy
- Conference Plan
- Special Teacher Plan
- Divided Period Plan
- Double Period Plan
- Periodical plan

* In Conference Plan, conferences are organised time to time. The problems and difficulties of children are sorted out by mutual consultations.
* In Special Teacher Plan, specialized teachers removes the problems, errors and difficulties of the children.
* In Divided Period Plan, two teachers supervise the activities of he children in the duration.
* In Double Period Plan, two periods are provided to the children to study the same subject-matter or topic. In the first period children are instructed to study after presenting the background of the divided topic. In the second period, the children study that subject and the teacher supervise their work.
* In Periodical Plan, children are instructed to do predetermined work. After some definite period, their progress is supervised by the teacher. Hence the teacher performs the task of supervision and guides them fortnightly, weekly or monthly.

Steps

* Introduction/prepration for their study.
* Instruction for the study.
* Supervision by the teacher.
* Development of Black-Board Summary.

Importance

* Every child gets opportunity to learn according to his abilities and capacities.

* This technique develops the habit of self study.
* It is based on the principle of activity and individual differences.
* The teacher's presence makes the atmosphere more disciplined.
* The teacher serves as a guide.
* Both the teacher and child remain active throughout the study.
* It develops group feeling in the mind of the child.
* There is no need of giving additional home work to the child.
* It helps to develop many qualities like self-reliance, hard-work and self-confidence.
* It develops habit of regularity in work and ensures sustained progress.

Precautions

* There should be more of freedom and facility for mutual exchange of ideas/views.
* The period for study should not be too long.
* The teacher must possess insight and resourcefulness.
* Emphasis should be given on the development of scientific attitude and mathematical reasoning.
* While selecting the topic, interest, attitude, needs and capacities of the child should be given due importance.
* Emphasis should be given on the development of the problem-solving abilities amongst the children.

The Analysis

Sometimes review is identified with drill work because they are both characterized by repetition and both aim at the fixation of concepts, relationships or reactions. Review aims not only at the fixation and retention of details but also at the thoughtful organization of the important things in a unit or a chapter in order that the relationship of the various parts to each other and to the whole unit may be understood clearly. While drill is mainly aimed at the automatization of relatively detailed processes and reactions.

The function of review is indeed to make recall more certain and more effective. In fact review means "re-view" or a new look, at the unit which has been studied, rather than through reducing reactions to the plane of automatic response. Review emphasises taught and meaning rather than habit formation, therefore, review and drill have some things in common, they also have certain differences. Both the review and drill are very important in the study of mathematics.

The children need to be taught that have to review material just as they need to be taught how to study. They cannot review effectively without definite instructions. The task of helping children to plan their review work is a responsibility of the teacher. Butter and wren, in their book entitled the Teaching of Secondary Mathematics (IV Edition) has written that:

"Review work may be incidental in the sense that it may be integrated with the other work of the course, or it may be specialized by making it the primary feature and objective of particular assignments. Both of these types of review are necessary for the most effective teaching and learning. Incidental type of review is especially valuable for the gradual building up and clarification of concepts through repeated reference and though continual re-application in those situations in which they play component parts. Though making the necessary associations of the ideas in the unit, he will be aided not only in remembering them but in understanding them and appreciating their interrelations. Hence, in order to minimise forgetting of the acquired knowledge, a systematic or periodical review is very necessary. Review can take the form of checking, verification or confirmation of the knowledge acquired by the children."

Other Tasks

Assignment is the work given to the students either before the lesson or after the lesson and it may be completed at school or at home. Assignment is a sort of undertaking or commitment on the part of the learner. The child undertakes upon himself the responsibility of carrying out the work assigned to him. Assignment should be brief, so that pupil will be more willing to try to do it. Assignment in mathematics includes two different kind of problems:

* Repetitive problems.
* Review problems.

Repetitive problems are based on new work. By assigning problems on several different topics, the teacher provides the child with variety in his assignment. Which might add some interest to the task of assignment. The repetitive problems serve to emphasize some aspects of what has been newly learned in the classroom that day? Thus these problems provides the child an opportunity to see if he has really mastery what was taught.

The review problems are that which spiral back over the skills and concepts learned in previous topics hence they also called spiral assignment. The spiral assignment contains both repetitive and review problems. These are the problems that donot allow the child to forget the mathematics he has learned previously. So these problems should be selected very carefully.

These problems may have some bearing on the work done that day in the class, or they may simply be review problems whose solution is intended to bring back the child's facility in working with previously learned material. Both sorts of review problems help prevent the forgetting phenomenon. In the daily assignments one or two verbal or word problem should be included and assignment should not be used as a pumitive device.

The problems involving the concepts should be included in the assignment. When the assignment is presented to the class at the end of the period, the teacher should know which problems have been touched upon in the classroom. It must be remembered that, if an assignment is worth giving then it should be worth checking. This enables the teacher to see which child is having problems with the work and at the same time, which problems are causing difficulties for the entire class.

The Purposes

* To solve mathematical problems.
* To prepare illustrations for a topic.
* To collect mathematical data.
* To solve siders based on a proposition.
* To understand a proposition or a group of propositions.
* To traceout the back ground of a mathematical problem/concept.
* To formulate problem on a topic/concept.
* To carry out some mathematical projects.
* To apply the mathematical knowledge in solving the problems.
* To create interest in mathematics.
* To develop the skills of problem-solving.
* To develop the habit of practice/exercise.
* To correlate the experiences and previous knowledge of the child.

The Characteristics. A good assignment should have the following characteristics—

* It should correlate experiences with the previous knowledge of the child.
* It should remove the difficulties of the child.
* There should be clarity and definiteness in assignment.
* It should be stimulating and direct learning activities of the child.

* Individual differences should be recognized while giving assignment.
* It should be motivating and interesting
* It should give proper reinforcements to the child.

How to Make an Assignment Effective. To make an assignment effective and interesting, following points may be considered:

* An assignment should not be a mere dictation of question but for its successful completion proper hints should be given to the children.
* An assignment should be insightful.
* It must be motivative, clear up doubts and mis-understandings.
* It should be a cooperative activity in which the teacher and pupils take an active part.
* Interaction between pupil and teacher is must in an assignment.
* Reference books, text-books and other treaching-learning material should always be used to stimulate and direct the pupils' assignment activities.
* An assignment should be activity-centred, need-based and interest-based.
* The teacher should aware of any unusual difficulties.
* The task of assignment should be pinpointed be cause vague and lengthy assignments are of no use to achieve better results.
* There should be advance planning of assignment work.

Mental Preparation

Brain storming is a democratic and problem-centred technique. It is based on modern theory of generalization of task.

In this technique the content is largely determined by the children. Brain storming creates situations for students and teacher interaction and both remain active in teaching. This technique encourages the creativity and orgamitity amongst the children. Brain storming is based upon the assumption that a child can learn better in a group rather than in individual study. By this the higher order of cognitive and affective objective can be achieved.

In this technique the teacher assigns a problem to all the children. All the children think over the problem independently and then they discuss and arrange a debate. The children are asked to express their on views and ideas which come to their mind frankly. It is not necessary that wether the ideas and views of the children are meaningful or not. The teacher writes children's view's and ideas on Black-board. In this way the problem is solved through Brain storming.

Hence Brain storming is based on the principle that the children can be provided with more and more knowledge through interaction. Therefore, such means are used which create movement in the minds of the children of the class for mutual consultation, logic, reasoning and discussion in order to solve some mathematical problems.

So the teacher should use brain-storming in the class-room as much as possible so that the qualities like self confidence, originality, creativity, reasoning etc. may develop in the mind of the child.

Importance

* It is a problem oriented strategy of teaching-learning.
* It helps to achieve the higher order of cognitive and affective objectives.
* It is a democratic technique of teaching.
* It provides more ideas and views of the child.
* It is more creative and encourages organility of ideas.

* It creates the situation for more independent study, thinking and reasoning.
* It increases the knowledge of the child.
* It makes class-room interaction more effective.
* It has both psychological and educational importance.
* The child selects ideas most likely to lead the solution so that habit of decision making is developed in the mind of the child.
* It develops problem-solving ability.

Summary

Techniques are not directly linked with the teaching objective but they are linked with the methods. Methods includes techniques and strategics of teaching.

Drill work in mathematics. Drill work is based on the psychological principles. It effort a convenient and fairly efficient medium for the rapid memorization of details and the automatization of the processes. Drill provides opportunity of self learning and improvement. Speed and accuracy in mathematics can not be possible without drill work.

Principles of Drill. Drill must be effective, motivated, according to abilities, capacities and interest of the child, drill exercise should be brief, specific etc.

Home Work in Mathematics. The home work in mathematics may consist of some problems based on facts taught in the class-room. By giving home work means creating in the children a school feeling at home. The nature and amount of home work should be given according to the capacities of the children.

Objectives of Home-Work. It utilizes the leisure time, provides the opportunity of independent work, application and practice of the gained knowledge, supplement the class-room teaching, serves as a link between parents and teachers, etc.

Correction of Home-Work. The correction of home work is very important. In order to do some justice to this task teacher may have sample checking every day. Stress should be given on neat and clean home work.

Oral Work in Mathematics. The value of oral work in mathematics is immeasurably great. It results in the saving of time and effort through omission of certain steps. It gives a quick and easy start in the process of learning. Oral questions make the lesson easily comprchensible and the process clear. Oral work must be supplemented by the written work.

Written Work in Mathematics. In order to attain exact precision and accuracy, written work is essential in mathematics. It enables the teacher to know the amount of work done by his pupils. It also helps in testing the knowledge imparted orally because simply oral discussions are not enough.

Group Work in Mathematics. In mathematics there is simple scope of group work. In case the teacher teaches by activities, projects, assignments or practical work, the pupils find many opportunities of group work. Some principles under lie in group work such as—principle of active participation, freedom for work etc.

Need of group work in mathematics. So consider, examine, investigate and analysise the various aspects of a problem, for table recitation, collection of mathematical data from the field etc.

Characteristics Group Work. Group work should be homogeneous, exchange of ideas and experiences, to make competitive cooperation etc.

Essential Constituents of Group Work. The teacher, the problem, the content, the group and evaluation.

Self Study in mathematics. It is a habit of independent study by which the children are able to solve the mathematical with their own efforts. It develops the sense of responsibility and regularity in children. It is individual's own independent study.

Importance of Drill Work. It develops sense of regularity, responsibility, hearistic and problem-solving attitude etc. and discourage role memorization.

How to Make Self Study More Effective. Habit of self study should be developed as early as possible, encourage the independent work, work of the child should be evaluated etc.

Supervised Study in mathematics. It is useful for the teaching of understanding level. In this technique both the teacher and child remain active. In this, every child has to devote his prescribed time for self-study. It creats a formal atmosphere for the self-study. The child learns according to his abilities & capacities. The teacher supervise the activities of the child.

Forms of Supervised Study. It may be in the form of conference plan. Special teacher plan, divided period plan, double period plan & periodic plan.

Steps for Supervised Study. Preparation for the study, instructions for the study, supervision by the teachers, development of Black-Board Summary.

Characteristic of Supervised Study. Child get opportunity to learn according to his, abilities, capacities, interests, develops habit of; self study, group feeling, regularity etc.

Precautions While Using Supervised Study. More freedom and facility for mutual exchange, teacher should possess insights and resourcefulness etc.

Review in Mathematics. The function of review is indeed to make recall more certain and more effective. Infact review means, 'Re-view' or a new look. It emphasises thought and meaning rather than habit formation. Review may be incidental and integrated. Both are necessary for the effective teaching and learning. In order to minimise forgetting of acquired knowledge, a systematic or periodical review is necessary.

Assignment in Mathematics. It is the work given to the child either before the lesson or after the lesson and it may be completed at school or at home. It includes two type of problems, (i) Repetitive and (ii) Review problems. The problems involving the concepts should be included in the assignments.

Brain Storming. It is a problem-centred and democratic technique of teaching mathematics. Brain storming creates situations for student and teacher interaction and both remain active. It develops creativity, originality and reasoning.

Importance of Brain Storming. It is problem centred democratic, more creative, encourages originality of ideas, increase the knowledge of the child, makes classroom interaction more effective, etc.

QUESTIONS

Essay Type Questions

1. What do you mean by Home-work in mathematics? Enlist the various principles of Home assignment. What points should be kept in mind while giving Home Assignment?
2. Write an essay on written work in mathematics.
3. Discuss the advantages and Disadvantages of Drill & written work in mathematics.
4. What do you mean by oral work in mathematics? what is the purpose and importance of oral work in mathematics teaching?
5. What is meant by techniques of teaching mathematics? Explain the utility of drill work in mathematics.
6. Distinguish between teaching mathods and teaching strategics: Enlist the various-techniques and strategies of teaching mathematics.
7. What do you understand by supervised study in mathematics? Explain in detail.
8. What is the place of Assignment and review in teaching mathematics? Discuss.
9. Discuss the place of drill and oral work in mathematics.
10. Writes notes on the following:

    (a) Self study in mathematics

(b) Brain Storming in mathematics
(c) Review in mathematics
(d) Merits and demerits of drill work in mathematics
(e) Home work in mathematics.
(f) Group work in mathematics.

Objective Type Items

Encircle the Correct Answer:

1. The form of drill work may be—

   (a) Oral (c) Home work
   (b) Written (d) All the above.

2. The Complementary written work is—

   (a) Oral work (c) home work
   (b) Drill work (d) None of these.

3. Which of the following is more helpful in the development of alertness—

   (a) Written work (c) Home work
   (b) Oral work (d) All the above.

4. Creativity and originality of ideas is developed in—

   (a) Home work (c) Written work
   (b) Brain storming (d) None of these.

5. Which is a problem-centred and democratic technique—

   (a) Brain storming (c) Drill work
   (b) Home work (d) All the above

Write 'True' for correct statements and 'False' for wrong statements.

(i) Teaching strategies are purposefully conceived and determined plan of action.

(ii) To exchange ideas, opinions, experiences etc. group work is useful.

(iii) Teaching strategies includes the techniques of teaching.

(iv) Reasoning power of students can be assessed by oral work.

(v) Through drill work confidence in teacher & pupil develops.

(vi) Written work = mental work + writing material.

(vii) In supervised study the mistakes and difficulties of child can be removed on the spot.

(viii) The supervised study and self-study develops the habit of independent study.

(ix) There is no difference between review and drill work.

(x) Review can minimise forgetting of acquired knowledge.

(xi) Assignment in mathematics should be brief and motivating.

(xii) Brain storming creates the situation for more independent study, thinking and reasoning.

9
Teaching Devices

We are facing the challenge of explosion of knowledge. The available explored knowledge is to be transmitted to our younger generation. In transmitting maximum quality of knowledge with less efforts and time, teachers require to use teaching aids because of the reason that teaching aids facilitate teaching effectiveness. Thus, teaching aids or audio-visual aids are added devices that help the teacher to clarify, establish, co-relate and coordinate various concepts, interpretations and appreciations. They enables him to make learning more concrete, effective, interesting, inspirational, meaningful and vivid. They also help in completing the triangular process of learning viz., motivation-clarification-stimulation.

Commenting on the use of audio-visual aids, the Kothari Commission 1964-66 observed that it should indeed bring about an educational revolution in the county. It further stated that the supply of teaching aids to every school was essential for the improvement of the quality of teaching.

The National Policy on Education, 1986 and as modified in 1992 has laid a great stress on the use of teaching aids, especially improvised aids, to make teaching-learning more effective and realistic.

Education, whatever be its goals or objectives, involves learning. Learning is modification of behaviour which is the result of post experience or prior activity. The basic learning experiences or the input of learning have to reach the pupil through his/her senses. As such, the senses along with the intellect are vital to learning. In one way senses appear to be even more important than cognitive interpretative abilities for learning as there can be nothing in the intellect which has not been transmitted through the senses.

Our senses are the gateways to acquire knowledge. We learn

1.0% through TASTE

1.5% through TOUCH

3.5% through SMELL

11.0% through HEARING

83.0% through SIGHT

We remember

20% of what we HEAR
30% of what we SEE
50% of what we SEE and HEAR
80% of what we SAY
90% of what we SAY and DO.

Basic Things

"The thing which I hear, I may forget.

The thing which I see, I may remember.

The thing which I do, I can not forget."

The Concept

According to B.C. Daint—Audio-visual Aids means that complete material, which helps to understand the written or oral subject matter in class-room or in other teaching situations.

According to Burton—Audio-Visual aids are those sensory objects or images which initiate or stimulate and reinforce learning.

According to Edgar Dale—Audio-visual aids are those devices by the use of which communication of ideas between persons and groups in various teaching and learning situations is helped. These are also termed as multi-sensory materials.

Good's Dictionary of Education—Audio-visual aids are anything by means of which learning process may be encouraged or carried on through the sense of hearing or sense of sight.

Required Items

Some of the importance of the proper use of audio-visual aids are given below—

Need & Importance

	→ Best Motivator
Solid and durable knowledge ←	
	→ First hand experiences
Follow maxims of teaching ←	
	→ Reduce verbalism
Saves time & energy ←	
	→ Activeness
Natural & easy ←	
	→ Development of scientific attitude
Vivid reality ←	
	→ Reinforcement
Variety ←	
	→ Develops imagination
Active Interaction ←	→ Simplification

The description of above points are as follows—

Best Motivators—They are the best motivators. The students work with more interest and zeal. They are most attentive.

Vicarious Experience—It is beyond doubt that the first-hand experience is the best type of educative experience. But it is neither practicable nor desirable to provide such experience to pupils. Substituted experiences may be provided under such conditions. There are many inaccessible objects and phenomena. So, in such cases, these aids help us.

Antidote to the Disease of Verbal Instruction—They help to reduce verbalism. They help in giving clean concepts and thus help to bring accuracy in learning.

Based on Maxims of Teaching—The use of audio-visual aids enables the teachers to follow the maxims of teaching like, concrete to abstract, 'Know to unknown' and learning by doing.

Clear Images—Clear images are formed when we see, hear, touch, taste and smell as our experiences are direct, concrete and more or less permanent. Learning through the senses becomes the most natural and consequently the easiest.

Helpful in Fixing Up New Learning—What is gained in terms of learning, needs to be fixed up in the minds of students. Audio-Visual aids help in achieving this objective by providing several activities, experiences and stimuli to the learners.

Encouragement to Healthy Classroom Interaction—Autio-Visual aids, through their wide variety of stimuli, provision of active participation of the students, and vicarious experiences encourage healthy classroom interaction for the effective realization of teaching-learning objectives.

Reinforcement to Learners—Autio-Visual aids prove effective reinforces by increasing the probability of re-occurrence of the responses associated with them and thus render valuable help in the teaching-learning process.

Positive Transfer of Learning and Training—Use of audio-visual aids helps in the learning of other concepts, principles and solving the real problems of life by making possible the appropriate positive transfer for learning and training received in the classroom.

Meeting Individual Differences—There are wide individual differences among learners. Some are ear-oriented , some can be helped through visual demonstrations, which others learn better by doing. The use of a variety of audio-visual aids helps in meeting the needs of different types of students.

Opportunities of Handle and Manipulate—Many visual aids offer opportunities to students to handle and manipulate things.

Helpful in Attracting Attention of Learners—Attention is the true factor in any process of teaching and learning. Audio-visual aids help the teacher in providing proper environment for capturing as well as sustaining the attention and interest of the students in the classroom work.

Saving of Energy and Time—A good deal of energy and time of both the teachers and students can be saved on account of the use of audio-visual aids as most of the concepts and phenomena may be easily clarified, understood and assimilated through their use.

Positive Environment For Creative Discipline—A balanced, rational and scientific use of audio-visual aids develops motivation, attracts the attention and interests of the students and provides a variety of creative outlets for the utilisation of their tremendous energy and thus keeps them busy in classroom work. In this way, the overall classroom environment becomes conducive to creative discipline.

Retentivity—Audio-visual aids contributes to increased retentivity as they stimulate response of the whole organism to the situations in which learning takes place.

It Gives Variety to Teaching and Learning—Mere Chalk and talk do not help. Audio-Visual aids give variety and provide different tools in the hands of the teacher.

Freedom For Learner—When audio-visual aids are employed, there is great scope for children to move about, talk, laugh, and comment upon. Under such an atmosphere the students work because they want to work and not because the teacher wants them to work.

Development of Higher Mental Abilities—Verbalism promotes memorisation. Use of audio-visual aids stirs the imagination, thinking process and reasoning power of students, and calls for creativity and inventiveness. Thus helps the development of higher mental faculties among the students.

Thus, the teaching aids enable us—

1. To make teaching effective
2. To make learning interesting and profitable
3. To quicken the pace of learning
4. To foster the development of knowledge
5. To economise teacher's effort.
6. To overcome possible hurdles during the act of teaching
7. To add variety and newness to the lesson
8. To simplify the complex phenomena.
9. To make teaching interactive
10. To develop inquisitiveness among the learner to learn further

Principles in the Use of Audio-Visual Aids

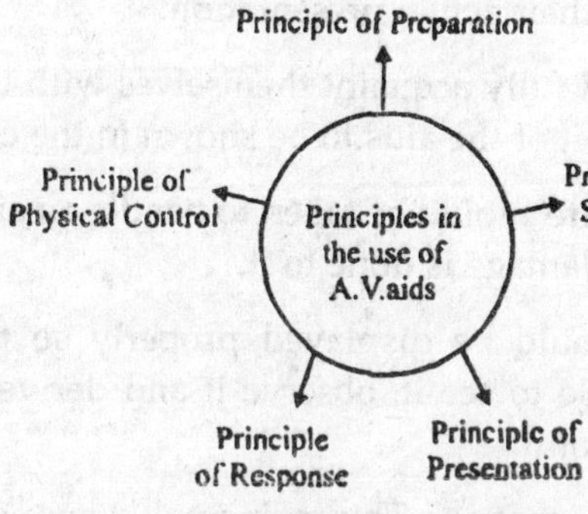

Principle of Preparation—This principle requires that following points should be attended to:

(a) As for as possible, locally available material should be used in the preparation of an aid.

(b) The teachers should receive some training in the preparation of aids.

(c) The teachers themselves should prepare some of the aids.

(d) Students may be associated in the preparation of aids.

Principle of Selection—Teaching aids prove effective only when they suit the teaching objectives and unique characteristics of the special group of learners. Following points may be kept in view in this regard:

(i) They should suit the age-level, grade-level and other characteristics of the learners.

(ii) They should have specific educational value besides being interesting and motivating.

(iii) They should be the true representatives of the real things.

(iv) They should help in the realization of desired learning objectives.

Principle of Proper Presentation—It implies the following points—

(i) Teachers should carefully visualise the use of teaching aids before their actual presentation.

(ii) They should fully acquaint themselves with the use and manipulation of the aids to be shown in the classroom.

(iii) Adequate care should be taken to handle an aid in such a way as no damage is done to it.

(iv) The aid should be displayed properly so that all the students able to see it, observe it and derive maximum benefit out of it.

Principle of Response—This principal demands that the teachers guide the students to respond actively to the audio-visual stimuli so that they drive the maximum benefit of learning.

Principle of Physical Control—Principle of physical control relates to the arrangement of keeping aids safely and also to facilitate their lending to the teachers for use.

Selection Standards

While selecting the audio-visual aids teachers should consider the following points in his mind—

1. They should be upto date and should have-desirable utility
2. They should be easily portable and its language should be easy.
3. They should motivate the learners.
4. They should be meaningful and purposeful and according to the age, intelligence and experiences of students.
5. They should be accurate, truthful and realistic.
6. They should be simple and integrated with learning.
7. They should be cheap and easily available.
8. As for as possible, they should be improvised.
9. They should be large enough to be properly seen by the students for whom they are meant.
10. Teaching aids should be according to the local needs of the students.

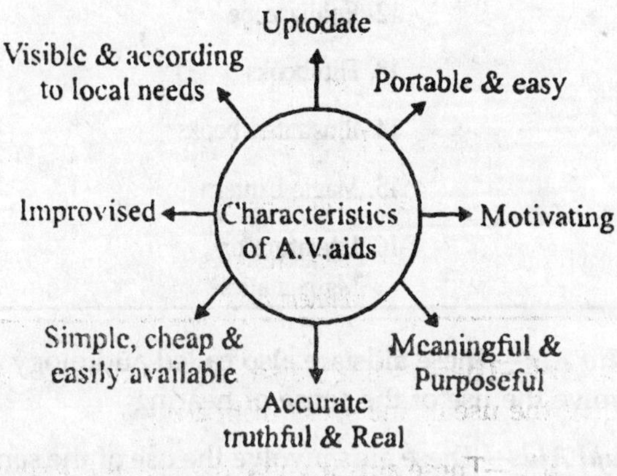

Classification of Teaching Aids—These can be classified as follows:

Classification Number—1

Teaching Aids		
Audio-aids	*Visual aids*	*Audio- Visual aids*
1. Language Laboratories	1. Chalk Boards	1. Films
2. Radio	2. Flannel boards	2. Printed material with recorded sound
3. Gramophone	3. Bulletin board	3. Sound Filmstrips
4. Tape recorder	4. Charts, Drawing, etc.	4. Television
	5. Magnetic boards	5. Video tapes
	6. Models	6. Computer
	7. Pictures and Posters	
	8. Film strips	
	9. Flash cards	
	10. Slides	
	11. Graphs	
	12. Epidiascope	
	13. Flip books	
	14. Illustrated books	
	15. Magic Lantern	
	16. Literature on Mathematics	

Audio Aid—These aids are also called audiology aids. These aids involve the use of the sense of hearing.

Visual Aids—These aids involve the use of the sense of sight.

Audio-Visual Aids—These aids involve the use of the sense of hearing and seeing/sight.

Classification No. 2

Teaching-Aids

Projected Aids	*Non-Projected*	*Aids Activity Aids*
(i) Films	***1. Graphic aids***	(i) Closed circuit
(ii) Film Strip	(i) Cartoons	Television
Projection	(ii) Charts	(ii) Computer
(iii) Coloured	(iii) Diagrams	Assisted
Slides	(iv) Flash Cards	instruction
(iv) Loop	(v) Graphs	(iii) Dramatics
(Coloured film	***2. Display Boards***	(iv) Demonstration
Cassette)	(i) Black board	(v) Experiments
(v) Slide Projector	(ii) Bulletin board	(vi) Projects
(vi) Epidiascope	(iii) Flannel board	(vii) Excursion and
(vii) Opaque	(iv) Magnetic board	Field trips
Projector	***3. Three Dimensional***	(viii) Programed
(viii) Overhead	***aids***	Instruction
Projector	(i) Models	
(OHP)	(ii) Mockups	
(ix) Liquid Crystal	(iii) Objects	
Display (LCD)	(iv) Puppets	
Panels	(v) Specimens	
	4. Audio Aids	
	(i) Radio	
	(ii) Recordings	
	(iii) Television	
	(iv) Video	

The Impact

All the learning experiences which can be utilised for classroom teaching are shown by Edgar Dale in a pictorial device 'Pinnacle Form' which he called the 'Cone of Experience'. If we go up the pinnacle from its base, we find that every aid has been arranged in the order of increasing abstractness or decreasing directness. In a simple language, it may be state that the 'cone' classifies the audio-visual aids according to their effectiveness in communication-aid at the base of the cone as most effective, relative effect gradual decrease. On the basis of relative effectiveness of teaching aids proposed by Edgar Dale is presented in the following manner.

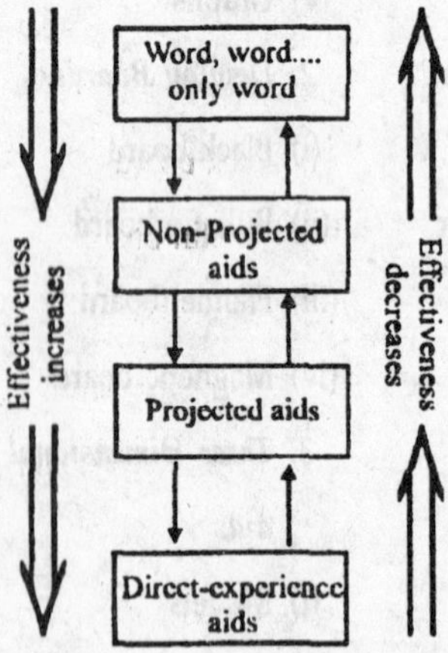

(Relative effectiveness of Audio-Visual aids)

Cone of Experience proposed by Edgar Dale is shown is following fig.

Audio-Visual Aids

Black Board. The Black board or the chalkboard, displayed prominently in most classrooms, is an excellent and inexpensive aids to instruction. Used essentially as an aid to visual presentation, the chalkboard plays an essential role in the logistics of teaching to a large group.

(1) It has been assured that all students can see the board from their seats the teacher has a lot of freedom in making the most of the chalkboard space.

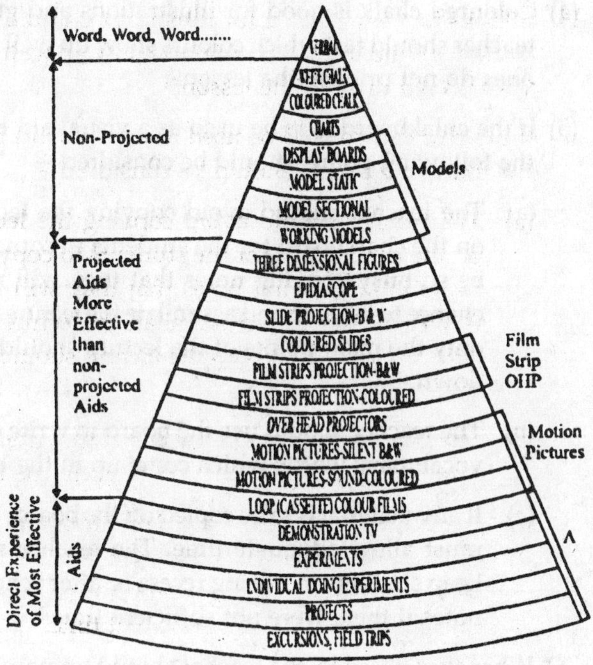

(Relative Effectiveness of Teaching aids)

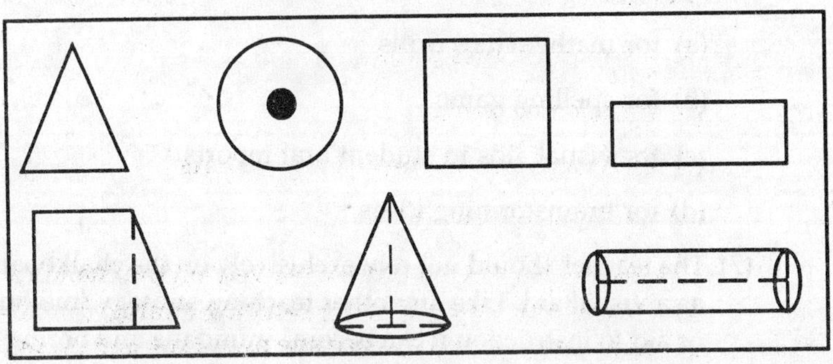

(2) In any case the teacher must print, write and/or draw in such a fashion that is legible and large enough that it can be seen.

(3) Any text and/or numerals must be written with white or yellow chalk. Avoid using rainbow colours for textural display.

(4) Coloured chalk is good for illustrations and graphs. The teacher should test which colours show up well and which ones do not prior to the lesson.

(5) If the chlakboard is to be used as a visual aid to a lecture the following points should be considred—

(a) The teacher should avoid copying the lecture notes on the chalkboard for the students to copy. They will be so busy copying notes that they will not have a chance to listen to and assimilate the lecture. Therefore, only the main points of the lecture should be copied down.

(b) The teacher should use the board to write down new vocabulary words which come up in the lecture.

(c) If any material is to be copied off the board, the teacher must allow adequate time. The teacher should not keep students in during recess or after school to copy notes if there were not sufficient time.

(6) Whenever possible, the teacher should prepare activities/lessons so that students actually get up and use the chalkboard :

(a) for mathematics drills

(b) for spelling game

(c) for visual aids in student oral reports

(d) for brainstorming ideas

(7) The teacher should not rely exclusively on the chalkboard as a visual aid. Like any other teaching strategy/method or aid to instruction it can become mundane and boring if overused.

The Black Board

1. Students and teacher should maintain the carefully black-baord i.e. a schedule of after-school cleaning may be set up by the teacher.

2. The teacher should also teach how to make notes as well as how to take notes from the chalkboard.
3. Legibility is important.
4. The teacher should make use of different colours of chalk but not so many that it becomes distracting or difficult to look at.
5. The teacher should not monopolize chalkboard use.
6. Students should be allowed to use the chalkboard whenever practical and appropriate.
7. The black board should be used for a variety of learning experiences. It can be used to display lecture notes such as to : present graphs, charts and illustrations; record comments during discussion; display learning centres; help students gain confidence in their skills; and help students gain confidence working with others.
8. The black board is usually used by the teacher to relay information to the student. The teacher records information on the blackboard the students write it down in his/her notebook.
9. Students can shut their brains off; the teacher does not teach—the student does not learn. Copying notes from the blackboard can be an effective segment of a lesson.
10. The teacher should supplement the learning experience with activities like discussion or debate in order to involve students in a true learning experience.
11. Students should also be taught the skills of note making and note taking.

Diagrams, Tables, Graphs and Charts. These come in the category of visual aids. Diagrams, tables and charts give a visual representation and summary of factual information. A diagram visually illustrates a fact, concept or generalization. A table provides a large amount of information in a condensed form. A graph illustrates statistical information in a single way. A chart visually illustrates large or small amounts of information.

1. The teacher should make use of every opportunity to enchance the lesson with visual illustrations. Therefore, whenever a diagram, table, graph and chart would assist students in their learning, the teacher should prepare visual aids and integrate them into the lesson.

2. The teacher must ensure that all students have the skills required to interpret the visual aids.

3. The teacher may have to prepare lessons or assignments so that students can practice and perfect these skills.

4. The teacher should have clear objectives for using visual aids and ensure that students have learned the necessary information presented in them.

5. The teacher should sketch out any visual aids prior to the lesson if he or she is going to draw the diagram, table, graph or chart during the lesson.

6. The teacher should give students adequate time to study and interpret any visual information before it is summarized by the teacher.

7. The teacher should not assume that students have assimilated and understood all the valuable information.

8. The teacher should link together the textual and visual information into a unified whole.

Precautions

1. The teacher should include examination questions on any relevant diagrams, tables, graphs and charts (if an exam is given). Such information is otherwise often overlooked during independent study.

2. The overhead projector is an excellent device for presenting visual information. Water soluble writing instruments make it easy for the teacher to correct errors and make changes during a lesson.

3. The teacher can teach and practice many inquiry skills through the use of graphs, tables and charts—drawing

inferences, interpreting the tables and drawing a conclusion, evaluating information and valuing.

Models—According to Hyman the model is a way to talk and think about instruction in which certain facts be organised, classified and interpreted.

Models are mainly representations, copies or images of real objects. They can be used to represent objectives, systems, concepts or ideas. Models may be concrete or two/three dimensional. Globes are common models found in the classroom. Models are prescriptive teaching strategies designed to accomplish particular instructional goals. (Paul D. Eggen).

Models are of several different types. The scale models of such objects as cars, buses, aeroplane, houses, wagons, ships are used to show the exterior form and shape of the original object. Working models show the operation of the various parts of the object.

Hence, models as a teaching technique, is highly motivating for students. Commercially produced models can be bought. Models may also be produced by teachers as well as students. Models can be used in all subjects and at all levels. Creating models is also correlating art with mathematics, social studies, science or any other subject. Models also contributes one of the requirement to justify them.

Importance of Models

1. Models can substitute for the real objects because many real objects cannot be brought to the classroom.
2. Teachers can use models to demonstrate an idea or concept to their students.
3. Students can create models to illustrate their understanding of what is being taught.
4. Models can be displayed in various formats around the classroom.
5. Models are also important for teaching disabled students-through the visual experiences.

6. The sectional type model can be dismantled to show the inner details.
7. Students can examine the parts and more questions could follow.

Precautions while Using Models

1. The teacher should provide an opportunity to think critically about a model. Does it serve the purpose for which it was intended?
2. All pupils have access to models and time to examine them.
3. If it is possible, pupils can be allowed to manipulate models and ask higher level questions.
4. All models should be adequately labelled.
5. It should develop scientific attitude amongst students.
6. Good storage facilities should be provided so that models can be kept in top-notch condition.
7. Models must be relevant to the lesson being taught.
8. The use of models become more effective if it is combined with other techniques such as verbal explanations and research.
9. It should make the teaching learning process effective & meaningful.

Film Strips. Film strips may be used for large groups or individualized instruction; for introducing a unit or for teaching a lesson. Filmstrips can be projected on a large screen for a group or they can be viewed by individual students on mini-viewers. Still pictures are projected and may or may not have written captions. Some filmstrips come with audio tapes or records with pre-recorded commentaries which accompany the visuals.

Use Film Strips

1. Teacher should ensure that all audio and video equipments are working properly.

2. Decide when would be the most suitable time to show the filmstrip.
3. Topical filmstrips should be closely linked to the content material being studied/and should not be shown in isolation. If filmstrips need to-be ordered, make sure this is done well in advance.
4. Once the filmstrip is in the teacher's possession, preview it. If the filmstrip has audio accompaniment, preview the filmstrip with and without it.
5. The teacher may discover that the audio accompaniment is less than stimulating. Uninteresting and monotone audio can spoil exciting visuals.
6. If the teacher decides that he/she will be the voice of the filmstrip, plan what will be said. This is a great opportunity to stimulate discussion.
7. Develop questions to ask the students. Moreover, this open-ended approach is more creative.
8. The teacher should relate the content of the filmstrip to the course content where appropriate.
9. After the filmstrip is viewed, the teacher should review and reflect on important points of the filmstrip.

Precautions

1. Relate the content of the filmstrip to the content of the unit under study. Make reference to filmstrips students have seen when appropriate.
2. Filmstrips are not made to be watched and then forgotten so the teacher must make the experience an exciting one.
3. Teachers should budget for preparation time (including previewing the filmstrip).
4. Students are increasingly becoming accustomed to fast moving high tech productions and may be bored with filmstrips.

5. Use non-captionalized filmstrips whenever possible. With this type of filmstrip, students rely on their own ability to interpret pictures without being influenced by prepared, "authoritative" text.

Overhead Projector (OHP). The overhead projector (OHP) is a popular teaching tool. Its primary function is to project still images (either teacher, student or commercially made) onto a flat vertical surface like a wall. The image to be projected on the wall is drawn or transferred on a standard sized (20 cm × 30 cm) overhead projector transparency (a kind of clear plastic paper). The transparency is placed on the OHP surface and after focusing, the clear image is magnified and projected on the screen/wall.

How to Use OPH ?

1. The teacher should have all transparencies to be used during a particular lesson ready and in the correct order.
2. The first transparency should be ready for viewing before the lesson beings. The teacher need only turn on the OHP at the appropriate time.
3. The image will be adequately magnified and focused so that the teacher will not have to interrupt the lesson.
4. The teacher should stand next to the OHP facing the class. He or she can refer to the transparency while students refer to the projected image.
5. The teacher should use a pen or similar object as a pointer and point to particular areas on the transparency without getting his or her hand in the way. If the pointer is placed on the transparency it is projected clearly on the screen or wall as well.
6. When the transparency is no longer applicable to the particular part of the lesson the OPH light should be turned off to avoid distraction and the next transparency placed on the OHP which will be turned back on at the apropriate time.

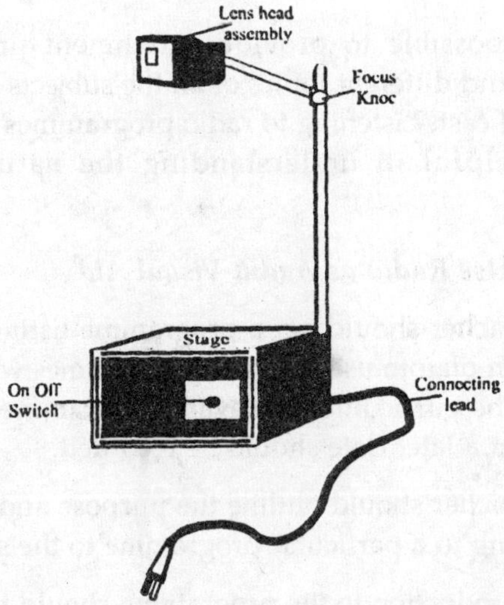

Precautions

* The OHP should not be used overused.
* The fan should be left on after the use of the projector so that the projector is cooled off.
* Although it is a time efficient and convenient teaching tool, like any thing else if over used, it becomes mundane and it looses its effects.
* The teacher should ensure that the OHP is in proper working order prior to its use during a lesson.
* The OHP light should be turned off, when the transparencies are no longer applicable to the particular part of the lesson.

Radio. According to watson," Radio is not an addition to education. Radio is something to be placed on top of education. Rather radio in education." Radio and other audio resources may either stand alone or be used as a component of the audio visuals. Audio tape and cassettes may be used to provide motivation, to convey information, to analyse verbal messages, to provide drill and practice or to teach a skill. It is easily accessible and radio broadcast is therefore, a home based education in one's privacy.

Hence, it is possible to provide enrichment programme in mathematics and different topics of all the subjects by the means of radio broad cast. Listening to radio programmes on education would be helpful in understanding the nature of audio programmes.

Procedure to Use Radio as Audio-Visual Aid

* The teacher should get a programme listing so that he/she can plan to use relevant programmes which coincide with the curriculum. Relevant programmes that can be used at a later date should be recorded.
* The teacher should outline the purpose and objectives of listening to a particular programme to the students.
* An introduction to the programme should be given.
* A radio programme guide can be used to select the programmes for recording.
* Students should be given an outline of what to listen for, and they should be instructed to take notes.
* The teacher must have the attention of all students prior to the beginning of the programme.
* Students could broadcast news current events, etc. from another country, and make their own commercials.
* Audio Commentary may be supported by projected visual aids, work books, photographs or simply figures drawn on paper.
* The teacher should review important points and conduct a culminating activities such as discussions, debates etc.

Importance/Advantages of Radio in Education

* The radio is a beneficial and inexpensive aid in the classroom.
* It gives us the current news of whole world.
* There are a variety of programmes relating to news, science,

mathematics, the arts, languages, weather, games and sports, etc.

* Radio programmes are broadcast many times a day.
* Radio programmes can be easily recorded for later use.
* It provides motivation to convey informations to analyse verbal messages.
* It helps in drill and practice or to teach a skill in mathematics.
* It provides many opportunities for students to develop speaking, writing, listening, critical thinking and other skills.
* It is a means of supplementing utilizing, correlating and modernizing the material of text books.
* Recorded audio cassettes used with work-books can bring about cognitive learning and also language learning.
* The audio resources (Radio) can penetrate the deepest in to the rural and urban areas.
* It helps to provide enrichment programmes in mathematics.
* It is a homebased education in one's privacy.

Precautions—Certain important considerations should be made before using radio as an A-V aid in a class :

* Because most youngsters have a short attention span, radio-programme based activities will generally work better with older students.
* Radio medium depends solely upon audio commentary and effects.
* Teacher should become aware of school broadcasts and special programmes relevant to their classes.
* Audio commentary should be supported by projected visuals.

* The teacher could take some time to discuss the history behind the development of the radio and visit a radio station.
* If the messages are identical through instructional design and developmental process, audio-resources may well be educationally meaningful.

Motion Pictures. The motion picture is unique in its ability to teach certain concepts because of the following important characteristics :

(a) It displays action. Because certain concepts involve motion it is futile to use a teaching aid which is unable to show action.

(b) Emotions and general attitudes toward specific issues can be generated using sound and special effects.

(c) It can relate us from the past.

Procedure to use Motion Pictures

Purpose
↓
Choice
↓
Order/reserve
↓
Preview
↓
Introduction
↓
Check
↓
Formulation
↓
Discussion

1. There should be some purpose for showing a film. There should be something about the film which enhances and enriches the lesson.

2. The teacher must choose a film with care and good critical judgment and should check film libraries and video stores.
3. Order/reserve the film as early as possible.
4. The teacher must preview the film before showing it to the class.
5. Once the validity of the film has been confirmed it should be introduced to the class.
6. Before class, all equipment must be checked and the film loaded so that it is ready to go. The screen and desks must be arranged to ensure maximum viewing by all students.
7. All distractions should be removed from the classroom.
8. The teacher and pupils should then formulate some questions for discussion.
9. After the film has been viewed, discussion and culminating activities are essential.

Precautions

1. The teacher may consider examining students on film content. If students know they will not be "tested" on its content it may be quickly forgotten.
2. The teacher must have some purpose in mind before the decision to show the film is made.

Television. It combines the best element of the radio and the potentialities of the film. The selected scientist can demonstrate a certain experience at one place and this can be seen at any corner of the world.

Television can be a valuable teaching/learning tool particularly in the social studies. Students see and hear about world events. The television allows the teacher to bring current events into the classroom and if students are encouraged to be critical in their interpretation of news and other programmes, television can be a valuable resource.

Procedure

1. The teacher and students must watch out for relevant programmes. Recording the relevant programme is better.
2. Introduce and discuss how it relates to the content of the class. If the programme is unrelated to the curriculum but the teacher feels it necessary and important for students to view it, introduce it as such.
3. If the programme is the introduction to a particular unit, allow extra time for questions immediately after showing it.
4. The teacher must preview the programme and make note of any inconsistencies, and/or errors. Students should be given the chance to discover for themselves any discrepancies before being informed about them.
5. If and when appropriate or necessary, provide as an introduction some biographical information about the people involved.
6. After all necessary preparations show the programme.
7. Schedule time for a question period.
8. At the end of programme students may be required to write short essay expanding on the topic of the programme.

Precautions

1. Remember that video-taped programmes can be stopped if a question is raised and selected scenes replayed if necessary.
2. Video tapes can also be kept to be played at a later date as a form of review.
3. If all teachers in a particular school collaborate, an interesting, comprehensive school video file can be built up in a short time.

Computers. It is the latest addition to the list of A-V aids. The use of computers is becoming more popular in science and mathematics education in the age of "information" and computer literacy, computers have found their way into the classroom faster than most of us thought would be possible. There is no denying the fact that computer as a teaching tool has made its impact on all curriculum areas. Computers provide more freedom to teachers and students-freedom to make mistakes without the fear of ridicule or personal embarrassment, computers have the potential of revitalizing education. Computers function as an excellent tool, which support the acquisition of skills, the learning of content and coming to terms with various factors involving the affection domain.

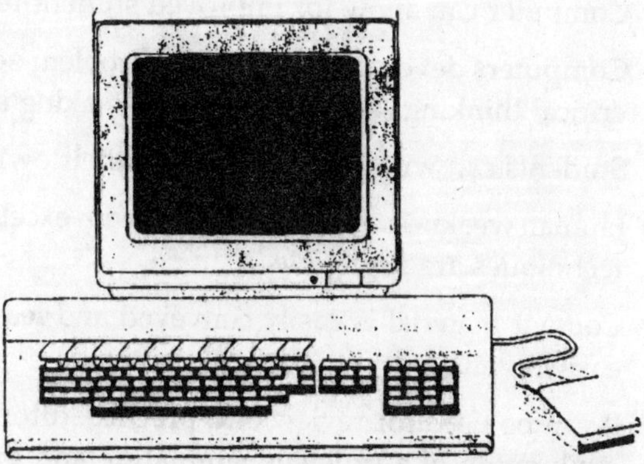

Computers and software are referred to as CA1 (Computer-Assisted Instruction) when they directly provide instuction to the student. This is, the computer/software functions as an aid to instruction. The most common uses of CA1 are drill and practice, tutorial, simulation games and problem solving. Thus, it is a significant tool to move educational practice into the 1990s.

Computers as A-V Aids

* The computers can store and retrieve information, conduct statistical analysis of data, simulate different situations, make graphs, charts, and tables and display them effectively, assist in composing, editing, and formatting

compositions and communicating with other informational networks.

* It can provide individualized, self paced instruction with easy access to enriched exercises or remedial work, if necessary.
* It can raise student performance in both cognitive and affective domain.
* As a motivational device, it can enhance interest levels and general positive attitudes towards school.
* It can provide immediate feedback.
* Computer can allow for improved student-teacher ratio.
* Computers develop inquiry skills, problem-solving skills, critical thinking skills and decision-making skills.
* Students can write programmes on their own.
* Human weaknesses which interfere with excellent teaching techniques are negligible.
* Content material is easily conveyed and learning of it is easily evaluated.
* It can be used for review and practice, tutorial work, for exploration of a problem, simulating and gaming or for providing entertainment from time to time.

Precautions

* All computer programmes must be previewed in a thoughtful and critical manner.
* The teacher should find specific information about the knowledge, skills and values being taught.
* The teacher must know how to use the computer effectively and how to evaluate software.
* The teacher should ensure that the software is appropriate to the grade level being taught
* The teacher should read all pamphlets and brochures supplied with the software package.

* The teacher must ensure that the computer system to be used for the programme has enough memory to run it.
* The teacher should use the guidelines in the selection of software.

LCD Panels. Liquid Crystal Display (LCD) Panels are an inexpensive way to project computer images as to a screen. The computer provides the text and graphics while a OHP provides the light and shines through the panel to project the image on the screen.

LCD panels are best suited for small and mid-size groups (up to fifty people). The computer can store "overhead transparency" content and project it electronically at the push of a key. New information can be displayed on command with the push of another key. You can make changes on the spot so LCD panels are ideal for interactive presentations.

Teaching Aids in Use

Some examples' are as follows—

Example

Area of a Circle—The following teaching aid may be developed and use to prove the formula for calculating area of a circle.

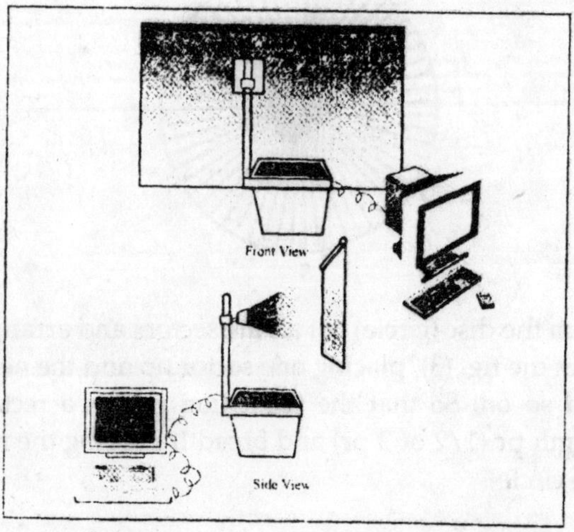

Preparation

(i) Draw a circle on card (Hard) board. To test the previous knowledge of the child teacher can asked about radius, circumference and diameter, etc. (Fig.)

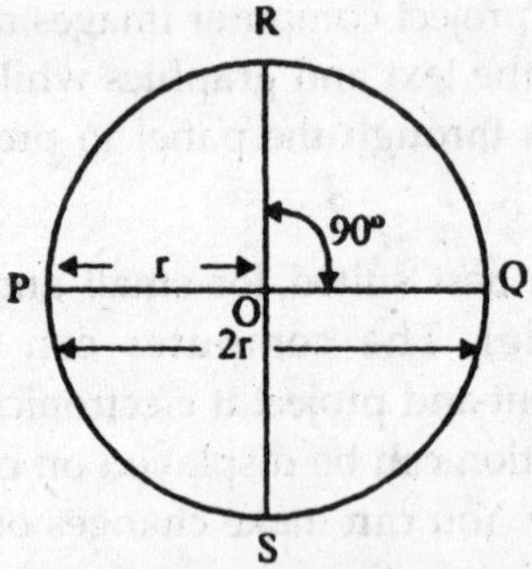

(ii) Then divide it into as many narrow sectors (even in number) as possible and cut out the circular disc very tiny arcs are considered straight line segments. Sectors are considred isoscles triangles with radius sides conceding with altitude. (Fig.)

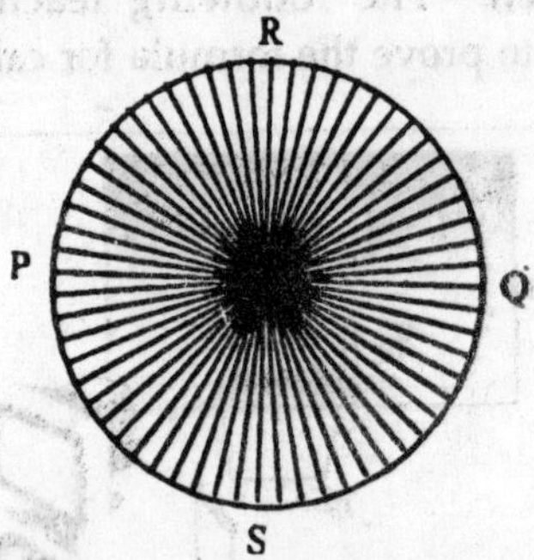

(iii) From the disc (circle) cut all the sectors and arrange them, as in the fig. (3), placing one sector up and the next down and so on. So that the formation makes a rectangle of length pr (1/2 of 2 pr) and breadth r (being the radius of the circle)

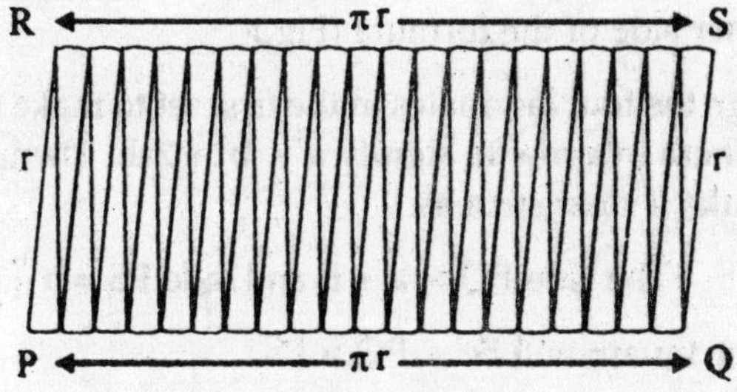

(iv) With the help of students teacher will find out the areas of the rectangle.

$$\text{Area of rectangle} = \text{Length} \times \text{breadth}$$

$$PQRS = \pi r \times r$$

****

Hence the area of circle will be equal to the area of rectangle formed as above.

$$\text{Area of circle} = \text{Area of rectangle PQRS}$$

$$= \pi r^2$$

or $$= \pi \times (\text{radius})^2$$

Thus students can generalize the above procedure and make their knowledge more durable and solid.

***Example* 2**—To prove the formula

$$(a + b)^2 = a^2 + 2\,ab + b^2,$$

we can develop the following material—

Preparation

(i) Giving values 3 and 2 units to a and b. Prepare two sets of these values.

(ii) Draw on the board squares of sides a and b and rectangles ab and ab and cut them out.

(iii) Cover them by three different colour paper, etc. Give it a plain coloured mount and frame.

(iv) Keep one set to represent one side and the other to represent the other side of the formula (Fig.)

(v) Arrange the four laminates in the first set to make $(a + b)^2$. Keep them in a row to signify $a^2 + b^2 + 2ab$. Then teacher can make it clear such as:

The side PQ = a + b and side PS = a + b

Area of square will be = PQ × PS

$$(a + b)^2 = a^2 + ab + ab + b^2$$

Or $$(a + b)^2 = a^2 + 2ab + b^2$$

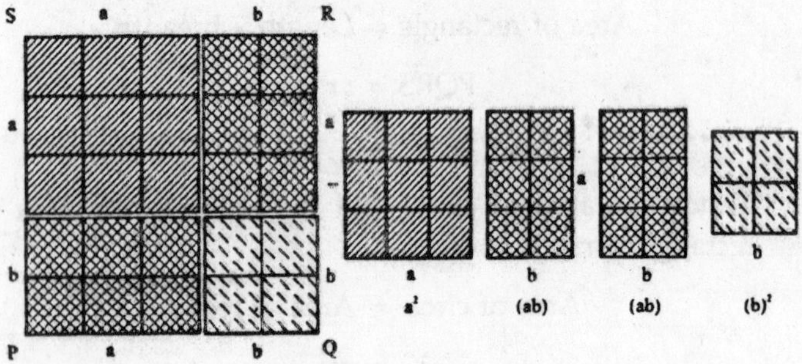

Set I *Fig.* Set II

Example 3

Extension of Pythagoras theorem to obtuse triangle, theorem,

Preparation

Following teaching aid can be developed and used :

(i) On a plywood board, paste a drawing paper.

(ii) On it, draw an obtuse triangle.

(iii) Describe squares on its three sides.

(iv) To have all integral numbers to deal with, take their sides to be 17cm, 9cm, 10cm (or in such ratio sets of magnitudes), Fig.

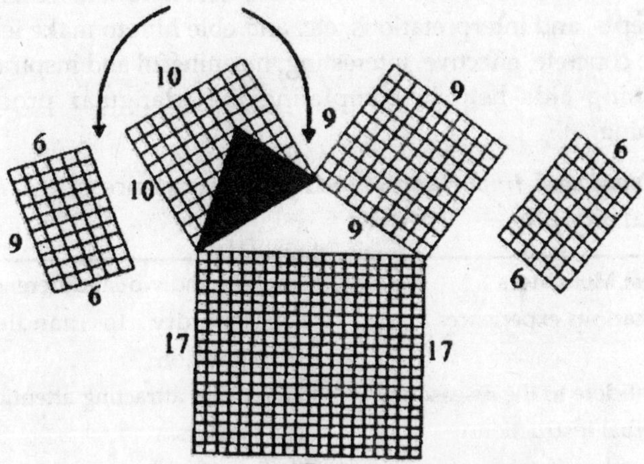

(v) Show 17^2 or 289 unit squares in the largest.

(vi) Colour them in various colours.

(vii) Produce the 9cm long side and erect on it the projection of the 10 cm long side (6cm).

(viii) Produce the 9cm long side and erect on it the projection of the 10 cm long side (6cm).

(ix) Prepare the rectangles of sides 9cm and 6cm.

(x) Colour them in the same colour.

(xi) Count unit squares and work out as follows:

Sq. pm side opposite obtuse angle		**Sq./on side-1**	**Sq. on side-2**	**Twice the Product of length and breadth**
		9^2 +	10^2 +	2 (9 × 6)
17^2	=			
289	=	81 +	100 +	108
289	=	289		
L.H.S.	=	R.H.S.		

Summary

Teaching aids or Audio-Visual aids are added devices that

help the teacher to clarify, establish, correlate and co-ordinate concepts, and interpretations, etc. and eble him to make learning more concrete, effective, interesting, meaningful and inspirational. Teaching aids help in completing the triangular process of learning.

Need and Importance. Need and importance of the Audio-Visual aids are —

* Best Motivators	* Meeting individual differences.
* Vicarious experiences	* Opportunity to handle and manipulation.
* Antidote to the disease of verbal instruction	* Helpful in attracting attention of the learners.
* Based on maxims of teaching	* Saving of energy and time.
* Clear images	* Positive environment for creative discipline.
* Helpful in fixing up new learning.	* Retentivity Freedom for learner.
* Encouragement to healthy classroom interaction.	* It give variety to teaching and learning.
* Reinforcement to learners.	
* Positive transfer of learning and training.	* Development of higher mental abilities.

Characteristics good teaching aids. Good teaching aids should be meaningful, purposeful, accurate, realistic, simple, cheap, easily available, upto date, easily portable etc.

Principles in the Use of Teaching Aids. Principle of preparation, selection, proper presentation, response and principle of physical control.

Classification of Teaching Aids. (i) Audio aids, video aids and audio-visual aids.

(ii) Projected aids, Non-projected aids and Activity aids or direct experience aids.

Relative Effectiveness of Teaching Aids

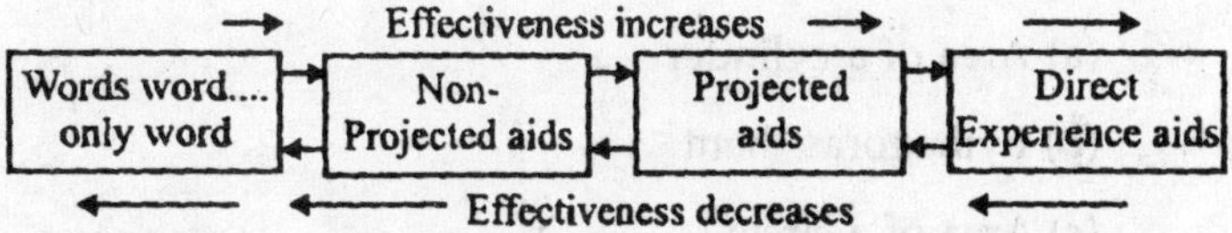

Some Importance Audio-Visual Aids in Mathematics—Black board, diagrams, tables, Graphs, Charts, models, film strips, OHP, Radio, Motion Pictures, TV, Computers, etc.

Preparation and Use of teaching Aids in Mathematics—Model of area of a circle, $(a + b)^2 = a^2 + 2ab + b^2$ and extension of Pythagoras theorem.

QUESTIONS

(A) Essay type Questions

1. What do you understand by teaching aids? What teaching aids would you use in teaching of mathematics to secondary level students? Explain by selecting any topic of your choice.
2. Discuss the need and importance of Audio Visual Aids in teaching of mathematics.
3. Black-board is considered as a visual aid. What precautions should be taken during the use of black-board in teaching of mathematics.
4. What do you understand by Audio Visual aids. What are the types of it ? Explain any two if them.
5. Write notes on the following —

   (a) Classification of Audio Visual Aids.

   (b) Selection of teaching Aid.

   (c) Use of radio and cinema as a teaching aid.

   (d) Projected and non-projected teaching aid.

   (e) Chart, model, film strips and epidiascope.

6. Prepare teaching aids to teach the following topics in mathematics.

   (a) Area of a cylinder

   (b) Pythagoras them

   (c) Area of a circle

   (d) $(a - b)^2 = a^2 - 2ab + b^2$

7. What do you mean by Audio-Visual aids? What is the need and importance of teaching aids in teaching maths? Explain any one of them.

8. What principle would you keep in mind while using teaching aids in mathematics? Give a brief classification of audio-visual aids.

(B) Objective Type Questions

Note I—Give the answer writing ***'True'*** *for* ***right*** *statement and* ***'False'*** *for* ***wrong*** *statement—*

(a) The history of mathematics can be taught to the children with the help of radio.

(b) After the film has been viewed, discussion is essential.

(c) Computer provides more freedom to teachers and students.

(d) The most use of computer is drill and practice.

(e) Tape recorder in an audio visual aid.

(f) Black-board is included in audio aid.

(g) Projected teaching aid is lesser impressive than the non projected teaching aid.

(h) LCD panels are not suitable for small and mid size groups.

Note II—Fill in the Blanks—

(a) 'Cone of Experience' was presented by...............

(b) Epidiascope is................type of teaching aid.

(c) News or informations are given are..............board.

(d) Diagram..............dimensional instrument.

Note III—Select the right choice—

(i) The most use of teaching aids in—

(a) Arithmetic
(b) Algebra
(c) Trigonometry

(ii) The most useful teaching aid in mathematics is—

(a) Visual aid
(b) Audio aid
(c) Audio Visual aid

(iii) The most effective teaching aid—

(a) Non-projected (c) Projected
(b) Direct experience (d) None of thesea

10
Prescribed Books

In each school subject text-book is an essential aid and has occupied a pivotal role in educating the children. A text-book helps in systematic teaching and learning. In a text-book the content organized in a systematic and specific manner. It gives direction to the class work and helps in evaluating pupil's progress. Thus a text-book is useful for both pupil and teacher. It influences the teaching-learning situations in a class-room. So it can be said that, "As the text-book, so the teaching and learning. Undoubtedly reading is an important means of communication and for the teacher's oral presentation, the text-book is the most widely used teaching instrument.

A text-book contains the subject matter according to a plan and with a specific purpose. Traditionally a text-book of mathematics has been an unavoidable instrument in teaching-learning process. Therefore, the text-book are the keys of knowledge and considered almost synonymous with schooling. These are the most influential instrument in determining the subject matter and the approach of teaching and learning. According to the report of Kothari Commission,"the question of text-books is the most important and urgent one for our country. Energetic on state and national basis is required to progress the preparation of high quality school text-books."

Significance and Utility

The text-book of mathematics is considered to be a course of study organized according to a set plan and a learning guide rather than a source book of information. In this support Hurl R. Duglas has emphasized that, 'In the analysis with great majority the text-book is a potent determinant of what and how they will teach.' Barr and Burton has also remarked that, the text-book is probably the most important tool in the country. Ragment has also defined text-book as. The text-book must be regarded as stractly supporting and supplementary to the teacher's lesson- while bacon has defined that, 'text-book' is a book designed for class romm use. Hence it can be concluded that, "the text-books are means to an end and not an end by itself."

The place of text-book of mathematics can only then be real if the mathematics teacher supplements in by his/her oral exposition, by reference reading, and by all his/her illustration. Text-books should be followed carefully and intelligently and not slavishly. A good text-book saves the time of both the student and the teacher. A good text-book probably is the cheapest and reliable source of information. It also serves as a reference book and teaching aid for the mathematics teacher. The need and importance of mathematics text-book can be summarised as follows—

* It serves as a guide for the teachers to proceed in an orderly manner according to prescribed syllabus.
* It stimulates the thinking and reasoning in the minds of pupils beside supplying necessary information.
* The pupils may have proper view of the subject matter to be studied.
* It can develope habit of self study in the students.
* It helps to complete the assigned home work at home.
* The teacher can use it as a reference book and teaching aid.
* With the help of text-book before hand planning of the lesson can be done properly by the teacher.
* With the help of text-book that learnt subject matter can be revised independently.

* It helps in improving teaching efficiency.
* It helps to solve the problems given in the exercise by understanding the solved examples.
* It helps the pupils to gain the power of understanding and interpreting fact and ideas given in the book.
* It helps to write the given assignments by collecting facts and information from the book.
* A teacher can provide guide lines to his pupils.
* It help to supplement class-work and home study by the pupils after the topic done in the class-room.
* It helps in saving time and energy.
* The mathematics teacher can assign home work & assignments to the pupils.
* It is probably a cheapest and reliable source of information.
* It helps the pupils to acquire the required information with speed and accuracy.
* It helps the pupils to make up their deficiency because of his failure to attend the classes.
* A text-book specifies the standards expected to be attained by a particular class or grade.
* It gives suggestions regarding the use of various teaching aids and activities to be undertaken by the pupil as well as the teacher.
* The text-book of lower classes with coloured illustration provide an incentive to learning and attracts the young learners.
* It can be used as a means of imparting new knowledge.
* It helps the teacher in teaching and correlating mathematics with other subjects and aspects.
* It is also essential for the critical appraisal of the content.
* It helps the pupils to do drill work.

Therefore, on the basis of above points it can be concluded that text-book of mathematics occupies an important and place in the classroom teaching. A good text-book of mathematics provides not only the content of mathematics but also determines the methods of teaching. Hence, the text-book of mathematics should not be used as the only source of instructional material. It should be used as an aid in teaching not a substitute for teaching. Moreover, no teacher can afford to work entirely without a text-book. Also, it is not a master to be feared, it is rather a servant to be ordered. It is a means and not an end in itself.

Main Features

The text-book have been criticized for numerous reasons. One reason being that text-books lack challenges for pupils. More demanding subject matter then must be printed in texts. If pupils read and study from text-books which are too easy, boredom sets in and a lack of challenge in evidence. On the other hand, text-book content too complex for students to understand makes for failure to learn. In the present time there is a great need of good text-books of mathematics but it is very sad to note that except a very few books we come across books of low standard. However, there are certain criteria for a good mathematics text-book.

According to hall Quest; A good text-book is—

(i) a source of knowledge.

(ii) a guide

(iii) an instruction to the pupil

(iv) a means of interpreting truth and

(v) a tool.

The characteristics/essentials of a good text-book of mathematics are as follows—

(A) The Author

* For the authors, certain minimum academic and professional qualifications may be prescribed.

* The authors should have a certain amount of experience of teaching the subjects.
* The author should consider and understand the real learning situations and difficulties of the child/learner.

(B) The Language

* The text-book of mathematics should be written in lucid, simple, precise and scientific language.
* The language in a mathematics text-book should be easy and within the comprehension of the students for whom the text-book is written.
* The sentences should be simple, short and correct.
* Also the sentences should be unambiguous and clear in expression.
* The mathematical terms must be introduced only after defining them clearly.

(C) The Content and its Organization

* The content given in the text-book should be according to the prescribed syllabus for the particular class or grade.
* The content (subject matter) should be presented in a very simple language with suitable examples.
* The subject matter should be arranged from simple to complex and concrete to abstracts.
* The content of the text-book should be consistent with pupils needs, interest and previous knowledge.
* The subject matter should be up-to-date and related to the daily life as well as experiences of the children.
* The statements of facts, principles, laws and the theorems must be correct.
* The content should also reflect the unknown and the uncertainties in mathematics.
* The topics and sub-topics should be illustrated with suitable pictures, diagrams and graphs etc.

* The major heading and sub-headings should be appropriate to the content.
* The presentation of subject matter should be more psychological and logical.
* The subjects matter should create interest in the pupil.
* The variety of topics should correspond to the variety of interests which the children are expected to have.
* The organization of content should be such that it retains learner's interest.
* A sufficient number of more difficult problems and project should be given for the more advanced or gifted children.

(D) Physical Aspects

For the physical appearance and get up of a good text-book due consideration be given to the following points—

* The shape and size of the text-book should be proportional neither too large (bulky & thick) nor too small. It should be handy.
* The cover design should be appealing and attractive.
* The get-up of the text-book should have psychological implications and attractive.
* The illustrations and diagrams should be bold, distinct and attractive.
* Paper and print of the book should be of a good quality.
* There should be no mistake in printing.
* The price of the book should be reasonable which the majority of pupils can easily purchase it.
* There should be proper marginal space around the printed matter of each page.

(E) Exercises and Illustrations

A good text-book not only teachers but it also tests. Therefore, there should be new thought-providing exercises.

* The problems should be graded in difficulties at the end of each chapter.
* The exercises should be such as to help to develop further concepts, desirable attitudes, technical skills and creative power of pupils.
* The exercises should develop thinking and reasoning power of the pupils.
* The illustrations should be attractive and useful.
* The pictures, diagrams and figures should be wheel drawn and realistic.

(F) Some general Characteristics

* A good text-book of mathematics should mention the audio-visual aids and other supplementary reading materials.
* Each chapter should be begin with a brief introduction and end with summary of the chapter.
* At the end of book there should be tables and appendices.
* New terms and concepts should be accurately and clearly defined.
* The problems and numerical examples should be graded according to difficulty level.
* It should facilitate the use of inductive, analytic, laboratory heuristic and problem-solving method of teaching of mathematics.
* The text-book of mathematics should satisfy the demands of the examinations, specially new type tests in mathematics.
* It should develop the interest, sense of appreciation and power of thinking, reasoning, observation and generalization.
* It should help the pupils to develop technical skills, scientific attitude and training in scientific method.

UNESCO planning commission has also prescribed a criteria of a good text-book as follows—

* A text-book, first of all meet the requirements of the prescribed syllabus.
* The facts, concepts etc., should be modern and with in the comprehension of the learners.
* The contents should contain only the established facts aiming at shaping integrated modern world out look.
* The content should be simple, brief, exact, accessible and definite.
* A text-book should help in linking up the subject with the daily life practice.
* The pupils should be equipped with the "know how" of utilizing the knowledge in every day life.

Utility of Text-Book for a Mathematics Teacher. The mathematics teacher should not consider that his/her work is confined to transferring the contents of text-book into the minds of the pupils. The text-book of mathematics should not be used as the only source of instructional material. But it should be used as means or aid in teaching. The text-book of mathematics should not be allowed to dominate the teaching programe. It is one of the many devices available to teacher for his/her teaching. But it is observed that most of the mathematics teachers become almost completely dependent on the text-books and take it as the only source of information. Therefore, over dependence on the text-book limits the advantages of its use. The contribution of text-book can be increased by creating situations where the pupils have a real purpose for turning to it. For an average maths teacher it is all his/her stock in trade. The greater; the capacity, professional training, knowledge and experience of mathematics teacher, the less he/she needs to depend on the text-books. However, no mathematics teacher can afford to work entirely without a text-book.

The text-book of mathematics may be useful for a teacher to perform the following activities—

* In selecting and organizing subject matter properly according to the level of the class.
* Text-book may be used to help to form right and exact understanding of fundamental laws, principles, formulae and theorems of mathematics.
* To develop scientific attitude in the learners.
* To develop understanding regarding open-mindness, co-operative attitude and scientific method.
* To arouse and maintain interest in mathematics.
* To acquaint the pupil with the wide variety of the application of mathematical knowledge.
* A mathematics teacher may use text-book for his/has self study. Dr. Thrug remarked that "A text-book is a teacher of teachers."
* To develop certain mathematical abilities and skills among students.
* To supplement meagre experimentation which can be performed in the class-room.
* A teacher of mathematics may use the text-book for class-room and home assignments.
* It is used for the construction of test papers by the mathematics teacher.
* It saves time of teachers as well as students.
* To lead the class-room discussion to accurate conclusions.
* To help the pupils for systematic and speedy revision of the content they have learnt.

Dr. Marlow Edigel, Prof. of Edu., North East Missouri State University, Kirksville U.S.A. in his paper Text-books and the school curriculum published in Experiments in education vol.xxiv, June-July 1996; has remarked that, "Quality text-book may be used to harmonize with diverse philosophies. The following distincts philosophies in the use of text-books may be emphasized.—

* To assist student to advise higher test score.
* To enable learners to solve problems.
* To aid in decision-making procedures.
* To attain ideas in a subject centered curriculum.
* To acquire vital content of the past which has endured in time and place.
* To reconstruct society so more may experience the good life. Teachers, supervisions and administrators need to experiment with diverse philosophies of teaching with the intent of guiding students to achieve more optically. Each student need to active as much as possible in all curriculum areas.

Moreover, a good mathematics text-book provides not only the contents of mathematics but also determines the methods of teaching. A mathematics text-book therefore occupies an important role in the teaching and learning process. Hence, the mathematics teacher should be familiar with the needs and characteristics of a text-book. In the words of Douglas— "The teacher and text-book make the school." Similarly Maxwell has also remarked that, "It is at least the medium through which the teacher presents a subject to the class. Thus the text-book should, however, not take the place of the teacher but should give the minimum level of knowledge which is unnecessary for the foundation of the child." Thus it is true that neither the text-book nor the teacher alone can be the best medium of instruction; but a good text-book and an experienced or trained teacher can make the teaching learning process more effective.

Summary

The text-book of mathematics is an essential aid and has occupied a pivotal role in educating the children. It is useful for both pupil and teacher. The text-books are the keys of knowledge and most influential instrument in determining the subject matter.

Need and Importance. The text-book is a means to an end and not an end by it self. A good text-book is probably the cheapest and most reliable source of information. It serves as reference book guide and teaching aid for the teacher. It helps-to complete home assignments, in planning, in improving teaching efficiency, to develop habit of self study, to make up their deficiency, to acquire knowledge etc.

Characteristics of a Good Text-book of Mathematics. There are certain criteria for a good mathematics text-book such as, the author, the language, the content and its organization, physical aspects, exercises and illustrations, and same general characteristics.

Utility. The text-book should not be used as the only source of instructional material. But, it should be used as a means or aid in teaching. Over dependence on text-book limits the advantages of its use. The text-book of mathematics occupies an important place in teaching-learning process.

QUESTIONS

(A) Essay type Question—

1. "Text-book of mathematics should be used as a means, but not as an end." Discuss this statement and describe what are the characteristics of a good text-book of mathematics.
2. What factors would you keep in mind while reflecting a suitable text-book of mathematics for high school level.
3. What is the importance of text-book in mathematics teaching? Explain the characteristics for a good text-book.
4. Write an essay on 'Text-Book of mathematics.'
5. What improvement would you suggest in mathematics text-book of high school or secondary classes?
6. How can a teacher use the mathematics text-book as a teaching aid?

7. Write short notes on utility of text-book for a mathematics teacher.
8. What are the essential characteristics of a good mathematics textbook. How a mathematics teacher should use the text-book? Discuss.

(B) Objective Type Questions

(I) Multiple Choice Items—

1. In the most useful text-book of mathematics—

   (a) There are many solved examples and some questions of exercise.

   (b) There are sufficient solved illustrations and more questions for exercise.

   (c) All the exercise question are solved.

   (d) All the above.

2. In the text-book of mathematics, the content should be developed—

   (a) in the order of exercise

   (b) in logical order

   (c) in problematic order

   (d) in all the above order

3. Characteristic of a good text-book is that it is—

   (a) comprehensive

   (b) formed by teacher

   (c) in simple and clear language

   (d) none of these

4. The organization of content is the text-book of mathematics should be—

   (a) according to the teacher

(b) accordings to the curriculum

(c) according to the students

(d) none of these

(II) True/False items

Write 'true' for right statement and 'false' for wrong statement—

(i) The formation of the text-book should be according to the examinations.

(ii) A teacher should use the text-book of mathematics as an end.

(iii) In the text-book of mathematics all the problems of an exercise should be of different type.

(iv) In the text-book of mathematics exercise questions should be according to the attitude of students.

(v) A text-book of mathematics should be written by the experienced teacher.

(vi) A text-book of mathematics is more important and useful for a teacher than the students.

11
Micro-teaching

The Concept

Micro-teaching has been describe as an innovation in teacher-education. Infact certain of its aspects have been in use from long time in various training situations. The term micro-teaching was first coined by A.W. Dwight Allen of the Stanford University in 1963 for developing teaching behaviours and teaching activities. These teaching behaviours or teaching activities are given the name of "teaching skills." It is a technique of training in which one learns the skills of teaching through a scaled-down process of teaching-learning. The main purpose of micro-teaching is to provide training of teaching skills to the pupil teaches.

1. Micro-teaching is a scaled down teaching encounter in class size and class time. —dwight Allen

2. A system of controlled practice that make it possible to concentrate on specific teaching behaviour and to practice teaching under controlled conditions. —Allen & Eve

3. Micro-teaching is most often applied to the use of closed circuit Television (CCTV) to give immediate feed-back of a teacher trainee performance in a simplified environment.

—Mc. Alease & Urwin

4. A teacher education technique which allows teachers to apply well-defined teaching skills to a carefully prepared lesson in a planned series of five to ten minutes encounters with a small group of real class-room students often with an opportunity to observe the performance on videotape. —Buch, M.B.

Main Features

On the basis of above definitions, the following characteristics or features of micro-teaching can be summarized—

* The plan for teaching is focused on micro events e.g. execution of the identified skills.
* It is scaled down teaching, which
  (a) reduces the class size, upto 5 to 10 students
  (b) reduces the duration of period upto 5 to 10 minutes
  (c) reduces the size of topic or content
  (d) reduces the teaching skills.
* Only one teaching skill is considered at a time
* It is individualized technique/device
* It provides the feedback for trainer's performance
* It is a training technique to prepare effective teachers.
* It is grouping of such desirable micro behaviours which constitute teaching skills. For example, the skill of asking questions involves micro behaviours consisting the following activities—
* Framing a question
* Thinking
* Standing position
* Facing the class
* Listening
* Asking the question
* Looking around for a response in the class
* Recalling the names of students
* Calling students by their names
* Recovering the response etc.

Skills for Teaching

Different educationists have mentioned various teaching skills based on their researches. Stanford University has identified the following skills—

* Stimulus variations
* Reinforcement of pupil participation
* Set eviduction
* Non verbal cues
* Probing questions
* Fluency in asking questions
* Lecturing skill
* Divergent questions
* Completing the communication
* Recognizing behaviour
* Planned repetition
* Use of examples
* Higher order questions
* Closure

Indian educationist Prof. Passi, B.K. (1975) has identified the following teaching skills—

* Writing instructional objectives
* Reinforcement of learning
* Introduction of lesson
* Silence and Non-verbal cues
* Fluency of questioning
* Increasing participations of students
* Probing questions
* Using Black-Board

* Explaining
* Achieving closure
* Illustrating with examples
* Recognizing attending beha'iour of the pupils
* Stimulus variation

The Procedure

Cliff and other-mentioned the three phases of micro-teaching procedure—

Knowledge Acquisition Phase. This phase involves the following two activities—

* Observation of demonstration skill
* Analyzing and discussing the demonstration

Skill Acquisition Phase. In this phase following activities are performed in the requer a given below—

* Micro-lesson planning
* Practicising the specific skill
* Evaluating performance

Transfer Phase. After acquiring the desired skill in the previous phase, the trainees are provided an opportunity to use the skill in normal class room teaching.

Various Stages

Micro-teaching cycle involves the following steps—

Identification of specific skill. A particular skill in terms of teaching behaviour is identified. After the identification, it is defined in the form of teaching behaviour for providing the knowledge and awareness of teaching skill.

Demonstration of the skill. The teaching skill is demonstrated by the teacher through the Video-Tape or film to the teacher-trainee.

Micro-lesson planning. The pupil-teacher plans a short lesson in which he practices the particular skill. Micro-lesson planning includes detailed preparation of micro-lesson plan, selection of media, preparation of audio-visual aids etc.

Teaching-session. The pupil-teacher teaches the lesson to a small group of pupils say 5-10. The skill taught by the pupil-teacher is observed by the supervisor and recorded on a video recorder audio reader or a closed-circuit television.

Providing feed back/for Evaluation. The recorded teaching is played back. The trainee is shown the video tape/audio tape to his own teaching activities. This is followed by discussions to provide the feedback. In discussions a constructive criticism is made an various aspects of lesson presented by the pupil-teacher. The awareness of his own teaching performance provides the reinforcement to the teacher trainee.

Replanning of micro lesson. The pupil-teacher replans the lesson in the light of discussions made in the previous step with the improvements considered necessary.

Reteaching session. The revised lesson is retaught with improved teaching to the same class for the same duration to practice the same skill.

Re-feedback or re-evaluation. The recorded teaching is replaced back for evaluation and further criticism. This is also followed by discussions to provide refeed back as in step V.

In this way the feedback is again provided to the teacher-trainee. Hence, this teach-reteach cycle is followed till the desire level of skill is achieved. The micro-teaching cycle can be shown as follows—

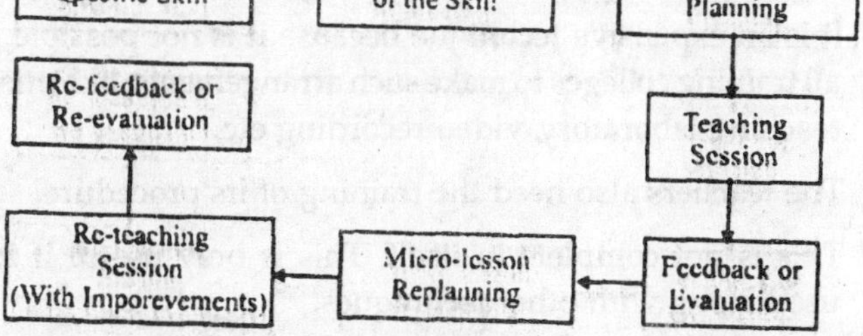

(The Micro Teaching Cycle)

Basic Principles. Basic principles of micro-teaching are as follows—

* Principle of enforcement
* Principle of continuity
* Principle of Drill and Practice
* Principle of Microscopic supervision and observation.

The Advantages

* It focuses on training for the accomplishment of specific skills.
* It expands the normal knowledge of results of feedback dimension in teaching.
* It is a real teaching.
* Micro-teaching enables pupil-teachers to view their own performance and provides opportunities to make self-criticism.
* It gives guide lines for improvement in teaching.
* It permits concentration on same specific skills.
* It provides immediate feedback to the trainees.
* It facilitates replanning, reteaching and refeedback till the desired skill is achieved.

The Limitations

* It needs more time for training
* It is only a simulated technique with a small group over a short period of time.
* It is an expensive technique because it is not possible for all training colleges to make such arrangements, like micro-teaching laboratory, video-recording etc.
* The teachers also need the training of its procedure.
* This is not complete in itself. This is only useful if it is used along with other techniques.

Simulated Teaching

It is also a teacher training technique. A number of techniques are being uses currently in India as well as in other countries for the modification of teacher-behaviour. Simulated teaching is also known as simulated social skill of teaching (SSST). Simulation may be defined as role playing in which the process of teaching is enacted artificially and an effort is made to practise some skill of communication. In simulated teaching pupil-teacher and the students stimulate a particular role and try to develop an identity with the actual class room environment. It is not actual teaching. Simulations are learning exercises that placed the students in roles similar to real world roles and in playing the game require them to make decision as if they were part of real situation. Hence, the whole simulated teaching programme becomes training in role perception and role playing. It is the basis of sensitivity training, role playing, sociodrama and psychodrama.

It can be defined as a mechanism of feedback devices to induce certain desirable behaviour among pupil-teachers by playing the role of t acher in their own group as an artificial situation of classroom teaching. Hence, Simulated teaching induces certain behaviour in artificial situations. In simulated teaching a pupil-teacher plays several roles such as; a teacher, as a observer (supervisor) and as a student.

It is assumed that through role perception the psychological appreciation of the classroom problems will grow and develop in pupil-teacher, a basis for handling the problems in the classroom the feedback mechanism can be used for the modification of social communication skills of the pupil-teachers. Thus some teacher behaviour are essential for effective teaching and the teacher behaviour can be identified and practised.

Procedure of Simulation—According to Flandres, the procedure of simulation involves the following steps—

Step. 1—Letters A, B, C, D, E, etc. are assigned to each pail teacher in the group. The role assignments are rotated by given letters so that each individual can get a chance to be an actor or observer.

***Step.* 2**—The teaching skill to be practised are discussed and topics of conversation that suit the skill are also suggested.

***Step.* 3**—After the selection and discussion of specific social skill, it is decided that who will intervene, who will stop the interaction and when it will be summed up? Thus the work schedule is decided.

***Step.* 4**—In this step, decision regarding the procedure of evaluation is taken. It includes the types of data to be recorded, method of recording, way of interpretation of data etc.

***Step.* 5**—After the preparation of all the steps, the first teaching/ practice session is conducted. The feedback is provided to all the pupil-teachers who participate in the practice session for their-performance. The session is followed by discussion and demonstration to provide feedback to the pupil-teacher by giving the awareness of his specific social skill of teaching. If necessary, the procedure of the second session is altered in order to improve the training procedure.

***Step.* 6**—After the first session, necessary changes are made in the teaching procedure. The topics are changed and also pupil-teacher, supervisor and teaching skills are altered to present a meaningful change to each actor to keep his/her interest as high as possible. In this way this cycle goes on till the pupil-teacher is trained in the specific skill

The process of stimulus teaching can be represented as follows—

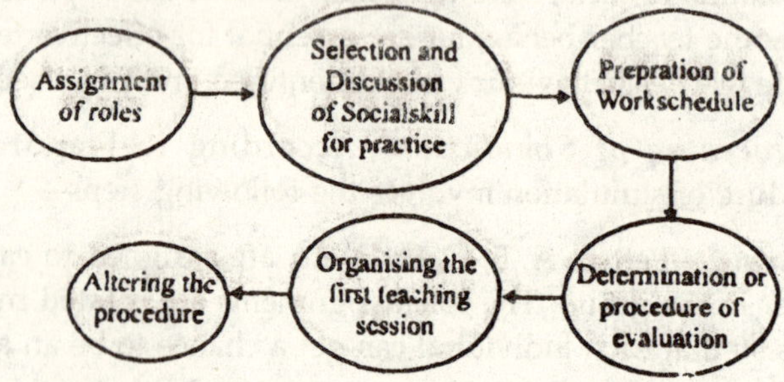

The Elements—The process of simulation consists of three roles; teacher, observer and pupil (student). Cruck shank considered that this teaching paradigm also includes three elements, such as—

* Dianosis
* Prescription
* Evaluation

These three elements can be shown with the help of the following diagram—

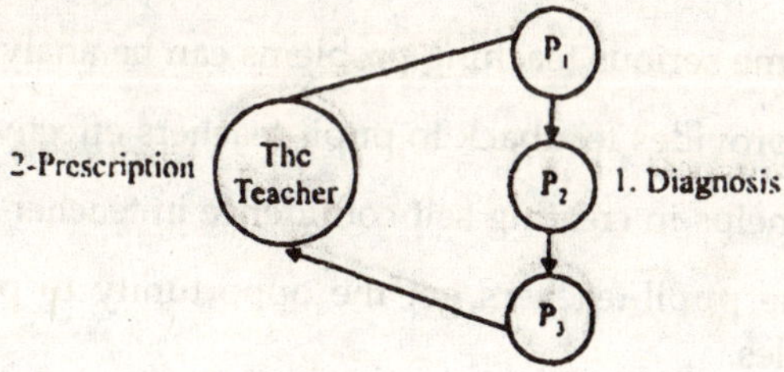

3, observation evaluation P1, P2, P3, are profit

Simulation Games

Simulation games are introduced for the purpose of introducing the elements or qualities of competition, cooperation and conflict as they normally occur in real-life situations. Hoover (1980) has mentioned the following steps in applying simulation games to teaching situations—

Identification of the problem to be used in simulation

↓

Development of the outline of the simulation game

↓

Identification of actors (role players) or terms simulation)

↓

Identification of game resources

↓

Playing the simulation games

↓

Conducting post-game discussions and analysis

The Advantages

* It establishes relationship between theory and practice.
* Some serious teaching problems can be analyse.
* It provides feedback to pupil-teachers effectively.
* It helps in creating self-confidence in teacher-trainees.
* The pupil-teachers get the opportunity to play various roles.
* It helps to modify teachers behaviour and acquiring class-room manners.
* It is useful techniques for slow learners.
* Role consciousness is developed in pupil-teachers.
* It increases the interest and enthusiasm of the pupil-teachers in the class-room teaching.
* This is also useful in research work.
* It promotes high level of critical thinking.
* It motivates students by making real-life situations exciting and interesting.

The Disadvantages

* Some times it becomes difficult to practise teaching skills for many pupil-teachers.
* It is not economical with regards to time, labour and money.
* It is difficult to play various roles by a pupil-teacher.

* This technique needs much preparation, so every teacher cannot opt extra work load.
* It is a training device/technique rather than a teaching device.
* It is quite possible that during an exercise, the observer may record incorrectly.
* It may be more effective; if used with other techniques of teacher-training like micro-teaching etc.

The Problems. Flanders' has suggested the following problems in using Simulated Social Skill Training (SSST)—

* The ability to ask questions either closed or open type of questions.
* The ability to summarize that what students have said previously.
* The ability to move the discussion to the next step in a logical sequences of problem-solving.
* The ability to use the ideas expressed by the students.
* The ability to make the constructive use of both the positive and negative feelings of the students.
* The ability to give reasons for use of praise or blame.
* The ability to guide constructive discussions.
* The ability to assist pupils to compare consequences of alternative actions-through speculation.
* The ability to organise pupils ideas in terms of teaching objectives. These are the same problems which are faced in stimulated teaching.

Hence, it may be conclude that simulated teaching or SSST can be a powerful technique in solving some of the problems of teaching and it can also help in imparting training of certain skills, which are necessary for teaching profession.

Summary

Micro-teaching is an innovative technique in the teacher education. It is a technique of training in which one learns the skills of teaching. It is a scaled down technique which reduced the class size, duration of period and size of topic or content. It provides immediate feedback for trainee's performance. Micro-teaching is a group of such desirable microbehaviours which constitute teaching skills. Micro behaviour contests various activities like; framing a question, thinking, standing position, facing the class etc.

Teaching Skills. Identification of skills by Stanford University and Indian educationist Prof. B.K. Passi.

Micro-teaching Procedure

* There are three phases of micro-teaching procedure—
* Knowledge acquisition phase
* Skill acquisition phase
* Transfer phase

Steps of Micro-teaching

* Identification of specific skill
* Demonstration of the skill
* Micro-lesson planning
* Teaching session
* Providing feedback /evaluation
* Re-planning of Micro-lesson
* Re-teaching session
* Re-feedback/Re-evaluation

In this way this teach-reteach cycle is followed till the desire level of skill is achieved.

Basic Principles of Micro-teaching. Principle of enforcement, continuity, drill and practice, Microscopic supervision and observation.

Advantages of Micro-teaching

* It focuses on training for the accomplishment of skills.
* It provides immediate feedback to the pupil-teacher.
* It permits concentration on some specific skills etc.

Disadvantages of Micro-teaching

* It needs more time and a very expensive technique etc.

Simulated Teaching. It is also known as Simulated Social Skill of Teaching (SSST). Simulation may be defined as role playing in which the process of teaching is enacted artificially and an effort is made to practise some skills of communication. It is not actual teaching. In simulated teaching a pupil-teacher plays several roles such as: a teacher, as a observer and as a student.

Procedure of Simulation. It follows certain steps—

* Assignment of roles.
* Selection and discussion of social skill for practice.
* Preparation of work schedule.
* Procedure of evaluation
* Organizing the first teaching-session.
* Altering the procedure.

Elements of simulated teaching. There are three elements of simulated-teaching, e.g. Diagnosis, prescription and evaluation.

Simulation Games. These are introduced for the purpose of introducing the elements/qualities of competition, cooperation and conflicts. Hoover has mentioned some steps in applying simulation games.

Advantages of simulated teaching. It establishes relationship between theory and practice. It helps in creating self-confidence, modifying teachers behaviour and acquiring class-room manners etc.

Disadvantages of simulated teaching. It is not economical, difficult to play various roles by a single teacher etc.

Problem in Using Simulating-teaching. Flanders' has suggest a number of problems in using simulated teaching.

QUESTIONS

Essay type

1. What is micro-teaching? Outline some teaching skills that can be practised and evaluated by micro-teaching.
2. Explain Micro-teaching. What are its unlading principles? Discuss its merits and demerits.
3. Can we modify teachers behaviour. Suggest some recent techniques for improving teaching skills. Explain any one of them.
4. Micro-teaching is a scaled down teaching. Discuss and justify the statement with appropriate arguments.
5. Explain the term 'Micro-teaching'. Describe its procedure.
6. Explain the term 'Simulated teaching'. Discuss its advantages and limitations.
7. What do you mean by 'Simulated teaching"? How does it help in the training of teachers.
8. What is simulated teaching? Discuss the various steps followed in simulated teaching.
9. Write Notes on the following—

(a) Various teaching skills

(b) Procedure of micro-teaching & Simulated teaching.

(c) Advantage and Limitation of Micro- teaching & simulated teaching.

(d) Place of Micro-teaching in training programme.

Objective type items

Write True for correct statement and False for Wrong.

1. In simulated teaching the participating teacher does not define the goal of simulation. (F)
2. Simulated teaching helps in acquiring class-room manners. (T)
3. Micro-teaching implies the usual class-room teaching ideas. (F)
4. The size of class is reduced in micro-teaching. (T)
5. Effective simulation gives the impression of the real situations. (T)
6. In simulating teaching the role of a teacher becomes that of an evaluator. (F)
7. In micro teaching the supervisor guides the trainees for better grip over the skill. (T)
8. In micro-teaching a single teaching skill is developed at a time. (T)
9. In simulated teaching the pupil plays three roles of teacher, student and observer. (T)
10. There is provision of immediate and effective feedback in micro-teaching. (T)

Answers :

1. F, 2. T, 3. F, 4. T, 5. T, 6. F, 7. T, 8. T, 9. T, 10. T

12
Curriculum Preparation

Concern over the mathematics curriculum in our schools is both wide spread and acute. It is found among layman as well as among professional people. The significance of this important current educational problem is emphasized by the work of committees representing the views of prominent professional organizations and by extensive experimentation being carried on for the purpose of discovering appropriate modification of curriculum content and instructional procedures. Today life is more complex than it was a hundred years ago, the pupil of tomorrow will be pupil of a more complex and intricate world than those of today. World is changing very fast creating new needs and new values and hence the mathematics curriculum which suited during over grandfather's time is not necessarily capable of meeting the present needs of pupil and society. Therefore, schools should exist to educate young persons for effective living in democracy consequently, education in democracy both within and without the school should develop in each individual the knowledge, ideas, habits, powers and interests whereby he will find his place and will use that place to shape both himself and society.

The 'What' and 'How' of mathematics have always been determined by its 'why'. These objectives are fundamentally important to guide curriculum constructors, textbook writers, teachers and other education officers and administrators. Now education is regarded as a dynamic process and so the aims and objectives have changed. It is not merely the course of study but it is the sum total of experiences of a pupil that he receives through various activities. It is much more than subject matter as it is traditionally conceived. Throwing light on the wider meaning of curriculum, the secondary education and commission (Mudalier commission) report (1952-53) that, "curriculum does not mean only the academic subjects traditionally taught in the school, but it includes the totality of experiences that pupil receives through the manifold activities that to in the school, in the classroom, library, laboratory, workshop, playgrounds and in the numerous infounal contects between teachers and pupils. In this sense, the whole life of the school becomes the curriculum which can touch the life of the students at all points and help in the evolution of a balanced personality." Hence curriculum includes all the learning experiences arranged and organised by the school inside or outside the class-rooms.

The curriculum word is derived from a Latin world 'currere', which means to run or 'Race course'. Thus curriculum means a cause to be run for reaching a certain goal'. Indeed curriculum is like a race course for the pupil. As a person runs to win the race in the same way a pupil (Child) undergoes various experiences to run through the curriculum to reach the educational goals. Therefore, etymologically it is clear the curriculum is that path or 'way' over which a child runs to achieve the aims of education. Hence in the wider sense curriculum signifies all those activities and learning experiences which a child undergoes in and outside the class according to his needs attitudes and interests. But in the narrow sense or according to old concept, the meaning of curriculum supposed to be a list of reading material. Reading material was generally called as study subject. In modern time, definitions of curriculum have become wide spread. These definitions in themselves not only include school subjects, but they write all other activities and experiences of the learner.

The Basic Issues

To make the meaning of curriculum more clear and comprehensive, some important definitions are as following.

According to Cunningham—"Curriculum is a tool in the hands of the artist (the teacher) to mould his material (the pupil) according to his ideals (aims and objectives) is his studio (the school).

According to Froebel—"Curriculum should be conceived as an epitom of the rounded whole of the knowledge and experience of the human life."

According to Crow and Crow—"Curriculum includes all the learner's experiences, in or out side school that are included in a programme which has been devised to help him to develop mentally, physically, socially, emotionally, spiritually and morally."

According to Shane, H.G. and Mc Swian, E.J.—"The psychological curriculum may be defined as the sum of experiences the learning, skills, habits and attitudes that the child has made a part of himself and that governs his behaviour as a result of the environment provided by the school."

According to Saylor and Alexander—"The total effort of the school is to bring about desired outcomes in the school and out of the school situation".

Thus, it is clear from the above definitions that curriculum is a means which gives right direction to the teacher, learner, examiners and authors. It includes learner's experiences in or out side school, attitudes, interest, etc., and help the pupil, to develop mentally, physically, socially, spiritually, emotionally as w ell as morally. Hence, organisation of learning experiences in a planned and systematic manner may be called curriculum. It is flexible, varied and progressive in the sense that it tries to meet the needs of the pupil as well as the demands of even changing society.

Purposes of Curriculum. John Dewey emphasize that education takes place in and through the society in which the teacher and taught both line. Thus it is the society which will determines the aims, content or curriculum and methods of teaching. Therefore, the process of education contains three poles. The teacher, the child and the society. As a matter of fact, education consists in the interaction of these three factors. Yet curriculum has a greater importance because without curriculum neither the teacher will be able to impart knowledge effectively nor the learner will be able to learn any thing correctly. Therefore, here we will discuss the various aims or purposes which a curriculum should achieve.

* To make pupil capable of understanding their national heritage and having faith in it. Along with it to evoke feeling for honour of an individual.
* To develop/prepare the all round personality of a pupil and to develop appropriate mental and emotional point of views and habits
* To develop knowledge and various skills in a child according to his abilities.
* To lay foundation for rich, useful and moral life so that the child may contribute for social welfare.
* To develop a unique judgement ability so that they may differentiate good and evil.
* To develop interest and abilities in child for search.
* To develop the thinking searching understanding and decision making abilities of a child for moral development.
* To promote and develop various constructive and creative abilities of child in conformity with the different stages of his development.
* To create new values for themselves by means of their resourcefulness, courage, behaviour and scientific attitude.
* To indicate aesthetic expression and appreciation in a child.
* To develop appropriate social and economic relations, so that the child may lead life in family, school and society.
* To develop vocational skills and to provide the child, knowledge of economic relations of human society.
* To promote international outlook and a sense of international brotherhood in the child.
* To create and develop faith in child for Indian republic and feeling of pride to make him aware with citizens rights and responsibilities.

Basic Principles

While the construction of curriculum in mathematics. The content should be related according to the changing needs of society in general and the subject, mathematics in particular. While constructing the mathematics curriculum following principles should be kept in mind—

Principle of Unity—While constructing curriculum in mathematics, we should include only those topics which are useful for a particular grade in many ways. In the first place, we should include those topics which are useful in our day to day life e.g. the four fundamental operations, tables percentage, profit and loss, areas, taxes, simpler nations of statistics, household accounts, graphs etc. Utility of a topic should be viewed in a broader perspective that is utility (i) in everyday life. (ii) in the study of other subjects, (iii) in various vocations, (iv) in appreciating the part played by mathematics in the development of civilization in its various aspects in commerce, trade, industry, engineering, physical & social science.

Principle of Community-Centralities—The child is to live in and for the society. He must be able to do well in society. So we should include those topics of mathematics which later to the needs, aspirations and ideas of the community. So curriculum must be shaped for the needs and welfare of the local community.

Principle of Flexibility—The aims of education and the aims of teaching mathematics to on changing. These aims depend upon the overcleaning society. Also the development and research in the subject necessitate changes in the curriculum. So we can not follow a rigid curriculum for all times. This has to be modified and revised from time to time.

Principle of Child Centruroides—Math matics is a vast subject, there are so many things which are useful to he students, we are likely to be over ambitious. While deciding upon useful content, we must not forget the children for whom that is meant. We should remember that curriculum is for the child and not the child for curriculum. Child interests, abilities, age level etc. should be kept in mind. The duration of the course, is another factor to be attended to. Moreover, there are individual differences in children. The same type of content may not be desirable for all. So there should be provision in the syllabus for various categories of students.

Teacher's Point of View—While framing or revising the curriculum, the teachers who are the real field workers should also be sought, they know the levels of students and the things which should to tought to the students. At present the curriculum is imposed on the teachers and as such, they don't realize the significance of changes in the curriculum if any.

Principle of Disciplinary Value—We know that mathematics is a subject which disciplines the mind. In the past this was the sole criterion to select the subject matter. This brought into syllabus much useless material. The pupils used to study certain Puzzles and riddles which had no particular utility. For disciplining the mind, one topic is as good as another. Unless and until a topic has some other values, it should not be included in the curriculum merely for its disciplinary value, Read useful problems train the mind better than unreal formal problems moreover, mental training depends upon the method of teaching.

Principle of Cultural Value—The subject of mathematics has played a great role in the advancement of culture and civilization. There may be curtain ideas which were pursued by the students of mathematics but these ideas may not be of any use now. But there are certain ideas and facts of mathematics which still form an integral part of modern culture and society. Such facts or ideas should be included in the curriculum. Their study will be a some of inspiration to the students.

Principle of Correlation—While organising the content in mathematics, we should arrange the topic in such a way that correlation of the subject is possible. Correlation can be of the following types—

(i) Correlation with life.

(ii) Correlation with other subjects.

(iii) Correlation among the branches of some subjects.

(iv) Correlations among the topics of the same branch.

(v) Coloration with craft or work experience.

In order to correlate teaching of the subjects, we must know—

(i) Day to day life activities.

(ii) The nature of topics included in the other subjects at the same stage.

(iii) The topics included in different branches of the subjects e.g. Arithmetic, Algebra, Geography etc.

(iv) The requiems of topics of the same branch of the subject.

(v) The nature of work experience or projects undertaken by the students.

Principle of Moderenisation—We should trace the curriculum according to the latest developments of the subjects and in accordance with the modern world. For this purpose the views of the subject specialists should be sought.

Principle of Preparatory Value—The content should include topics which prepare the child (a) for university education (b) for life. There is only a small percentage of students. Which go up to the university stage whereas for most of the students, school is a terminal stage. Thus the requirements of the college course need not dominate the school curriculum. We must see that those who leave the school for good, are as fully equipped as possible. So we should include the topics and materials which are useful for a wide variety of vocations.

However, there are topics which can be learn from the point of view of higher learning and which may also be useful for the second category of students. Such topics prepare a sound background for any type of further learning or course. So these topics must be included in the curriculum.

Thus we see that while constructing curriculum for a grade, a number of considerations are to be kept in mind. Utility should provide the chief criterion of curriculum construction, of course the latest trend in the subject. The needs of community, the needs of students and above all, the views of the teachers should be given due importance in any programme of curriculum construction in mathematics.

Recommendation of Secondary Education Commission. Secondary Education commission (1952-53) has suggested following principles of curriculum construction in mathematics

* Principle of variety
* Principle of flexibility or elasticity.
* Principle related to proper utilisation of leisure time.
* Curriculum should be correlated with life.
* It should be based on dinasified activities
* It should be according to the needs of the society.

The Foundation

It is clear that curriculum is positively correlated with the needs and requirements of the society for which it is formulated, Organised and developed. There are four important basics of curriculum construction :

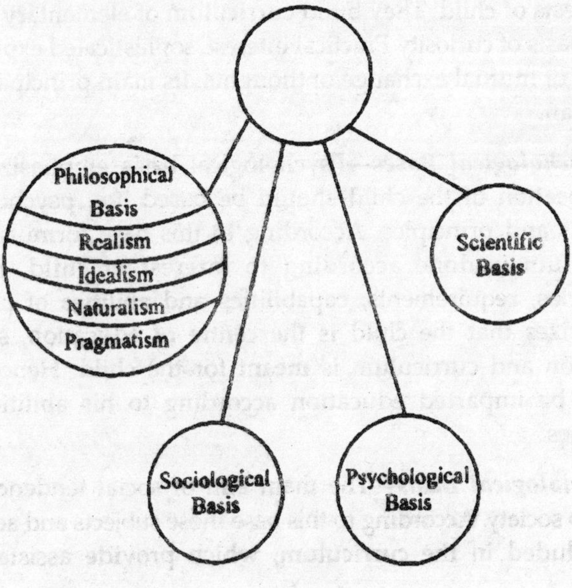

Philosophical Basis—Construction of curriculum is done for achieving objectives of education. The curriculum is determined in different forms. Here we are throwing light on the curriculum construction according to the following philosophies :

Realism—It includes those activities in curriculum through which knowledge can be obtained in real situations of life. Realistic curriculum is developed according to utility and needs. Subjects concerning day to day activities are included in realistic curriculum.

Idealism—The main aim of curriculum assumes thoughts, eternal values and ideas of man. Idealism provide principal place to literature art, music etc. in curriculum. In idealistic curriculum humanistic subjects are emphasized.

Naturalism—Free development of individuality of child is one of the major aim of education. Due to this reason, naturalists are supporters of providing unlimited liberty to the child for self-expression. In naturalistic curriculum science subjects occupy main place.

Pragmatism—Pragmatic curriculum is based on subjects of utility. Construction of pragmatic curriculum is done according to interests of child. They build curriculum of elementary classes on the basis of curiosity Practical interest, sophisticated expression, interest of mutual exchange of thoughts. Its main principal being utilitarian.

Psychological Bases—Psychological basis emphasizes that the education of the child should be based qon psychological methods and principles. According to this base formulation of curriculum is done according to interest of child, natural tendencies, requirements, capabilities and abilities of child. It emphasizes that the child is the centre of education, so both education and curriculum is meant for the child. Hence child should be imparted education according to his abilities and capacities.

Sociological Basis—The main aim of social tendency is to develop society. According to this base those subjects and activities are included in the curriculum, which provide assistance in developing appreciation of sociability. This tendency emphasizes inclusion of social qualities in children so that they also contribute their best to social welfare and advancements.

Scientific Basis—According to this base, more importance is given to the scientific subjects in curriculum. Its supporters hold the view that it is only after the study of scientific subjects that man can lead a complete life. It opposes literary education and proposes practical and useful knowledge. It promotes scientific attitude towards life and society.

Different Types

There are various types of curriculum in mathematics. In brief they are as follow—

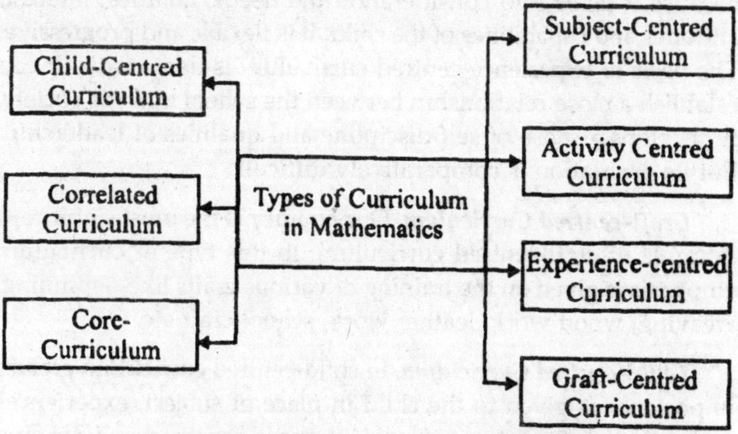

Various Types of Curriculum in Mathematics

Subject-centrad Curriculum. Subject-centered curriculum gives more emphasis on subject matter in place of the child. This is also called Book-centrad curriculum because it lays emphasis on bookish knowledge and learning. It is based upon a clear specific ideology of education and sociability. It can achieve an effective correlation among various subjects. It facilitates testing and examination. Subject-cetnred curriculum is unpsychological in nature because it pays no consideration to the needs, interests, attitude, capacities and abilities of the child. Its content is definite and predetermined. Subject-centered curriculum cannot lead to wholesome development of the personality of child.

Activity-centred Curriculum. In activity-centred curriculum various activities are emphasized in a specific manner. In support of this John Dewey expressed his views emphatically that by means of activity-centred curriculum, a child will develop interest in useful and purposeful activities which will promote his developments to the fullest extent possible.

Experience-centred Curriculum. In experience-centred curriculum, experiences are regarded as more important for the development of a child in comparison with emphasis on subject and activities. It necessarily needs very capable and intelligent teachers for its implementation. It is a psychological in nature because it takes into consideration the needs, abilities, interest, attitudes and capabilities of the child. It is flexible and progressive. The basis of experience-centred curriculum is democratic. It can establish a close relationship between the school and the society. It develops a sense of self discipline and qualities of leadership. But its evaluation is comparatively difficult.

Craft-centred Curriculum. Our country is the most significant example of craft-centred curriculum. In this type of curriculum emphasis is given on the training of various crafts like—spinning, weaving, wood work, leather work, school craft etc.

Child-centred Curriculum. In child-centred curriculum greater importance is given to the child in-place of subject, experiences and activities. Such type of curriculums is constructed according to the needs, capacities, attitudes, interest, hobbies, and physical as well as mental level of the child. Thus it helps in harmonious development of personality of child. Kinder-garten, Montessori, project and heuristic method etc. are the examples of child-centred curriculum. Hence, it is constructed on the basis of psychological principles and theories.

Correlated Curriculum. Correlated curriculum is more a methodology rather than a type of curriculum construction. This signifies the intimate connection and correlation of various subjects in the curriculum. Correlaterd curriculum emphasizes that instead of presenting knowledge in segments (parts), it should be presented as an integrated whole through integration and correlation.

Core-curriculum. In the core curriculum, some subjects are grouped together as essential and compulsory subject and many other subjects become optional. Study of the compulsory subjects, known as core-curriculum, is necessary for all children, and out of the optional or elective subjects, a child is free to select one or more according to his needs, interests and abilities. Core-curriculum aims to develop both individual and society. It is child-centred and gives practice and experiences to solve social problems. Thus according to it so many subjects are taught together and the child becomes a dynamic efficient and socially useful individual.

The Drawbacks

The main defects of existing curriculum are as follows—

1. There is no conformity with the aims and learning experiences of teaching mathematics.
2. It is subject centred and topical.
3. The approach in curriculum construction is not pragmatic.
4. It is not constructed according to the social and cultural values of teaching mathematics.
5. So many rules, principles, concepts and problems are not all connected with our daily life.
6. In the existing curriculum separate content is written for Arithmetic, Algebra and geometry. It shows that they are not correlated with each other.
7. At Primary stage only arithmetic is included in the curriculum.
8. A number of topics and problems that have been included are dull, uninteresting and useless.
9. The curriculum of primary, upper primary, secondary, and

senior secondary (intermediate) stage are not correlated carefully, so that the contents of many topics are separated in higher classes.

10. Teaching of geometry in class 6 is not according to psychological principles.
11. It does not give commercial and technical training to the pupils, so they are unable to utilize their knowledge.
12. No place is given to practical work in mathematics.
13. Present curriculum emphasizes on examination.
14. Present curriculum is not flexible.
15. There is main emphasis on exercise and revision, but it is not high lighted that which part of the content should be revised.
16. In mathematics curriculum there is no pace with social progress.
17. There are no creative activities in existing mathematical curriculum.
18. It is devoid of mathematical activities like mathematics clubs, Hobbies etc.
19. It outfits the different age groups, the capabilities interests of different age groups are not taken in to consideration while framing the mathematics curriculum.

In this way after critical evaluation or study of mathematics curriculum we find out that present mathematics curriculum is bookish, theoretical, unpsychological, and overcrowded, so there is a need of improvement. The curriculum should be child centred, activity centred and useful to the children.

According to Secondary Education Commission (1952-1953) Report, the defects in present mathematics curriculum are as follows :

1. Present mathematics curriculum is narrow in conception.
2. It is bookish and theoretical.

3. It is not related to daily life of children.
4. Its content is voluminous and not rich and significant.
5. It is examination ridden.
6. It has lack of technical and vocational subjects.
7. In this curriculum the individual differences of children are not taken in to accounts.
8. There is no attention towards interests and needs of children in the curriculum.
9. The construction of curriculum is unpsychological.
10. The execution of curriculum is not effective.
11. There is no attention towards the needs of children as well as society.

According to Kothari Commission (1964-66) there are following defects in the existing curriculum:

1. Present mathematics curriculum is inadequate. It does not consist all experiences of pupils.
2. Existing mathematics curriculum is not useful and there is lack of creative activities.
3. Existing mathematics curriculum is overpacked.

In this way critical appraisal of existing mathematics curriculum can be made on the basis of following points:

1. Relation between content and teaching objectives.
2. Comprehensiveness of the content.
3. Selection and organisation of subject matter.
4. Child centeredness of content.
5. Theoretical and practical aspects of the content.
6. Correlation in subject matter.
7. Utility of content is relation to examination and evaluation of pupils.

Guidelines for Reforms

From the above discussion it is clear that the existing curriculum of mathematics has many defects. This curriculum has failed in its task of promoting complete and harmonious development of the child. The existing curriculum needs and early reorientation on the lines suggested as follows—

* While constructing the curriculum due importance should be given to the aims and objectives of teaching mathematics.
* Cognitive, affective and Psychomotor domain must be considered while determining the objectives.
* Curriculum should consist of variety of physical and intellectual activities which are necessary for proper adjustment to the social and physical environment.
* There should be the provision for practical work so that learning by doing may tape place in the learning mathematics.
* Oral and home work should be given due importance with written and drill work in mathematics.
* Content should be organised in logical and psychological order.
* While constructing curriculum child's needs, interest, attitudes, abilities and capabilities should be considered well.
* Curriculum should be flexible and should fulfill the varying needs of the child and the society.
* It should include the content which helps in the appreciation of the work and contribution of great mathematicians.
* The learning experiences should be organised in order of difficulty i.e. from simple to complex.
* It should solve the problems of livelihood of the child.

* In the mathematics curriculum various topics and activities should not remain isolated, but they should form an integrated whole.

* It should provide education for useful utilization of leisure time. The Kothari Commission (1994-1966) has also suggested a member of recommendations to overcome the defects of existing curriculum. Some important recommendations suggested are given below—

* There should be periodic revision of curriculum.

* School curriculum should be upgraded through research and advancements.

* It should be under taken by University departments of Education, Training institutions, Boards of School Education and State Institutes of Education.

* Schools should be given freedom to devise and experiment new curriculum which suited to their needs.

* The preparation of test books and teaching-learning material should be under taken on a large scale.

* To revise the curriculum, Orientation programmes for teachers should be organised.

* The Subject Teacher's Associations (STA) in different school subjects should be formed, so that it may help to stimulate experimentation and the upgrading do curriculum.

* Curriculum should be child centred and should develop the natural interests, aptitudes and capacities of child and satisfy his needs.

National curriculum framework for School Education, NCERT Document (2000) has also suggested a number of recommendations to improve the curriculum. Some of the major recommendations are as follows—

With their increasingly ubiquitous presence within and outside the school, Information and Communication Technologies

(ICT) have begun to challenge what schools (all over the world) try to teach and the whole basis of assessing the knowledge and skills that-students acquire. The process of education can no longer ignore the social and psychological impacts of the technology that structures information and the possibilities that global information sharing opens up. Furthermore, that these technologies affect the way people think and learn has been widely recognized.

Integration of ICT into schools, therefore, has a strong pedagogical rationale and is a natural sequence in the evolution of the schooling process. But this integration has several implications, which clearly make the following demands :

1. The educational planner looks beyond the current class room devises updated plans for education in an electronic environment and expands his designs so that the computer becomes more than a subject of study and is not merely integrated into an existing curriculum. It becomes, instead, an integral part of the scowling process.
2. The educator accepts the broad general principles that he is challenged with. These are :
   * Creation of framework for enhancing learning opportunities that computer-based learning material and accessible resources offer;
   * Access to information, shared educational goals and pedagogy;
   * Access to professional development opportunities for teachers which would enable them to act as facilitators of learning;
   * Flexible curriculum models which would embrace interdisciplinary and cross-disciplinary thinking; and
   * Development of attitudes that are value-driven, not technology— driven.
3. The curriculum developer re-defines his role. All innovative experiments in the areas of media production,

interactive video and multimedia computer software are curriculum development processes. They come to naught without active participation of the curriculum developer.

4. The teacher adopts an instructional design that helps learners master heuristic and algorithmic strategies for tackling new problems using the computer and communication technologies, wherever possible, as apposed to strategies that aim at mastery of discrete units of fixed knowledge.

5. A method of evaluation and assessment of what students learn in ICT-rich environment supported by the computer and communication technologies must evolve, for this environment is going to cause perceptible shifts from:

   * Traditional learning atmosphere to a climate of values that encourages exploration, problem-solving and decision-making;
   * Didactic classroom teaching to participatory and interactive group learning;
   * Linear, sequential reasoning to search for patterns and connections;
   * Mastery of fixed body of knowledge to understanding a web of relations between the parts of a whole; and
   * Collection of information to processing of information, leading to knowledge management skills.
   * The traditional tests cannot measure the skills and abilities that result from these shifts.

6. It is only with new skills and perceptions that the teacher can assume his/her new role as a facilitator of learning and implement and maintain innovations in the classroom. This calls for a new definition of pre-service courses and effective training and orientation programmes for those who are already in the job. The new courses should help teachers acquire skills of using information technology as well as making the best use of computer in curriculum transaction.

7. The management system for vocational educational has to be developed in strength, structure and task delineations.

8. A sound programme of vocational education requires extensive and broad-based preparation through work education and pre-vocation education during the first ten years of formal schooling.

Elementary and Secondary Stages

According to National Curriculum Framework for school education, NCERT (2000). Some new thrust areas may also need to be added in the light of the changes all around. School education in the present scenario has to have the main thrust on the following :-

* Inculcation and sustenance of personal, social, national and spiritual values like cleanliness and punctuality, good conduct, tolerance and justice; a sense of national identity and respect for law and order and truthfulness.

* Elimination of poverty, ignorance, ill-health, chastises, dowry, untouchability, and violence, and ensuring equity, health, peace and prosperity.

* Thinking, experiences and innovations which are rooted in the Indian-tradition and ethos and relating these with global thinking.

* Establishing uniformity of structure of school education, i.e., 10 + 2 + 3 throughout the country.

* Broad-based general education to all learners up to the end of the secondary stage to help them become life long learners and acquire basic life skills and high standards of Intelligence Quotient (IQ), Emotional Quotient (EQ), and Spiritual Quotient (SQ).

* A common scheme of studies for the elementary and secondary stages with emphasis on the skill of 'learning how to learn' with flexibility of content and mode of

learning to suite all learners including those with special needs.

* Inclusion of Fundamental Duties and the core curricular areas at all the stages of school education.
* Human Rights including the right of the child, especially those of the girl child.
* Ensuring the minimum essential level of the acquisition of knowledge, understanding and skill at all stages, commensurate with the learners abilities and the societal context.
* Freedom, flexibility, revance and transparency in the section of content, transaction and procedures at different stages of school education.
* Nurturance and sustenance of multiple talents and creativity among all learners in various domains of knowledge.
* Shift of emphasis from information-based and teacher centred education to process centred and learner friendly education.
* Development of a responsive and supportive system of evaluation.

Development Method

While organizing the curriculum in any subject generally two methods are adopted. They are-

* Topical Method
* Spiral Method

Topical Method. Topical arrangement means that a topic should be finished entirely at one stage. It takes the topic as a unit. Topical arrangement requires that easy and difficult portions of a topic should be dealt with one stage only which is not psychological. In this system the topic which is dealt with earlier receives no attention later and so there is every likelihood of its being forgotten. The main defect in the topical method is that it introduces in the curriculum a large mass of irrelevant material for which the pupil finds no time and no immediate need or the use of which can not be appreciated by the pupil at that stage. They are introduced with a view to make the teaching of the topic complete and through. Hence topical method demands that a topic once taken should be finished in its entirety, so that this is not more useful for lower classes.

Spiral Method. Spiral method of curriculum organisation is based on the principle that a subject can not be given an exhaustive treatment at the first stage. This method demands the division of the topic or the subject into a number of smaller independent units to be dealt with in order of difficulty suiting the mental capacities of the pupils. Spiral method has got the advantage of providing opportunities for revision. If topics are taught thoroughly before going on to the next ones, certain proteins are not taught at an early stage when the pupils feel the need for them or when they can very well appreciate their use. Therefore, topics should be graded according to difficulty. Each part should be introduced at a stage when it is needed and when the pupil has attained the stage of development which would enable him to understand and appreciate its use. Hence we should see to the combination of things which can be best learns together.

For example, the best stage for teaching equations in algebra is the stage when we are dealing with the inverse problem in arithmetic. Similarly $V = L \times B \times H$ is easier than area of a circle or a triangle. Thus this is a practical method of organizations of curriculum.

Concept and Meaning of Curriculum. Curriculum is not merely the course of study but it is the sum total of experiences of a pupil that he receives through various activities. The curriculum word is derived from a Latin word 'Curere', which means 'to run' or 'Race Course.' Thus it means a course to be run for reaching a certain goal. Thus curriculum is that way over which a child runs to achieve the aims of educations.

Definitions. 1. Cunningham 2. Rebel 3. Crow & & Crow 4. Shane, H.G. and MC Swairn, E.J. 5. Saylor & Alexander.

Purpose of Curriculum. So develop knowledge, various skills, judgement abilities, interest, thinking, reasoning, under-standing, new values, arithmetic expression, appreciation, social and economic relations, vocational skills etc.

Principles of Curriculum Constructions in Mathe

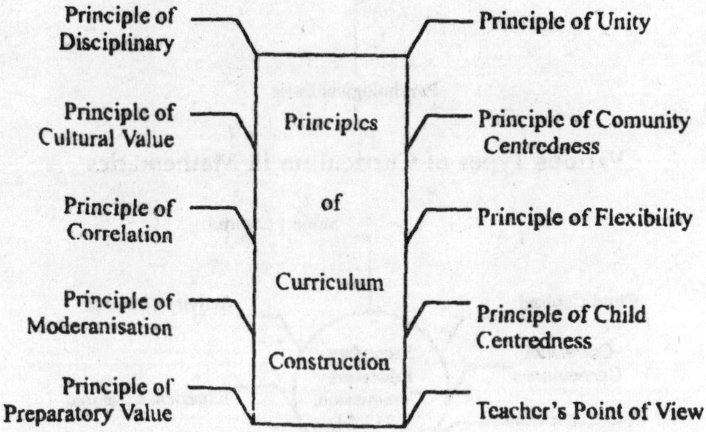

Principles of Curriculum Construction According to Secondary Education Commission (1952-53)

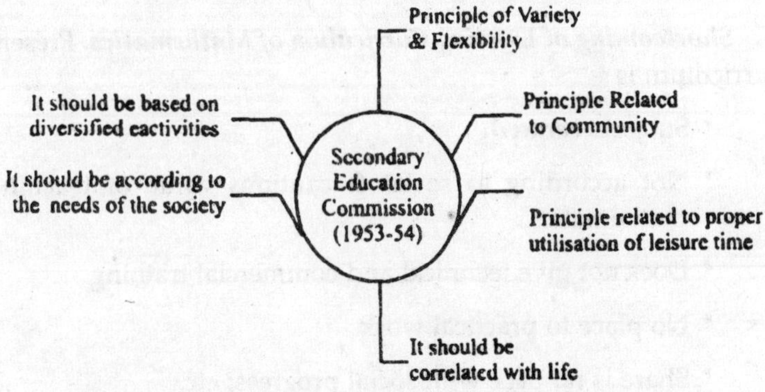

Basis of Curriculum Construction in Mathematics

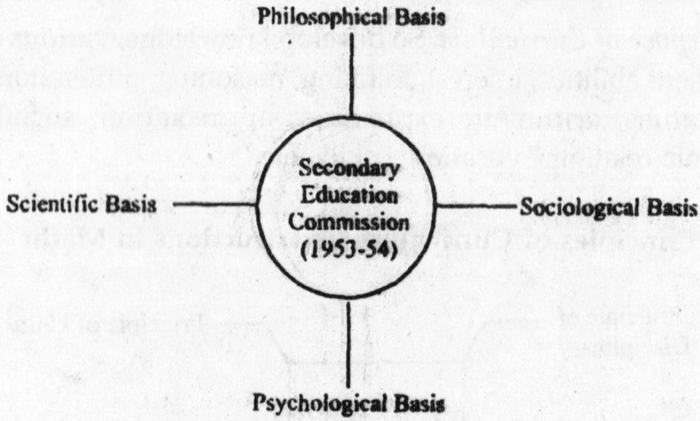

Various Types of Curriculum in Mathematics

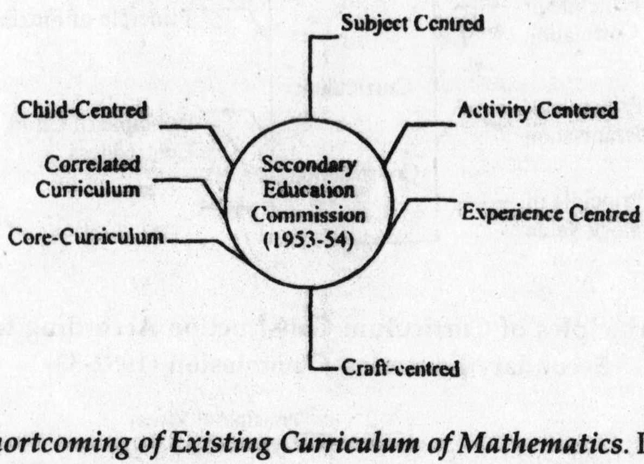

Shortcoming of Existing Curriculum of Mathematics. Present curriculum is

* Subjects centred
* Not according to social & cautions value of teaching mathematics.
* Does not give technical and commercial training.
* No place to practical work.
* Share is no pace with social progress; etc.

Shortcomings According to Secondary Education Commission (1952-53). It is bookish, narrow, theoretical, examination ridden, lack of technical & vocational subjects etc.

Shortcomings According to Kothari Commission (1964-66). It is in adequate, lack of creative activities, over packed etc.

Suggestions for Improvement in the Existing Mathematics Curriculum

* General suggestion
* Suggestions according to Kothari commission (1964-1966)
* Suggestion according to National Curriculum Frame work for school Education, NCERT, Document (2000).

Organisation of Curriculum in Mathematics at Elementary and Secondary Stages.

* Indication and sustenance of personal, social, national and spiritual values.
* Elimination of poverty, ignorance, ill health etc.
* Broad-based general education for all up to secondary stage etc.

QUESTIONS

A. Essay Type Questions

1. What points would you bear in mind while framing a curriculum in mathematics at secondary stage? Critically comment on the existing curriculum and give suggestions for its improvement.
2. Define curriculum. What points must be kept in mind while constructing mathematics curriculum?
3. Define the term 'Curriculum'. Explaining the basic principle of construction of mathematics curriculum at school level.
4. Explain the detail the principle of curriculum construction in mathematics.
5. Give a critical appraisal of existing curriculum of mathematics at secondary level in your state. Give your suggestion to improve it.

6. Discuss the need and importance of curriculum. Explain different types of curriculum.
7. What do you mean by organisation of curriculum ? Illustrate the various methods of curriculums organization.
8. How does curriculum differ from syllabus? Enlist the syllabus of mathematics at secondary (High school) stage.
9. Write notes on the following—
   (a) Different types of curriculum.
   (b) Defects or shortcoming of existing curriculum.
   (c) Principles of curriculum construction given by secondary Education Commission 1952-53.
   (d) Syllabus of mathematics at upper primary stage.
   (e) Rate of mathematics teacher in the construction and execution of curriculum.
10. Discuss the various types of curriculum in mathematics? What are the basis of curriculum construction in mathematics?

B. Objective Type Question

1. Multiple Choice Items

1. The word 'curriculum' is derived from—
   (a) Latin language (c) French language
   (b) German language (d) None of these
2. Organization of curriculum on the basis of topics is called—
   (a) Spiral method (c) Concentric method
   (b) Topical method (d) None of the above
3. Curriculum means—
   (a) Subject-matter
   (b) Activities and experiences in school situations
   (c) Topics from different concepts
   (d) All the above

4. In subject centred curriculum more emphasis is given on—

   (a) Subject matter (b) Child
   (c) both a & b (d) None of these

5. In which type of curriculum emphasis is given on the training of various crafts—

   (a) Child-centred (b) Experience-centred
   (c) Craft-centred (d) All the above

2. *True/False Type Questions*

1. Spiral method of curriculum construction is more effective than topical method.
2. Teachers usually follow mathematics syllabus not the mathematics curriculum.
3. Subject-centred curriculum is also called text-book-centred curriculums.
4. In spiral method the topic/ subject matter is divided into a number of independent units.
5. Topical method demands that a topic should be finished entirely at one stage.
6. The present curriculum of mathematics is topical and subjects centred.

13
Curriculum Development

Curriculum development is a process in which different components such as formulation of a curriculum policy, curriculum research, curriculum planning, its implementation and then its evaluation play an important role. The curricular framework generates creative thinking at various levels of decision making such as at the national, state regional and district levels. It provides a great deal of flexibility to provide space for local specificity and contextual realities. In evolving the curricular policy the views and participation of all the stakeholders from parents to teachers and various other members and interest groups of the society are fully well ensured.

International experiences have shown that neither the completely centralised approach nor the totally decentralised approach to curriculum development has really been successful. The countries which at one point of time had tried the decentralised approach to curriculum development subsequently reverted back to some kind of a nationally developed centralised curricular policy.

The impact of school curriculum is so crucial for national and state policies that in most of the countries of the world this responsibility is shouldered by various government and national level organizations and agencies. In fact, no country can afford to ignore the curriculum development process.

The Backdrop

The NCERT emerged as a nodal agency at the national level in the area of school education. It was involved directly in the process of curriculum development and preparation of textbooks. This was gradually followed by the establishment of the State Institutes of Education, State Textbook Boards, and the State Councils of Educational Research and Training (SCERT) for providing technical support to research and development activities related to the formulation of curriculum and the preparation of textbooks at the state/union territory level.

The publication of *The Curriculum For the Ten Year School—A Framework* in 1975, and Higher Secondary Education and its vocationalisation in 1976 by the NCERT gave concrete shape to the efforts for restructuring of school education and the adoption of the 10 + 2 pattern as recommended by the Education Commission (1964-66). The NCERT then developed supporting syllabi and textbooks to be used as models by states and union territories. The Curriculum for the *Ten Year School: A Framework* (1975) provided an impetus to the teaching of environment studies, science and mathematics as part of the general education curriculum from the primary level.

The National Curriculum for Elementary and Secondary Education—A framework brought out by the NCERT in 1988 responded to the major thrusts and recommendations highlighted in the *National Policy on Education* (1986) and the *Programme of Action* (August 1986) by incorporating the socio-cultural, political and economic considerations as well as some important pedagogical concerns.

The pedagogical issues highlighted in the *National Policy on Education* (1986) were also adequately reflected in the 1988 curriculum framework. Emphasis was also laid on continuous and comprehensive evaluation as well as on utilisation of media and educational technology. In its totality, the curriculum framework of 1988 has contributed to the development of a national system of school education by ensuring uniformity of levels and standards. In addition to this, realisation of the goals enshrined in the Indian Constitution was one of the major objectives of the 1988 curriculum. As in the year 1975, comprehensive guidelines were again developed for preparing detailed syllabi for different stages of school education. The state governments also took steps for developing their own curricula, syllabi and instructional materials.

The basic features and main thrusts of the 1988 curriculum framework stem from the policy documents on education (NPE 1986, and POA 1986). While briefly reviewing he implementation of the various thrust areas, one finds that improvement was evident in a number of areas like strengthening and restructuring of teacher education, National Literacy Mission, and improvement of Science Education in Schools it is felt that much still needs to be done. Of the several thrust areas, only a few could be implemented and that too in a limited manner. A centrally sponsored scheme like 'Operation Blackboard' providing science kits, musical instruments etc. as a one time support should have created much better impact. Obviously, efforts for developing a national system of education as envisaged by the policy makers have to be strengthened further.

Over the last decade, changes in every walk of human endeavour have been much greater in magnitude and impact as compared to those during the earlier five or six decades. The educational and social demands have changed. In fact, education and learning have undergone a transformation. India and many other countries have looked critically on their education systems and have come out with a frank and honest assessment thereof. *The Challenge of Education* (India, 1985), *A Nation at Risk* (USA, 1983) and *Learning to Succeed* (UK, 1993) have looked hard at their national systems of education. At the International level the UNESCO document (1986), *Learning: The Treasure Within* has also taken a critical look at the total educational scenario and made long range meaningful suggestions.

Within the ambit of systems and structures, curriculum design has an important role to play. It is generally accepted that in education, curriculum renewal and development is an ongoing process and no national can afford to go slow in the matter. The curriculum must meet the learner's needs, societal expectations, community aspirations and international comparisons. (National Curriculum Framework for School Education, NCERT 2000, Document).

Main Aims

The emphasis on the 'learner-centred approach' necessitates careful determination of the objectives of education to be achieved at a particular stage/class in keeping with the norms of physical, mental, social, and emotional development of the learners of the relevant age-group. However, the level of achievement with regard to a particular objective will be rising from one class to another in a spiral fashion. Therefore, school curriculum has to aim at enabling learners to acquire knowledge, develop understanding and inculcate skills, positive attitudes, values and habits conducive to the all-round development of their personality, young girls and boys, are to be empowered through education to increase their capability. Paradigm shifts are therefore necessary to support a curriculum that values the interaction of the process and the content. In NCERT's National curriculum france work for School Education 12000 document; it is highlighted that school the following objectives school curriculum has therefore, to help to generate and promote among the children—

* Language abilities of listening, speaking, reading, writing and thinking and communication skills—verbal and visual-needed for social living and effective participation in the day to day activities;
* Mathematical abilities to develop a logical mind that would help learners to perform mathematical operations and apply them in every day life;
* Scientific temper characterised by the spirit of enquiry, problemsolving, courage to question and objectivity leading to elimination of obscurantism, supersition and fatalism, while at the same time, sustaining and emphasising the indigenous knowledge ingrained in the Indian tradition;
* Understanding of the environment in its totality both natural and social, and their interactive processes, the environmental problems and the ways and means to preserve the environment;

* Understanding of the positive and the negative impact of the processes of globalisation, liberalisation and localisation in the context of the country;
* Qualities clustered around the personal, social, moral, national and spiritual values that make a person humane and socially effective, giving meaning and direction to life;
* Knowledge, attitude and habits necessary for keeping physically and mentally fit and strong in perfect harmony with the earth, water, air, fire and the sky;
* Qualities and characteristics necessary for self-learning, self-directed learning and life-long learning leading to the creation of a learning society;
* Capacity not only to process information but also to understand, reflect and internalise and develop insight;
* Willingness to work hard, entrepreneurship and dignity of manual work necessary for increasing productivity, obtaining job satisfaction and creating wealth generating systems;
* Acquisition of pre-vocational/vocational skills;
* Appreciation of the various consequences of large families and over population and need for checking population growth; and
* Cultivating proper understanding of and attitude toward healthy sex related issues and respectful attitude toward members of the opposite sex.
* Understanding of the diversity in lands and people living in different parts of the country and the country's composite cultural heritage;
* Appreciation of the sacrifices and contributions made by the freedom fighters and social workers from rural, tribal and weaker sections from all the regions of the Indian society, particularly India's freedom struggle and social regeneration, and readiness to follow their ideals;

* Appreciation for the need of a balanced synthesis between the change oriented technologies and the continuity of the country's traditions and heritage;

* Knowledge of and respect for the national symbols and the desire and determination to uphold the ideals of national identify and unity;

* Deep sense of patriotism and nationalism tempered with the spirit of *Vasudhaiva Kutumbakum.*

Various Stages

There are four stages of curriculum development in mathematics:

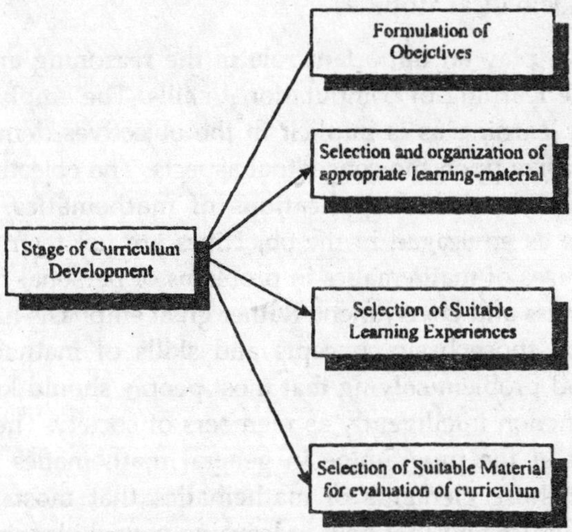

Formulation of Objectives—The objectives of teaching mathematics formulated and determined in behavioural terms. While formulating and determining objectives following points should be kept in mind—

* That the set of objectives formulated should indicate both the desired behaviour and the type of situation in which it is to occur.

* An objective should be expressed in terms of desired pupil behaviour rather than of teacher behaviour.

* An objective should be specifically stated so that it is possible to infer some appropriate learning activities.

Selection and Organisation of Appropriate Learning-Material—The selection of suitable content depends to a great extent on those basic considerations that underlie in the formulation of objectives. The objectives recognize four significant aspects of mathematical learning—

* Concepts or meanings
* Computational skills
* Problem-solving (reasoning), and
* Mathematical attitudes.

Concepts play an important role in the reasoning and also facilitate the learning of computational skills. The emphasis on meaningful learning as is implicit in the objectives demand in turn, emphasize upon the conceptual aspects. The objectives lay emphasis on the social applications of mathematics. Social applications as envisaged in the objectives are not restricted to traditional uses of mathematics in problems of personal finance, home, business and government. Rather great emphasis has been placed upon those basic concepts and skills of mathematical thinking and problem-solving that most people should know in order to function intelligently as members of society. Therefore, the content of the programme in general mathematics should include all those elements of mathematics that most people occassionally use and that help in learning new skills which the future will demand for many of them.

Thus, an analysis of the objectives clearly shows the importance of concepts in effective learning of mathematics, in usefulness of mathematics and in preserving the nature of mathematics. A second force that has guided the choice of content is the new thinking which now going on in school teaching. A few of the recommendations taken into consideration are as follows—

* Greater attention should be given to the nature of mathematics. We have been teaching mathematics to great

extent form the point of view of its use as a tool or of its utility with emphasis on developing skill in computation by the application of fixed rules or in mechanical manipulations of symbols. Emphasis is necessary on basic properties of number system, formal properties of operations, axiomatic exposition, rules of education and more precise definition. Also the use of clearly defined terminology and the employment of precise symbolism through the language of sets should be accepted.

* The time spent on Arithmetic should be saved by not including Arithmetic as a separate entity. Problems and topics of social usefulness that were so far included under arithmetic should not be used as the basic pattern for organisation and presentation of mathematical subject matter.

* In Algebra, today, much time is spent on a large number of complicated and necessary sums requiring only mechanical manipulations such as factorization, H.C.F. and L.C.M., square root, ratio proportion, elimination, surds, indices etc. All these should be discarded here. Emphasis should be given on basic ideas such as variable, functions, relations, equation and inequalities and the development of an appreciation of the structure of algebra stressing the commutative, distributive and similar other properties and axioms.

* In view of the fact that the utility of Euclid's geometry has been seriously questioned, it has been suggested here that greater emphasis may be put on the axiomatic structure and the nature of proof. Basic ideas, such as symmetry, similarity, congruence, inductive discovery and deductive proof, meaning of 'if and only if, 'if then, theorem and converse of a statement, definition and postulates, should be stressed in keeping with the modern spirit of the subject.

* No sharp distinction is desirable between Algebra and Geometry. Analytical methods should be used throughout the Geometry. Also, whenever possible, Plane and Solid Geometry should be treated together.

* Trigonometry should be related to Algebra and much of the work on identities, solution of triangles, etc. should be eliminated. Greater emphasis should be given to the study of trigonometric and logarithmic functions.
* The idea of co-ordinates should be introduced early as much work in Algebra and Geometry now needs to be integrated through the use of co-ordinates and graphic representation.
* Statistical notions, such as averages, mean, median, mode, dispersion, etc. and probability should be introduced in consideration of their growing usefulness in life.

In the NCERT's document; National Curriculum Frame Work for School Education (2000); following curricular areas have been suggested in mathematics:

One of the basic aims of teaching mathematics in schools is to inculcate the skill of qualification of experiences around the learners. Toward this, carrying out experiments with numbers and forms of geometry, framing hypotheses and verifying these with further observations form inherent part of mathematics learning. It would also include generalising these findings with proof and developing competence to solve problems. Mathematics helps in the process of decision-making through its application to real life situations in familiar as well as non-familiar situations. It contributes in the development of precision, rational and analytical thinking, reasoning, positive attitudes and aesthetic sense. Apart from being a distinct area of learning, it helps enormously in the development of other disciplines which involve analysis, reasoning and quantification of ideas. Study of mathematics also provides ample opportunities for making conjectures, testing and building arguments about their validity and also in asking new questions. Understanding of the basic structure of mathematics leads to a much better appreciation of the scope and power of mathematics. The mathematics curricula must develop an appreciation and understanding of the contribution of Indian mathematicians along with that of others. This would develop a sense of self-esteem and self-confidence amongst the learners.

While determining the curriculum in mathematics for the secondary stage it must be kept in mind that majority of learners would leave school at the end of the stage. They would need to apply mathematical skills and competencies in their work situations. A smaller number of students, of course, would go for higher education. The curriculum therefore needs to strike a balance between the learning requirements of both the groups.

Primary Stage—In the first two years of the primary stage, i.e., in Classes I and II children need to form some basic pre-number concepts related to size, length, mass etc. They need to sharpen their skills of classification, grouping and sequential thinking. These provide them a sound foundation for learning numbers and developing competency of addition and subtraction. Content of mathematics will be built around the immediate environment of the child. In classes III to V, the child should be introduced to numbers and fraction as a concept. The four fundamental operations—addition, subtraction, multiplication, division, and computational skills related to them need to be mastered on numbers and fractions. The concepts of length, mass, capacity, money, time, area and volume be developed along with the units of measuring these. The child should gain familiarity with geometrical forms and figures and be able to appreciate patterns and symmetry in the environment. Simple applications of arithmetical processes should find an important place.

At Upper Primary Stage—The upper primary stage should be confined mostly to the study of essentials of mathematics for day-to-day life. The students should acquire knowledge and understanding of facts, concepts, principles of mathematics needed for daily use, practical geometry, simple mensuration, descriptive preliminary aspects of statistics and fundamentals of algebra. The geometrical concepts should be introduced and verified experimentally using variety of models and instruments. The students may be encouraged to gain proficiency in oral/mental maths useful in day-to-day life activities as well as solving problems with accuracy and speed. Further the students should be able to read and interpret data from statistical graphs/charts/diagrams, and develop skills of drawing, model making and measuring.

At Elementary Stage—The quality of teaching/learning process of mathematics at the elementary stage should enable students to attain the mastery level. Remediation and proper evaluation should constitute an integral component of teaching-learning of mathematics at this stage.

At Secondary Stage—At the secondary stage, the teaching-learning of mathematics has to serve two complementary purposes. Firstly, the aim should be to further enhance the capacity of the students to employ mathematics in solving problems that they face in their day-to-day life. Secondly, a systematic study of mathematics as a discipline has to be started here and continued further. The curriculum may include the study of relevant arithmetical concepts, number system, algebra, geometry, trigonometry, coordinate geometry, mensuration, graphs, statistics etc. The idea of proofs should be developed with thrust on deductive reasoning. Emphasis is to be laid on wider applications of mathematics by way making data based problems pertaining to actual data on population, agricultural, environment, industry, physical and biological sciences, engineering, defence, etc. Also the students should attain proficiency in presenting information available in their environment in the form of graphs and charts, and be able to do calculations with speed and accuracy. Further the students should acquire the ability to solve problems using algebraic methods and apply the knowledge of simple trigonometry to solve problems of heights and distances etc. The history of mathematics with special reference to India and the nature of mathematical thinking should find an important place. The students may be encouraged to enhance their computational skill by the use of *Vedic Mathematics*.

Mathematics learning should be imparted through activities form the very beginning of school education, i.e., from the primary stage itself. These activities may involve the use of concrete materials, models, patterns, charts, pictures, posters, games, puzzles and experiments. The importance of using learning aids needs to be stressed.

To help exploration of mathematical facts through

experimentation, a mathematics corner could be set up in the existing science laboratories. For this existing science laboratories need to be converted into science-cum-mathematics laboratories. This may be done by involving students and teachers by mobilising community resources to this end. This should be treated as an exploratory centre for science and mathematics. Indigenous experiences and innovations in mathematics, based on real life situations, be given an important place.

Selection of Suitable Learning-Experiences—The achievement of the objectives already elicited and further clarified into behaviour changes depends upon suitable and well organized learning experiences which are presented to the pupil in order to produce effective learning. The concept of learning-experience as it emerges from the thinking about the learner and the learning principles accepted as the basis for objectives, can be broadly described as a desired change in the mental makeup of a child and it can be brought about through, "Activities leading to the discovery of connections, relationships and meanings which have significance in the directing or ordering of conduct. Learning-experiences, as envisaged here, place great importance on the pupil and the learning situation, instead of on the leather and the content. The proper organisation of learning experiences depends upon a number of factors such as—

* Age, needs and previous experiences of the learner.
* Needs of a particular community
* Abilities of the children
* Facility available in the school
* Readiness, maturity and capabilities of the child.
* Attention and interest of the learner.

Each teacher should feel free to adjust the objectives, content and activities to suit his requirements. The pattern of his teaching should, however, always follow the sequence which may be summarized as follows—

* Select the objectives and clarify them in terms of pupil behaviour.

* Select and organize suitable content for these objectives and behaviours.
* Select appropriate learning situations and activities for the pupils.
* Evaluate the outcomes of these activities.

The following criteria should be kept in view while selecting and organizing learning experiences—

* Learning experiences should be appropriate to behaviour changes defined under objectives.
* They should be suitable for the content area.
* They should be practicable.
* They should be adequate and effective.

It is difficult to lay down specific criteria for judging practicability, adequacy and effectiveness of learning experiences. Much reliance is therefore, put on the judgement of the teachers who framed them.

1. Learners feel more at home while learning through learning experiences.
2. Learning process becomes easy, convenient and more interesting.
3. It takes care of the learner's need, age, mental and maturity level etc., hence they learn more quickly.
4. Learning experience may be retained longer in the memory of learners as learning by doing.
5. It is based on psychological principles of learning so it is easily accepted by the learners.
6. Difficult concepts can be taught easily and effectively.
7. Learning experience includes series of successive steps as stages, therefore, the learners can learn progressively.
8. Since the learners learn though practical experiences-they fell more satisfied.

9. It provides strong motivations and stimulates for further learning.
10. The learner will get practical experience to solve certain problems which may creep in during the activity.
11. Learning experience provides opportunity for effective learning.

***Selection of Suitable Material for Evaluation of Curriculum*—** Evaluation and curriculum are regarded as closely related parts of the same educative process, not as distinct and seperate functions. No curriculum can therefore, be said to have been planned without laying down some basic principles of evaluation. Evaluation comes in at the planning stage when objectives are identified. The needs, interests, attitudes and abilities of child should be kept in mind while selecting suitable material for evaluation of curriculum.

The institutions responsible for imparting pre-service teacher education in the country-can play a vital role in bringing about reform in evaluation practices. For this, they will have to make evaluation a core component in their curricula and review the existing ones thoroughly. Apart from undertaking research they will also have to conduct in-service teacher orientation programmes in evaluation for the teachers belonging to the schools in their vicinity. National agencies like the National Council of Educational Research and Training, the proposed National Evaluation Organisation and the Council of Boards of School Education need to undertake the following tasks:

* Laying down the expected levels of attainment in each curricular area of all the stages of school education.
* Developing conceptual materials and prototypes on child-centred, activity oriented and competency based teaching-learning materials;
* Generating various kinds of tests, which could be meaningfully employed for assessing cognitive and non-cognitive learning outcomes, and making them available to the state agencies;

* Conducting orientation programmes for key resource persons;
* Organising training programmes for paper setters of different boards;
* Inventing and suggesting logistics of maintaining records and reporting of results;
* Conducting research for finding out better ways and means for evaluating learning outcomes.
* Conducting achievement surveys for obtaining census-like data; and
* Dissemination of information.

State agencies like Directorates of Education, State councils of Educational Research and Training, DIET's and voluntary agencies will have to shoulder the responsibility of assisting and guiding schools in developing and selecting appropriate instructional materials and selecting suitable transactional strategies with a view to realising the educational objectives. Besides, they must also help schools develop tests which can be used for assessing cognitive and non-cognitive learning outcomes and organize regular in-service training programmes for their teachers. They also have to provide to schools the logistics for maintaining student's records, conducting achievement surveys, undertaking innovations, conducting research besides monitoring the progress of individual schools and providing them necessary feedback and guidelines. At the secondary level, evaluation should lay stress on testing the understanding and application of concepts rather than testing the rote memory of the concepts.

Hence, curriculum development essentially is a ceaseless process of searching for qualitative improvement in education in response to the changes taking place in the society. As such, it is not a static but a dynamic phenomenon. A meaningful school curriculum has to be responsive to the society, reflecting the needs and aspirations of its learners. Even in the new millennium, some of the country's important societal concerns would remain unchanged because these could not be addressed adequately in the past. At the same time, many new concerns have emerged in response to the fast changes in the social scenario of the country as well as the world. The curriculum has to lead to a kind of education that would fight against inequity and respond to the social, cultural, emotional, and economic needs of the learners. This would not be possible just with the element of mediocrity and ordinariness in the entire educational endeavour. Nothing short of excellence in every aspect of school education is the first imperative for meeting the multifarious challenges of today and tomorrow. In other words, the curriculum must stand on the three pillars if relevance, equity and excellence.

Conclusion. Curriculum development is a process in which different components such as formulation of a curriculum policy, curriculum research, and curriculum planning. The curricular frame work generates creative at various levels of decision making. It provides a great deal of flexibility. Curriculum development is to identify the concepts or topics which constitute essential mathematics and analyse them into specific learning points (NPE, 1986).

Gradual Development

* The NCERT emerged as a nodal agency at the national level in the area of school education. This was gradually followed by the establishment of the SIE, State text-book Boards and SCERT. The curriculum for 10 years school: A framework (1975) provides an impetus to the teaching of environmental studies, science and mathematics.
* The National Curriculum for Elementary and Secondary education; a frame work by NCERT in 1988 responded to the major thrusts and recommendations highlighted in NPE, 1986 and POA, 1986.

Educational Motives

To generate and promote-language abilities, mathematical abilities, scientific temper, understanding of environment, etc—

Stages of Curriculum Development—There are four stages of curriculum Development—

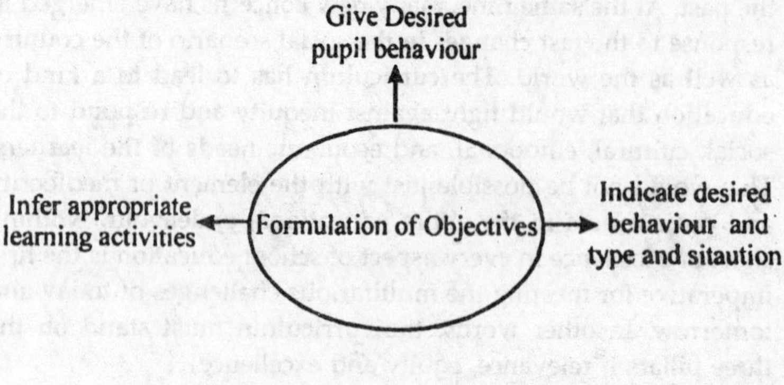

Stage 1

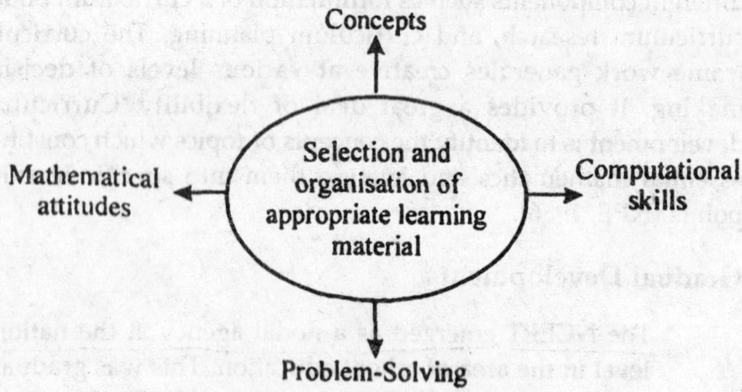

Stage 2

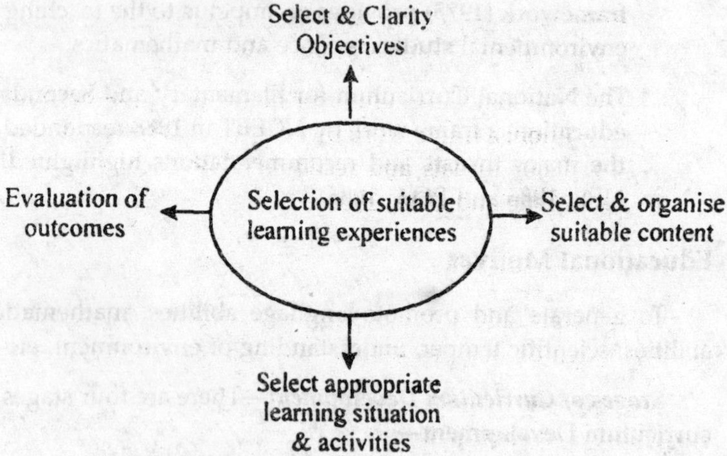

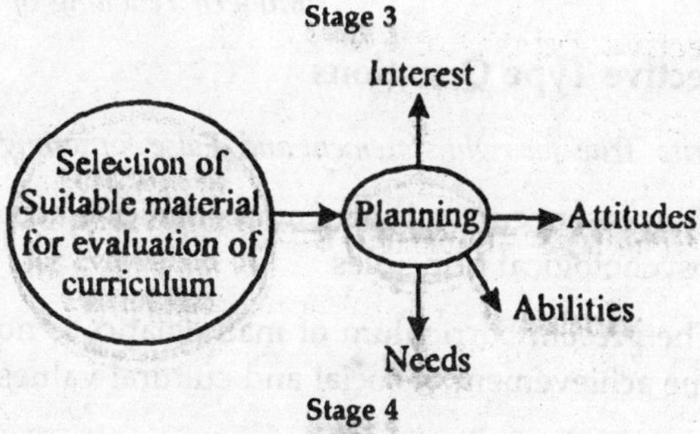

QUESTIONS

(A) Essay Type Questions

1. The existing school syllabus of mathematics has outlines its utility. Discuss.

2. Explain the various considerations in the selection of content and learning experiences for developing mathematics curriculum at High School stage.

3. Write a brief essay on the "Development of New Curriculum in Mathematics."

4. Illustrate the various stages of development of curriculum in mathematics.

5. What are the historical perspectives of curriculum development? Discuss the curricular areas in mathematics suggested by the National curriculum frame work for school Education.

6. Write note on the following—

   (a) Selection and importance of learning experiences.

   (b) General objectives of school education.

   (c) Selection and organization of learning material.

7. Discuss the criteria for selection of appropriate learning-material and learning-experiences.

(B) Objective Type Questions

Write 'True' for right statement and 'False' for wrong statement—

1. The present curriculum of mathematics is according to the psychological principles.
2. The present curriculum of mathematics is not helpful in the achievement of social and cultural values.
3. Objective should point out towards the desirable behavioured and conditions in which it has been completed.
4. The organization of suitable learning experiences depends upon the available facilities in schools.
5. First of all, objectives are formulated for the construction of curriculum.
6. The SCERT provides technical support to research and development activities related to the formulation of curriculum.
7. The National Curriculum for Elementary and secondary education. A frame work brought out NCERT in 1986.
8. The curriculum must meet the learner's need and societal expectations.
9. The mathematics curriculum should develop an appreciation and understanding of the contribution of mathematicians.
10. Attention and interest of the child must be considered while selecting suitable learning experiences.

14
The Measurement

Evaluation is defined as a process of collecting evidences of behavioural changes and judging the directions and extents of such changes. This means that evaluation is free neither from instructional objectives nor from the teaching learning. In fact, it is intimately related to objectives and learning activities on the one hand, and improvement of instructions on the other. The desired changes in children represent the purpose or end of instruction, while the evaluation procedures and learning experiences provided to children are the instruments or means related to these ends. The relationship between educational objectives variations learning experiences and evaluation techniques can be diagrammatically represented as follows—

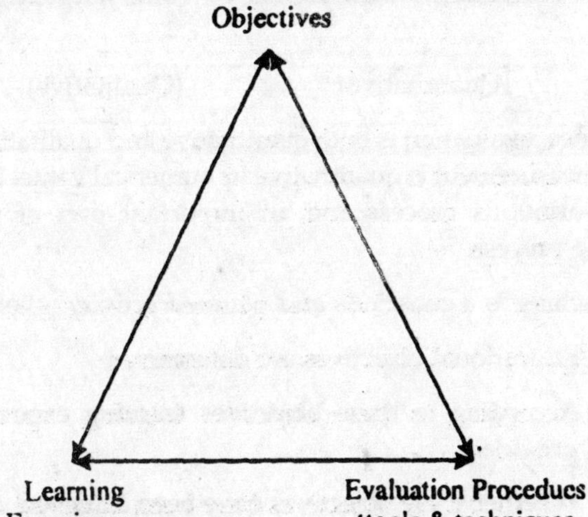

Triangular relationship between Objective, Learning Experiences and Evaluation : It is clear from the above triangular relationship that :

* All the three steps are inter-related.
* The objectives of teaching constitute a pivotal step on which both learning experiences and evaluation techniques are based.
* Evaluation is a natural step involved in teaching-learning process.
* Evaluation based on objectives of teaching and learning experiences evaluates the objectives also at the same time.

Therefore, in classroom, teacher organizes suitable teaching learning activities in order to promote desired expected changes in behaviour. The learning experiences offered in classroom, are directly related to the predetermined in functional objectives. Thus, the teaching-learning activities are objective based not content or text-book based. The extent to which the teaching-learning activities result in experiences which lead to the realization of particular objective is determined by pupil evaluation. The evaluation may be classified as follows :

Evaluation = Measurement + Value Judgement

↓ ↓

(Quantitative) (Qualitative)

Hence, evaluation is both quantitative and qualitative process while measurement is quantitative or numerical value. Evaluation is a continuous process and an important part of teaching - learning process.

Teaching is a conscious and planned activity where

1. Educational objectives are determined
2. According to these objectives learning experiences are provided.
3. Whether these objectives have been achieved or not.

Thus evaluation is interwoven with the teaching learning process.

The Concept

The most comprehensive definition of evaluation according to N.C.E.R.T. is—Evaluation is any systematic, continues process of determining :

(i) The extent to which specified educational objectives previously identified and defined, are attained.

(ii) The effectiveness of the learning experiences provided in the classroom;

(iii) How well the goals of education have been accomplished.

Georgia and Adams—"To evaluate is to ascertain the value of some process or thing. Thus, educational evaluation is the paning of judgement of the degree of worth whiteness of some teaching process or learning experience.

Quillen and Hanna—"Evaluation is the process of gathering and interpreting evidences on changes in the behaviour of pupils as they progress through school."

Dandekar—"Evaluation may be defined as a systematic process of determining the extent to which educational objectives are achieved by the pupils."

Goods—According to goods, "Evaluation is a process of ascertaining or judging the value or amount of some thing by careful appraisal."

Muffat—"Evaluation is a continuous process and is concerned with more than the formal academic achievement of pupils. If is interested in the development of the individual in terms of desirable behavioural changes in relation to his feeling, thinking and actions."

Bradfield and Moredock—"Evaluation is an assignment of symbols to a phenomenon in order to characterise the worth of value of a phenomenon usually with reference to some social, cultural or scientific standard."

In Encyclopedia of Education Research. Evaluation is defined as, Evaluation is relatively a new technical term, introduced to designate a more comprehensive concept if measurement that is implied in conventional tests and examinations.

Hence it is evident from the above definitions that:

* It is wider concept that testing, measurement and examination.
* Teaching-learning process becomes dynamic & self-developing.
* It is a continues as well as comprehensive process.
* It is directly related teachers of education.
* It helps in determining the potentialities and interests of children.
* On the basis of day to day record, it becomes easy to know the present status of the children.
* It improves the attitudes habits, appreciations, interests, manipulative skills and understanding of the children.
* It helps the teachers in diagnosing children's difficulties.
* It involves self-appraisal by the children and their success and failures.

Aims and Objectives

Keeping in view the concept and definitions of evaluation, we may list the following purposes and functions of evaluation :

* To determine the present status of the children in the teaching-learning process.
* To motivate the children for better learning
* To provide basis for guidance and councilling to children.
* To determine the rate of progress of the children.
* To collect evidences for improvement in curriculum.

* To diagnose children's weaknesses and strengths for further instructions.
* To measure the examination system.
* To improve the efficiency and success of the teacher.
* To measure the behavioural changes of the children.
* To discover innovative and effective methods of teaching.
* The classify the children in different categories.
* To improve the teaching techniques and strategies.
* To provide basis for remedial teaching on the bases of strengths and weaknesses of the children.
* To encourage teachers for action research.
* To give reinforcement and feedback to both the teachers and pupils.

Main Features

1. Evaluation implies a systematic process which omits the casual uncontrolled observation of pupils.
2. Evaluation is a continuous process. It goes hand in hand with the teaching-learning process.
3. Evaluation emphasise the broad personality changes and major objectives of an educational programme.
4. Evaluation is more concerned with the growth which the student has made, than with his status in the group.
5. Evaluation includes all the means of collecting evidence on students behaviour.
6. Evaluation is continuous, and integral part of all training and Testing.
7. Evaluation is descriptive as well as qualitative.
8. Evaluation is a co-operative process involving students, teachers and parents.

9. To assess the students and their complete development brought about through education is evaluation.
10. Evaluation is corrective Noun. It not only labels the child with defects but suggests measures for improvement also.
11. Evaluation is purely objective centered.

The Characteristics

* It measure the direction and extent behavioural changes.
* Evaluation is quantitative and qualitative estimation of specific changes in children's behaviour.
* Evaluation is diagnostic so that it may provided basis for remedial teaching.
* Evaluation is a continuous and comprehensive process.
* Evaluation offers feedback to the entire educational system.
* Evaluation is pupil oriented.
* Evaluation is activity based.
* Evaluation may be used to improve instructions, curriculum, methods and examinations etc.

The Procedure

Evaluation process involves the following steps :

[I] Selection and Formulation of objectives

[II] Defining objectives in terms of behavioural changes

[III] Selection of tools and techniques of evaluation.

[IV] Use of tools and techniques and making results

[V] Interpretation and generalisation of results.

[VI] Feedback the results for improvement of teaching learning Process.

Motives and Purposes

The objectives to be tested are selected and formulated in

advance before conducting evaluation. A mathematics teacher must be very clear about the instructional objectives towards which instruction are geared. Each objective when specified provides basis for construction of test items.

After determining and formulating the objectives to be tested, teacher should define them clearly in terms of expected changes in pupil's behaviour.

Tools and Techniques

Selection of suitable tools and techniques depends upon the types of evidences required. Tools and techniques must provide evidence on the teaching objectives to which they are concerned. They should also satisfy criteria of a good measuring rod or good evaluation.

After selecting and developing the tools, teacher applies them is testing situations. She scores or other evidence regarding the behavioural changes are recorded. On the basis of recorded evidences and informations conclusions and drawn.

The evidence which we get through various tools and techniques of evaluation are not meaningful to the learner the teacher or the parents unless the scores are interpreted properly. This requires analysis in terms of objectives to rate progress of an individual's comparative performance in the class. Such an analysis provides useful data on the level of achievement.

Process of Learning

On the basis of analysis of test results or evidences recorded, pupil progress may be made to the pupils and their parents. This is necessary for parents to know child's self evaluation strengths and weakness of their ward for proper diagnosis and to overcome the re-teaching or remedial teaching that may be arranged.

Evaluation and Examination

Generally, examination and evaluation are used as synonyms and mutually interchangeable. But the fact is that they carry different functional meaning that they cannot be replaced by another. The difference between evaluation and examination is as follows.

Examination	Evaluation
1. It is a narrow concept.	1. It is a wider and compre-hensive concept.
2. It only aims to determine the achievement of child in a particular subject in a specific period e.g. annual, half yearly, monthly etc.	2. It is a continuous process and aims to determine the achieve-ment of children in overall activities.
3. It gives quantitative data or informations.	3. It gives quantitative as well as qualitative data or informations.
4. It is used for classification and promotion of children only.	4. It is used for classification, diagnosis, prediction and guidance to the children.
5. It is less reliable and valid than evaluation.	5. It is move reliable and valid.
6. It is mainly, oral, written and practical i.e. quantitative techniques.	6. It involves the use of various tools and techniques of evaluation i.e. both quantitative and qualitative techniques.
7. Examination confines to the memorization of knowledge only.	7. It does not confines to memorization.
8. It is informative.	8. It is formative.
9. It can examine cognitive domain only.	9. It can evaluate all the three domains.
10. It does not improve curriculum, methods etc.	10. It improves curriculum, method etc.

The Difference. Difference between evaluation and measurement are as follows :

Evaluation	Measurement
1. Evaluation is wider and more inclusive concept.	1. It is narrow and less inclusive concept than evaluation.
2. It is quantitative and qualitative process.	2. It is quantitative/numerical only.
3. It is a continuous process.	3. It is a part of the evaluation process.
4. Emphasis is laid upon broad personality changes and major objectives of an educational programme.	4. Emphasis is upon single aspect of subject matter/achievement.
5. It interpretes, explains and analyse the data provided through measurement.	5. It merely provides data needed for evaluation.
6. It is a lengthy process.	6. It is not a lengthy process.
7. It is helpful in making significant prediction and diagnosis.	7. It is not helpful in prediction and diagnosis.
8. If gives both numerical and descriptive results regarding change in pupil's behaviour.	8. It gives only numerical results regarding change in pupil's behaviour.
9. Remedia teaching is possible.	9. Remedial teaching is not possible.
10. It is more reliable, valid and objective.	10. It is not.
11. It is laborious and time consuming process.	11. It is not more laborious.
12. Comparative study is possible. (Individual & group comparison)	12. Comparative study is not possible.
13. Objectives of all the three domains can be evaluated.	13. Only the objectives of cognitive domain can be measured.
14. The teaching-learning process can be up improved and modified.	14. Teaching-learning process can not be improved and modified.

Summative Forces

Formative Type. When the students are said to be in well state regarding knowledge, the process of teaching applied to learn any thing is called formative and the method of judging how much the reactions of teaching are made to students is evaluation. Therefore, the purpose of formative evaluation is to monitor the instructional process to know that learning process is taking place or not. It is designed only to enhance the teaching-learning process and not designed to make final judgements. Hence, in formative evaluation teaching process is made and learning is judged. The process works upon in a long term, so it is called continuous evaluation in which unit tests, class tests and assignments are the essential components.

Pupils weakness is diagnosed through class room teaching. Hence formative evaluation is continuous feed back to both the teacher and the student, that determines success and failure of learning. Through feed back, process of learning to children is made successful to a great degree and learning difficulties that a child faces, are also identified and diagnosed. In one hand, formative evaluation provides feedback to children; on the other it apart feed back to teachers also, so as to, modify instructions to prescribe remedial work therefore it can easily be said that formative evaluation brings improvement in child's learning and also removes the drawbacks that are committed during teaching and learning process, hence teaching-learning process is better enchanced through this evaluation. It can also be said that formative evaluation gives the relevant information during class room teaching-learning process. It joins the three teacher, pupil and the planner and direct feed back to the three.

According to Tanner (1972), "Formative Evaluation refers to the use of tests and other evaluative procedures while the course and Instructional programme is in progress."

Groxlund (1976, PP. 489-94) pointed out that the specific use of formative evaluation is to plan corrective action for overcoming learning difficulties or deficiencies to aid in motivating learning and to increase retention and transfer of learning. Needs of classroom group and corrections in learning deficiencies are made through periodic testing and evaluation of pupils during the instructions.

Both criterion referenced and norm-referenced tests are designed in formative evaluation to mastery in content. These are the tests given at the end of learning unit, such tests are also called interim tests, unit tests, learning tests and quizes.

So, in a nut-shell, Formative Evaluation is primarily useful in identifying learning errors, planning correct action for over coming learning deficiencies, motivating learning process, providing practice, minimizing test anxiety and to enhance the academic achievement to children at the stages of formative Evaluation.

Formative Type

* It provide informations to teachers for modifying instruction and teaching.
* It helps to prescribe group and individual remedial programs.
* It is helpful in monitoring pupil's learning progress.
* It provides feedback to both the teachers and pupils.
* It facilities retention and transfer of learning.
* It enables the teachers to adjust their instruction according to the need of the students.
* It helps the teacher for correcting learning deficiencies.
* Formative evaluation also reinforce the learning/of high achievers.
* It helps is better performance is the simulative evaluation.
* Formative test can also be used as a self-evaluation devices by the children.
* It provides immediate feedback to the children.
* It is also helpful in diagnosing child's strength and weaknesses.

Summative Evaluation. When Formative Evaluation takes its last steps, there is an urgent need of Summative Evaluation, hence it can also be said that summative Evaluation is a later process occurs in the end of a session or term to measure the achievement of pupils. Overall results of teaching-learning process can be obtained through this short of evaluation. It simple words where Class tests, Unit tests Quizes and learning tests are the parts of Formative Evaluation, then Term tests. Annual Tests and External Examinations conducted by school or public agency are the essential parts of summative Evaluation. Hence, Summative Evaluation is either External type or Internal type Evaluation.

In other words, it can also be said that Formative Evaluation serves refinement purpose during teaching-learing process, but summative Evaluation may be said the evaluation of refined product. When student be come fully familiar with the whole syllabus, and test of the whole syllabus is made, summative Evaluation takes place. Thus summative evaluation occurs in the end of academic year session to promote students to next class. Hence Summative Evaluation becomes Part and Parcel with future point of view. It is identification document of failure and success of the class indicated. Promotion to the next class is also done through this document. Hence summative Evaluation gives birth to a certificate that bears the whole year work out. Hence summative Evaluation is inevitable and has to remain an integral part of the whole evaluation process.

Each educational situation need to be examined to arrive at a proper balance between formative and summative evaluation. Summative Evaluation may be seen in three different ways National curriculum frame work for school education. 2000); the three ways are known as follows.

* By assessing the progress of student with reference to their own selves (Self Referenced)
* By assessing the progress of student with reference to criteria set by their teacher (Criterion - referenced)
* By assessing the progress of student with reference to the progress made by their peer group (Norm - Referenced)

To conclude, Evaluation must be such type so as to bring all-round development in children. Hence both kind of evaluation should be made keeping all necessary point in view. Both kind of valuation bring a great change in educational system. Where quality is a matter, both type of evaluation should be applied stepwise for the improvement of quality of school education.

The Difference

Formative Evaluation	Summative Evaluation
1. The purpose of formative evaluation is to diagnose the strength and weaknesses of the pupils.	1. The purpose is classification and promotion of students.
2. Evidences secured by it are used for further improvement of instruction and students better progress.	2. Its results are used for certification and passing judgement on pupils achievement.
3. Its focus is on improvement of pupils' achievement.	3. Its focus is on measurement of pupil's achievement.
4. It refers to continuous evaluation by means of unit tests, assignments etc.	4. It refers to term tests, annual tests and external examinations.
5. It is an integral part of teaching-learning process.	5. It is treated as an end of the course activity.
6. If provides continuous feedback to both pupil and teacher.	6. It does not provide feedback.
7. It is done during the course of instruction.	7. It is done at the end of academic session/years.
8. It gives relevant informations which helps to improve classroom instructions.	8. It provides the overall results of the teaching-learning process.
9. Its results are used for providing remedial measures and enrichment programmes for slow and gifted learners respectively.	9. Its results are used for classification placement and prediction for future success.

Summary

Measurement. Measurement involves the process of quantification and is a formal process which is used in planned and objectives way. The direct measurement is used in physical and Biosciences while measurement is indirect in psychology and education.

Main landmark of measurement. Ernest Heirick Webar (1795-1818), Alexander Bain (1818-1903), Francis Galton (1822-1911), Wilhelm Wundt (1832-1920), Mckeen Cattle (1860-1944).

Historical Development of Education and Physical measurement.

* Development of physiological and experimental psychology.
* Darwaian Biology
* The clinical concern for the maladjustment and undeveloped individual.

Prognosis, Prediction, Compression, Diagnosis, Research

* *Scales of measurement.* Nominal ordinal, interval and Ratio Scale.
* *Evaluation in mathematics.* Evaluation = Measurement + Value judgement It is both quantitative and qualitative. It is continuous process and an integral part of teaching - learning.
* *Purpose and functions evaluation.* To motivate the child, to provide basis for guidance, to diagnose, to measure efficiency & behavioural changes of the children et.
* *Important Aspects of education Evaluation.* It is a continuous process, emphasises the broad personality changes, more concerned with the growth of the child etc.
* *Characteristics of a good evaluations programme.* It is a diagnostic, continuous & comprehensive, offers feed back, pupil oriented, activity based, etc.

* ***Process of evaluation.*** Selection and formulation of objectives - Defining objectives in behavioural terms - Selection of tools & techniques - Interpretation & generalisation, feedback the results,

QUESTIONS

(A) Essay type Question :

1. What do you understand by 'Evaluation'? Explain the functions and process of evaluation.
2. Explain the meaning of evaluation. Describe its aims and functions.
3. What is the importance of evaluation in mathematics teaching? Explain the characteristics of a good evaluation programme.
4. What is evaluation? How does if differ from examination?
5. What is difference between measurement and evaluation? Describe the different levels of measurement.
6. What is the relationship of evaluation with objectives and learning experiences? Give in brief the process of evaluation.
7. What are the aims of purpose of evaluation in mathematics teaching? Explain the process of evaluation.
8. Write notes on following :

   (a) Levels of measurement

   (b) Formative and Summative evaluation

   (c) Process of evaluation

   (d) Need and importance of evaluation in mathematics.

   (e) Difference between measurement and evaluation.

   (f) Difference between formative & Summative evaluation.
9. Write as essay on measurement and evaluation in mathematics teaching.

10. Write an essay on 'Historical development of measurement.'
11. What do you understand by measurement? Describe its needs and importance in mathematics teaching.
12. Differentials between qualitative and quantitative measurement.
13. Knowledge of measurement and evaluation is essential for effective teaching. Critically examine this statement.
14. Give a description of the main scales measurement.
15. What are the main scales of measurement. Explain any two of them.
16. What do you understand by formative and summative evaluation? What is the importance of formative evaluation?

(B) Objective Type Questions

(a) Multiple choice items

1. The most reliable scale of measurement is

   (a) Ratio (b) Ordinal
   (c) Interval (d) Nominal

2. To provide the marks on the basis of presence forms :

   (a) Interval scale (b) Nominal scale
   (c) Ratio scale (d) Ordinal scale

3. Evaluation is closely related with :

   (a) Content (b) Evaluation strategies
   (c) Objectives (d) Process of learning.

4. Evaluation should be done in teaching of mathematics :

   (a) At the time of providing experiences of learning

   (b) At the time of clarification of objectives

   (c) After the clarification of objectives and providing the experiences of learning.

(d) At all the above levels.

5. Evaluation is done by :

   (a) Measurement (b) Formulation of values
   (c) Grading (d) All these

6. Prognosis has the administrative function such as :

   (a) Classification

   (b) Promotion and gradation of students

   (c) Selection

   (d) All the above.

7. The locate specific learning and instructional difficulties is the main aim of

   (a) Prognosis (b) Comparison
   (c) Diagnosis (d) Prediction

True/False Questions

Write "True" for right statement and "False" for wrong statement.

1. Those tests are not reliable which are formed by a teacher.
2. Evaluation is qualitative and quantitative.
3. The objective of evaluation and examination is same.
4. Absolute zero point is found in physical measurement.
5. Educational measurement is relative.
6. The first laboratory for standing psychological relations was established by Wilhelm Wundt.
7. Origin of species book was published in 1859 gathered data based upon the intelligence of school going children.
8. J.M. Rice is associated with objective type tests.
9. Seguin established a special school for gifted children.

15
The Evaluation

Measurement is related to Human race right from the dawn of civilization.

Man's innate curosity motivated him to make an attempt to know his surroundings and to define or describe these attributes.

But it was totally impossible to describe all other attributes in totality. Therefore the need of *SCALE DOWN* arose.

Measurement is thus related to one attribute.

Examples : Measurement of Height, Weight, Intelligence etc.

Measurement is very essential in the study of science. Science is collection of information and observation about the natural or physical phenomena. Mathematics is a universal language which can be easily and powerfully utilized by any science, its technology is unlimited yet well definite. It is easily possible to communicate, correctly and objectively through measurement. Which can also be manipulated in thoughts. The objective description is called measurement, is a useful mean to obtain these goals.

J.P. Guilford has defined this term as— "Measurement means the description of data in terms of numbers."

Campbell defines measurement as the—"Assignment of numerals to objects or events according to certain rules is called measurement."

According to Stevens—"Measurement is the process of assigning numbers to objects according to certain assigned rules."

According to Bradfeild and Moredock—"Measurement is the process of assigning symbols to the dimensions of a phenomena in order to characterise the status of the phenomena as precisely as possible."

A still more elaborate and wider definition has been given by Nunnaly.—"Measurement Consists or rules for assigning numbers to objects in such a way to represent quantities of attributes."

An analysis of the above definitions of measurement given by Nunnaly reveal the following main properties of measurement.

* The process of measurement involves assigning of numbers according to certain rules. Therefore, it is a quantitative process. A number is a kind of numeral which has some quantitative meaning.

Number are not assigned by investigator according to his own wish, but according to certain fixed and explicit rules.

(a) One type is where the rules are explicit and obvious, e.g. while measuring the length of the cloth in feet or inches, the rules for assigning numerals are quite clear.

(b) But for measuring the extroversion trait of personality or the intelligence of a child i.e. psychological, sociological and educational attributes, the rules are generally vague and less explicit.

* Measurement is always concerned with certain attributes or variables of features of an object.

These attributes or features of the object are measured and not the object itself, e.g. one would measure the aptitude, intelligence attitude of a person and not the person himself.

Numerals are used to represent the quantity of the attribute in the process of measurement.

In other words, measurement involves the process of quantification. The extent of the particular attribute present in a particular object is represented by quantification.

Measurement is the formal process which is used in planned and objective way.

The direct measurement is used in physical and bio-sciences while measurement is indirect in psychology and education.

Thus, measurement is of two kinds :

1. Measurement in Physical Sciences. (Direct measurement)
2. Measurement in Behavioural Sciences. (Indirect measurement)

It is simple and precise process of quantification in which physical traits of the objects are perceivable and measured directly. The measuring instrument is placed along the trait e.g. height is measured by placing the metre along the height of a person. The characteristics of physical measurement are

* The units are fixed and definite
* Here the entire quantity can be measured e.g.; the entire length of cloth can be measured and expressed in meters or centimeters.
* There is the reference point in physical measurement. It is also known as absolute measurement.
* Physical measurement is direct.

It involves indirect process of measurement, therefore the process of measurement in behavioural science is difficult as well as complex.

The trait is not directly measured by the scale but the trait is measured indirectly by the behaviours.

* There is no fixed unit of measuring any trait and characteristics.
* In the behavioural science a trait or variable is defined in several ways and there are several theories available to explain the nature of variable.
* The behavioural science measurement is relative as the zero has no meaning in this measurement.

Psychology of 1850 was still in large measure a part of philosophy. Course dealing with man and his action presented under this title:

Moral Philosophy, and discussed in an arm chair fashion the nature of the mind and the soul.

The nearest approaches to psychological measurement were a few scattered experiments by physicists and physiologists on the measurement of the ability to make sensory discriminations and the speed of simple elementary responses.

By 1900 psychology had felt the impact of the physical and biological sciences and was staving mightily to become a science itself. It was shaking off the ties that bound it to philosophy and forming new alliances with the biological sciences. It had adopted the experimental method and was measurement conscious. Measurement is the basic tool in experimentation and psychology was expanding its measurement technique in all directions. The record since 1900 is the record of the attempt to expand and adopt measurement techniques to cover all aspect of human behaviour.

The three main streams combined to yield the vigorous measurement movement is psychology and its spread about education. These are

1. The psychology and physiological that had its main growth in Germany in 19th century.
2. Darwinian biology, and
3. The clinical concern for the maladjusted and underdeveloped individual.

The Backdrop

In 1850 psychology was considered as independent science. The following landmarks have revealed by the review of the literatures.

Biologists and physicists were pioneers in conduction experiments, phycology started getting for measuring behaviour.

Psychology became measurement concise as a result of their experiments.

(1) Earnest Heinrick Wabar (1795-1878)	Discrimination of vision, hearing and experimental approach
(2) Alexander Bain (1818- 1903)	(1) The senses & intellect (1855) (2) The emotions & will (3) Philosophical approach
(3) Francis Galton (1822-1911)	(1) Statistical study of individual difference (2) Correlation-technique was developed (3) Non-experimental speculation
(4) Wilhelm Wundt (1832-1920)	(1) First laboratory of psychology (1879) at Leipzig University. (2) Physiological methods were employed (3) Emphasis on the study of vision, hearing, senses & reaction.
(5) Mckeen Cattle (1860-1944)	Range of Individual difference.

As a matter of fact, the history of psychological and educational measurement during the period 1850 to 1900 was nourished by the three major influences namely psychophysics, Darwinian biology and clinical practices.

The early historical development of mental measurement reveals that it was developed in two independent direction :-

The Field of Psychophysics—It is the foundation stone of modern psychology.

Modern Testing Tradition—It was interested in individual difference.

Measurement has a wider application not only in the field of science and technology but also in psychology and Education. The proof of measurement are found in China, Jordan and Egypt.

According to Dubois (1965)

People who were aspirants of public office or civil service were examined through achievement and proficiency test.

Three main streams combined to yield the vigorous measurement movement in physiology and its spread through education. These were :

(i) Development of physiological and experimental psychology that had growth in Germany.

(ii) Darwanian Biology

(iii) The clinical concern for the maladjustment and underdeveloped individual.

The physiologists were mainly interested in measuring the process of seeing, hearing, speed of conduction etc.

The first laboratory for studying psychological reaction was established in 1879 by wilhelm wundt at the university of Leipzig.

This laboratory flourished and developed into excellent centre for the measurement of human relation.

Darwin was a biologist and his theory of evolution resulted in the growth of psychological measurement.

In 1959 Origin of species book was published.

According to the theory of evolution *"member of same species are not alike.'*

Darwins work was developed by sir francis galton. Galton was interested in the study of individuals difference.

Karl Pearson later developed several techniques for statistically unleashing the data on individual differences of human ability which provided good stream for psychological measurement.

Pearson Method (r) is know as Product Moment Method.

Supearman Method (P) is know as Rank-Difference Method.

Galton Whistle and Galton Bar used sensory motor test to establish mental ability and the laboratory test was known as Anthropometic Test (1883) in Entrand.

Clinical studies growing out of medicine, psychiatry and

social welfare institution in western countries provided impetus for the growth of measurement.

Alfred Bint gathered data based upon the intelligence of school going in 1905 children.

Development in Nineteenth Century	
1845	Horace Mann suggested the use of written examination. He was secretary of Massachusets board of Education and editor of Common School Journal.
1864	George fisher devised Scale book and it proved to be first Objective Examination. It helped in assessment in field of mathematics, grammar, spelling, history, drawing etc.
1890	Dr. J.M. Rice encouraged objective testing. He concluded that students devoting 30 minutes daily for 8 hrs to study spelling were as good as those studying it just for 15m in. a day.
1897	Ebbinghavs developed intelligence test which considered (a) Arithmetic computation (b) Sentence completion.
1838	Esquirol differentiated between insane and feeble minded by the use of language.
1837	Seguin established special school for mentally defective children.
1806	Charles Bell wrote 'Anatony of Expressions' which disproved the fact of Lavater (1772) that mental ability could be measured on the basis of facial expressions.

The 19th century, particularly of second half hand witnessed the development of number of scientific tools and innovations in physics, chemistry and scientists were of the opinion that those physical methods could also be successfully tried in measuring psychological properties.

Development in Twentieth Century	
1905	First intelligence test took place by Alfred Binet Group intelligence test is of two types: (a) Army alpha test. (b) Army Beta test.
1908	First arithmetic reasoning test by Stone
1909	Thorndike developed handwriting scale Mc Call laid emphasis on New type of objective tests.
1920	Mr. Call advocated the construction and use of teacher made informal objective test. Taylor developed and modified technique of objective test construction. Cattell used the word mental test, speed of moving, weight discrimination, Reaction time and Memory to know intelligence.

Origin of Statistical Methods	
1600 A.D.	Theory of Probability was considered as a matter of chance.
1654-1705	Book on Statistics by Bernoulli.
1667-1754	Moivre discovered Normal Probability Curve.
1812	Laplace wrote book on probability and has given proof for least square method.
1777-1865	Gauss applied normal probability curve in practicals Gaussian Curve.
1796-1874	Quetelet pointed out use and importance of statistical method for data of biology and social science.

Practical Aspects

The function of psychological and educational measurement can be used to answer the following questions.

1. What a person can do? Achievement test (Prognosis) What is a person can not do? Diagnostic test (Diagnosis)
2. What a person will do? Aptitude test (Prediction)

What a person can learn or develop into in future can be predicted with the help of aptitude test while in the achievement test our interest is in what he has learn in the past.

So the functions of measurement are :

Prognosis—The prognosis has the administrative function such as

Classification—Promotion and gradation of students.

Selection—Measurement helps in the selection of suitable students for different courses. Various entrance tests are devised to serve this purpose.

Grading—Measurement helps in assigning ranks to students in a group. Usually the terminal examinations of course serve this purpose.

Guidance—Evaluation helps to serve the purpose of giving guidance and thus helps in making decisions about courses and careers.

It is only after successful measurement, that a teacher can discharge his duties of giving guidance property. The teacher has to guide and counsel the students at every stage which is possible through measurement only. Rousseau was of the opinion that a child is like a book whose every page has to be studied by the teacher. The impact of the saying is that the teacher should give educational and psychological guidance and counselling to the pupils which cannot be achieved without successful measurement.

Prediction—Whenever a test is given to two persons the relative difference between the performance of the person is known. But this fact would be of no significance if it is not used to predict the future performance of the two individuals.

Prediction is helpful in pupil gradation and placement. Placement of pupil is one of the most difficult situations faced by supervisors and teachers. Prediction is also the ultimate justification for the achievement test used for grading in schools. The grades are helpful in the prediction of future activities of the student. The scores of the students are also helpful to a teacher in deciding the method of teaching, e.g. if a teacher is rocevers good results by the used of a particular method in a class. Them she can anticipate similar results of instruction from another class. Without the predicting function, grading would be an act of crying over split milk.

Comparison—A very important field of psychology is the area of individual differences. There are individual difference in almost all traits e.g. knowledge, intelligence, personal traits etc. The main aim of psychological tests is to compare these individual difference. Galton gave great importance to such studies and tried to find out the causes of individual differences.

Results of an exam conducted on students of various class be compared to each other.

This comparision helps in diagnosing the various problems faced by students. Another comparison that is even more useful is that between the attainment of a class at the beginning and the end of a term or a year's work, or at shorter intervals in the course of a term.

Diagnosis—The main aim of diagnosis is to locate specific learning and instructional difficulties, and if possible to determine their cause. As a medical science several instruments are used for diagnosis as thermometer, stethoscope, microscope etc. so that objective of correct diagnosis is made, similarly in education of psychology several tests and instruments are used for diagnosing purpose. Still educational diagnosis is not as objective in a medicine.

The two main functions of educational diagnosis are

* Diagnosis of general difficulties.
* Diagnosis of specific weaknesses.

Diagnosis not only helps in finding out the problems faced by students but also help in finding remedies for them. If a student is weak in solving problems based on trigonometry then remedial teaching can be arranged for him.

Research—The psychological tests are also used widely for research purposes e.g. in equating the two groups on intelligence or on some personality dimensions may be interested to know whether special coaching effects the intelligence score or not for all such purpose tests are employed.

Thus we can say,

There is no phase of life where there is no influence of measurement.

Measurement colours each and every phase of mankind. Measurement has always been an integral unknown part of Man's civilization and will remain so.

Evaluation Standards

Measurement involves quantification and assigning of numerals. Stevens has defined that measurement is a process of assigning symbols or numerals to the objects according to certain agreed rules. Helmstadha has also definined measurement as "Measurement is the process of attaining a numerical description of the extent to which a person or thing processes some characteristics." A convenient scheme for classifying measurement scales according to the

* Levels of refinement
* Degree of accuracy
* Complexity and
* Sophistication

There are four scales of measurement known as :

* Nominal scale
* Ordinal Scale
* Interval Scale
* Ratio Scale

It is common to distinguish four level or scales of measurement which have been most clearly delineated by Stevens. From lower to higher levels we have Nominal, ordinal, internal and ratio scale of measurement. These scales are distinguished in terms of several criteria.

Classification Scale

It is the lowest level of measurement/refinement. The only operation possible is counting.

It is simply classification of items into two or more categories without any extent or magnitude. We make use of symbols and numbers just to classify on the basis of quantity the only rules for assigning numbers are that all numbers of any class will have the same number and that no classes shall be assigned the same number.

* Boys and girls.
* Pass and fail.
* Male and female.

Limitations

In Nominal Scale :

1. Mathematical operations cannot be applied
2. Magnitude cannot be assigned.

Various Scales

Each object is assigned on the basis of rule to one of a set ordered categories.

The categories are arranged according to the amount of trait or characteristic that each category represents. This is also known as *Ranking Scale* No mathematical operation is involved except greater than or less than it is good for quantitative description.

Uses : This scale if frequently used is schools :

1. For prize distribution.
2. To provide motivation by the technique of competition.
3. By asking the questions, the teacher considers the place of the student in class.
4. Selection of teacher's in school according to their performance, qualification and merits.
5. Distributing trophies to players according to their performance.

e.g. Suppose we have five persons. Although we do not know their heights yet it is possible for us to arrange them in order of their heights. We can call the tallest person as No. 1, next to him No. 2 and the smallest as No. 5.

Thus, they can be ranked according to height.

We can also rank them according to some other traits, for example fairness of their colour or their fatness or weight etc. Thus, without knowing the exact quantity of the variables, we can compare them.

This scale gives us only the order, but gives no idea of amount or magnitude of difference between the two scales. These ranks cannot be added or subtracted like gram and centimeters.

Limitations

1. There is neither an absolute zero, nor the units of measurement uniform throughout.
2. No arithmetical operations is permissible except the interpretation of greater than or less than or ranking method.

Thus, an ordinal scale is useful when it is possible to express a characteristic quantity actively but impossible to define units of measurement which are equal to all points on the scale.

Thus we can say that, most of the measurement in education can be done mostly at the level of ordinal scales, unless we make assumptions about the uniformity of units.

The fundamental difference between a nominal and an ordinal scale is that the nominal scale incorporates the relation of equivalence only while ordinal scale incorporates the relation of equivalence as well as greater than. This relation is flexion.

The interval scale is more precise and refined as compared to nominal and ordinal scale. This scale thus has all the characteristics and relationship of the ordinal scale.

It involves refinement but the difference between the consecutive points in the scale are equal over the entire scale. This is also called equalunet scale. Linear transformation source of measurement of temperature is

$$\frac{C}{100} = \frac{C-32}{180} = \frac{R}{80}$$

$$\frac{C}{5} = \frac{C-32}{9} = \frac{R}{4}$$

°C	0	10	20	30	40	50
°F	32	50	68	86	104	122

If we want to calculate the ratio of ΔC and ΔF at any place then we get,

$$AC = C_3 - C_2 = 20 - 10 = 10$$

$$\Delta F = F_3 - F_2 = 68 - 50 = 18$$

$$\therefore \quad \frac{\Delta C}{\Delta F} = \frac{10}{18} = \frac{5}{9}$$

Similarly, $$\frac{\Delta C}{\Delta F} = \frac{C_4 - C_3}{F_4 - F_3} = \frac{10}{18} = \frac{5}{9}$$

We can also say that tow objects having assigned numbers of 5 and 10 are as for apart on the scale as two other. Objects having assigned numbers of 15 and 20. In equation form this statement may be stated as Q – P = S – R. In this scale (2)

Zero is not fixed but arbitrary, it does not show absence of trait.

e.g. If a child gets zero in mathematics test it does not mean that he knows nothing. It implies that he cannot do correctly any of the problem. A person getting 60 marks is no doubt an intelligent, than a person with 30 marks. We can compare the difference between marks.

Thus, an interval scale gives us morden as well as equal interval and plays an important role in teaching and learning and curricular innovations.

Ratio Scale. It is most refined level of measurement and has a defined zero point and uniform units of measurement.

It is scientific, reliable land widely developed scale. It has the characteristics of interval scale. The data in this scale can be subjected to arithmetic operation. Such operation are permissible on the numerical values assigned to the objects in the data as well as on the intervals between numbers e.g length measured in inches of feets.

$$\frac{10}{5} = 2$$

or $$\frac{10}{5} \times \frac{4}{4} = 2 \text{ will be equal}$$

it is unique upto the multiplication of positive constants. In a ratio scale the ratio of any two scale points is independent to the unit of measurement. So there scales have absolute zeros.

Limitations

* Units are arbitrary
* Calculations are unique upto multiplication of positive

constants. The various scales of measurement may be compare as follows :

Scale Characteristics	Nominal Scale	Ordinal Scale	Interval Scale	Ratio Scale
Refinement	**Lowest**	**Less Refined**	**Refined**	**Highest**
Mathematical Operations	only Counting	Ranking less than or greater	Addition Subtraction	All
Units	No units	Compansion		No

16
Lesson Planning

Planning is essential not only in teaching but in all spheres of life. In the teaching profession planning is often connected with lessons. Planning of a lesson is an important equipment of a teacher in a school or in a college. A lesson plan is strictly individual; it is indeed the creation of the teacher who plans out the lesson plan. A plan is a work of art involving much imagination and study. The plan is an unfolding of the teacher's soul, it contains the life-blood of the teacher. Lesson plan is a kind of discipline, which has to be learnt in the training college.

A lesson is not mere giving of instructions, or mere doing out of facts. It becomes an occasion for learning, thinking and understanding as well as judging. Lesson planning constitutes essential learning experiences for all teachers in training because pre-planning is essential for quality teaching. But it raises an important issue: how lesson planning is to be done? The question has two dimensions, viz;

1. What is going to be the broad pattern of lesson plan?
2. How much and what kind of details in their lesson notes are to be required by the pupil-teacher.

Therefore, lesson planning is an essential pre-requisite for good teaching, the structure of the plans should vary with different teaching learning situations and with the needs of different groups of pupils. More over, whatever way you plan a lesson, lesson planning is an essential part of the teacher's work. If the teacher has planned his lesson both wisely and too well he will enter his class with confidence and with an easy conscience.

However, the lesson plan is a good servant but a bad master. It is a means to an end not an end by itself. The teacher should be able to discard his plan if a sudden situation demands it.

R.L. Stevenson states the importance of lesson plan as, "To every teacher I would say, always plan out your lesson beforehand but do not be slave to it." Ryburn also said, "To teach we must use experience already gained as starting point of work". Hence, the lesson plan reflects the intelligence, ability, capacity, resourcefulness and personality of the teacher. Lesson planning provides awareness to the structure and content with which teacher is involved in the direction to achieve the objectives.

Basic Principles

1. "Daily Lesson Planning involves defining the objectives, selecting and arranging the subject-matter and determining the method and procedure." —***Bining and Bining***
2. Lesson Plan is the title given to a statement of the objectives to be realized and the specific means by which these are attained as a result of activities during the period. —***Bossing, M.L.***
3. We may define lesson plan as a draft of the lesson put upon paper with all the important points whether of matter or method clearly marked. —***Joseph London.***
4. Lesson must be prepared for, there is nothing so fatal to a teachers' progress as unpreparedness. —***Davis***

Thus it is clear from the above definitions that lesson planning is the programme of the teacher which indicates the objections, subject-matter, learning experiences, audio-visual aids, methods and techniques etc. Generally, there are three levels of Planning.

* Weekely planning
* Monthly planning
* Annual planning

These levels may be plans as—

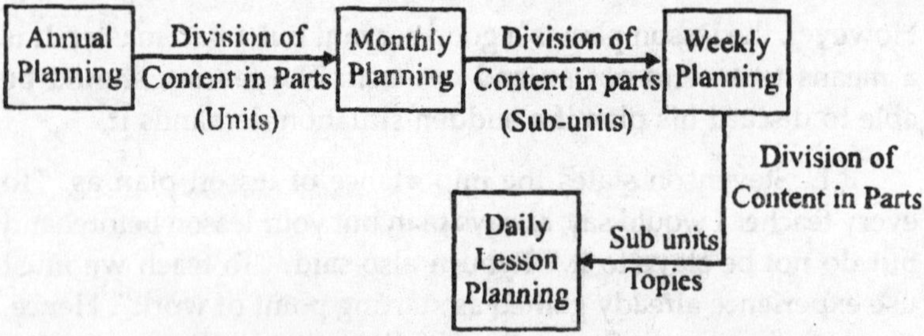

Some principles of planning are as follows—

Plan Should be Flexible. The plan should be concrete and specific as well as it should also be flexible. Each child is different in his ability, experiences, needs, his interests and each has his own attitudes. Necessary extension, revision and reorganization of plan is a favourable index of the quality of teaching.

Plan Should be Specific in Nature. A plan should give specific information as to how the teaching-learning process is expected to move forward. There should be specific provision for the anticipated procedures.

Plan Should be Realistic

(a) The mathematics teacher should do the task of planning in the real sense.

(b) The level of educational development must be taken into account.

(c) The amount of time anticipated should be examined carefully.

(d) The mathematics teacher should assess his teaching resources carefully.

It should be linked with the previous knowledge of the child. It should contain suitable subject matter.

Various Approaches. The main approaches to lesson planning given below.

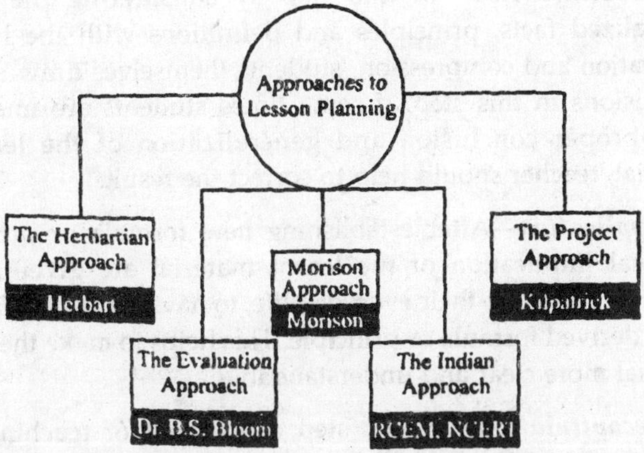

Various Approaches to Lesson Planning

Various Approaches

Herbartian formal steps for lesson planning are as follows:— (i) Preparation (ii) Presentation (iii) Association & comparison (iv) Generalisation (v) Application (vi) Recapitulation.

Preparation—In this state simply a ground is prepared. Student is made ready to learn something new. Nothing new is total to the child. Child's previous knowledge is tested in such a way that curiosity may arouse for learning something new in the mind of the child. This should be done by linking their previous knowledge with the new learning material.

Presentation—Before coming to the second step, aims of the lesson are made clear to the students. The methods and techniques employed are related to the subject matter. Material is presented to the students in an orderly manner with suitable examples, taking in account the understanding power of the child. Proper question answer technique is employed to develop the subject matter with mutual participation of the teacher and taught. Proper illustrations and aids are used according to the needs.

Association—In this step new ideas and knowledge is compared with the known similar facts to arrive at proper generalisation, to establish principle or to derive definition. It is the most important step in the process of lesson planning.

Generalisation—In this step by considering the above generalized facts, principles and definitions with the help of association and compression, students themselves draw out the conclusions in this step, if some times students are unable to have proper conclusion and generalization of the learning material, teacher should help to correct the result.

Application—After establishing new formula or principle, practical implication of the learnt material are given to the students, related to their everyday life, to have actual verification of the derived formula or principle. This helps to make the learnt material more clear and understandable.

Recapitulation—In this step assessment of teaching and learning material is done. By putting objective type questions to the students at the end of teaching. If need arise corrections are made. Finally home work is assigned to the students related to the subject matter taught.

According to Mr. Arora—

"These herbartian steps are not the final. There are numerous topics of teaching mathematics. Each and every topic can not be taught and explained by following these six formal steps rigidly. Change may be brought about in explaining and presenting the subject material according to the requirements." The Herbartian steps have also been discussed by many other educationists and writers like—Introduction, preparation, presentation, organization, comparison, association and evaluation or application.

This approach is also known as Dewey and Kilpatrick approach because it was developed by W.H. Kilpatrick and John Dewey. They gave stress on self activity, social activity and real activities of life. The basis of this approach is project method, so that its steps are same as project method. The steps of project method are listed in brief on next page.

The details of above steps are given in the project method of teaching mathematics in the previous lesson.

- Creating the situation
  ↓
- Proposing & Choosing the Project
  ↓
- Planning the project
  ↓
- Execution of the project
  ↓
- Evaluation of the project
  ↓
- Recording of the project

Dr. B.S. Bloom is the originator of this approach. According to this approach, teaching-learning activities must be objective centred Bloom also considered education as a tripoar process. Three poles are-objectives, learning experiences and change of behaviour. Evaluation includes all activities of teaching and not only pupil performance. Pupils' performance is evaluated and measured in terms of learning objectives and not achievement of the content. It may cover cognitive, affective and psychomotor learning out comes. Hence this approach is objective centred rather than content centred. Following are the steps in evaluate approach—

1. Formulating educational objectives expected behaviour and changes
   ↓
2. Creating Learing-Experiences
   ↓
3. Evaluating the change in Behaviour

The description of above steps is given in the chapter, the aims and objectives of teaching mathematics.

According to evaluation approach the format of the lesson plan may be as follows —

Teaching Point	*Objectives & Expected Behavioural Changes*	*Teaching-Learning Situations*		*Teaching Method & Technique*	*Evaluation*
		Teacher's Activities	*Student's Activities*		

Approach for India

This approach was developed by the Regional colleges of Education, governed by N.C.E.R.T. (Delhi). Now these colleges are known as Regional Institute of Education. So this approach is called Indian approach to lesson planning. In this approach importance is given to teaching objectives, teachers' activities and pupils' evaluation. Learning experiences are also considered while preparing lesson plan.

The basis of this approach is Bloom's taxonomy of objectives. N.C.E.R.T. has classified cognitive objectives in four categories in place of six categories, as given by Bloom. These categories have been discussed in the previous chapter; aims and objectives of teaching mathematics. This approach includes the following three steps—

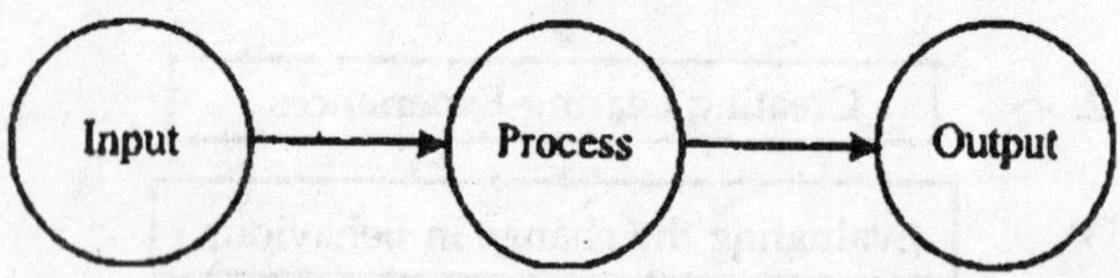

Input. Input includes the determination of Expected Behavioural Outcomes of the child. These are known as EBO's. With the help of EBO's teaching objectives are written in behavioural terms of the child by using 'mental abilities' as suggested by RCEM.

Process. To achieve the determined EBO's teaching is organized. To achieve the objectives, the teacher organizes teaching strategies and teaching material. Teaching strategies includes both teacher's and students activities. Thus teaching learning situations are created by the teacher. These all activities may be known as learning Experiences.

Output. This includes the real behavioural changes amongst students. These are called Real Learning Out Comes (RLO's). For RLO's teacher uses the various tool and techniques of evaluation. The evaluation of the child is based on EBO's.

Formale of Lesson Plan according to N.C.E.R.T.—

Input	*Process*		*Output*
(EBO's)	*Learning Experiences*		*(RLO's)*
	Teacher's Activities	*Student's Activities*	

Morrison's Approach. This approach is given by Henry. C. Morrison. It is based on units. Morrison's approach is known as ***'Cyclic Plan of teaching'***. There are following five steps—

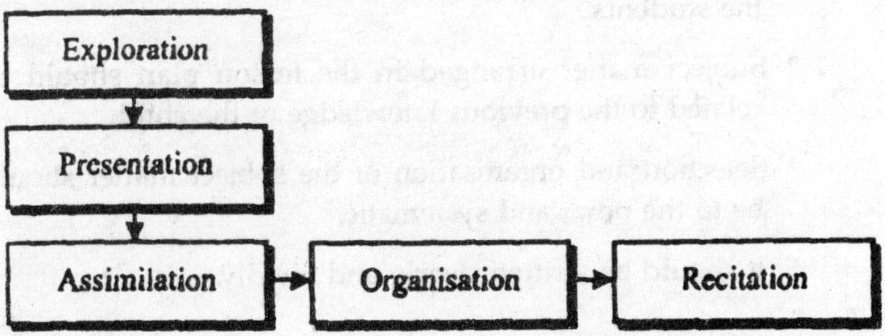

Morrison gives main stress on assimilation aspects while Herbart Process the presentation aspects of the teaching.

Only the theoretical knowledge of lesson planning is given here in this chapter. Detailed lesson plans are given in the appendices, at the end of the book, so that students will be able to prepare the lesson plans.

Main Features

* Subject matter in the lesson plan should be according to the time for teaching at the disposal of the teacher.
* Provision of homework related to the subject matter taught should be there.
* It should provide maximum participation of the child in the teaching and learning process.
* In the lesson plan there should be proper provision of the teaching aids and good illustrations.
* In the lesson plan there should be proper provision of recapitulation to have view of evaluation of the subject-matter tought to the students.
* In the lesson plan there should be provision of summary of whole subject matter.
* Lesson plan should be child centred.
* Example quoted to teach and explain the subject matter should be related to the everyday life of the child.
* Method, procedure and techniques applied for teaching should be according to the age and the mental level of the students.
* Subject matter arranged in the lesson plan should be related to the previous knowledge of the child.
* Selection and organisation of the subject matter should be to the point and systematic.
* It should be written clearly and vividly.

* Vague and irrelevant material should be avoided.
* It should clearly state the aims and objectives of the subject matter.
* It should be in written form, in good hand and bold letters.

Preparatory Steps

The teacher should consider the following points while preparing lesson plan in mathematics—

* The mathematics teacher should have mastery and full command over the subject-matter.
* The teacher should have the abilities to write objectives in behavioural terms.
* He should plan the lesson according to the psychological needs of the child.
* The teacher should have the awareness of individual differences of the children.
* The teacher should have the skills for the effective use of Blackboard.
* He should have the competency and abilities to choose appropriate methods, strategies, techniques and audio-visual aids.
* He should have the abilities of content analysis.
* The teacher should be able to construct the criterion test for evaluating child's performance.
* Previous knowledge of the child should be kept in mind before preparing the lesson.
* There should be proper co-ordination among the various components of the lesson.
* Lesson plan should be based on the needs, interests, nature of content and mental level of the children.

The Merits

* It help the teacher to understand the objectives & desirable change in the child properly.

* It helps in creating interest amongst student towards the lesson.
* It guides the teacher, what and how he must teach.
* The content is organised systematically.
* The lesson plan stimulates the teacher and student to think in an organised way.
* Lesson Plan establishes proper correlation between the new and old knowledge.
* It compells the teacher to think about the use of teaching aids.
* It develops self-confidence in the teachers.
* It inspires the teacher to improve the further lessons.
* It helps the teacher in evaluating his teaching.
* It also helps the teacher to select appropriate method & techniques of teaching.

The Demerits

* The teaching process becomes more difficult.
* There is lack of flexibility in lesson planning.
* Teacher cannot work/teach independently.
* More time is required to plan a lesson.
* Some times simple matters become complicated.
* In new or odd situations teacher feels himself helpless.

Various Stages

Major steps involved in a lesson planning are as follows—

General Entries—Subject, sub-subject, class, date, period, duration of the period, Name of the school and topic of the lesson (Only heading is written, topic is written after teacher's statement).

General Objectives

Specific Objectives and expected change in behaviour.

Teaching/Audio-visual aids

Method and Technique of Teaching

Previous knowledge of the Child—Previous knowledge and experiences related with the new knowledge or topic of the lesson.

Introduction—Testing of previous knowledge through questions.

Statement of Aim—Statement of teacher related to the topic e.g. today we will study............................(the name of the topic).

After Teacher's statement—The topic is written ***on the blackboard.***

Presentation of lesson—The following format may be followed—

Teaching Point	*Teaching Learning situations*		*Black-board Summary*	*Evaluation*
	Teacher's Activities	*Pupils Activities*		

This format is a speciman, not a universal format of lesson planning. It may differ from teacher to teacher as well as college/ University to other college. The format is different from the point of view of organization of contents, the steps remain same.

Teaching Point—The points (subject matter) to be taught in the class by the teacher. The content of the lesson is divided into small parts. Then each part is treated as teaching point. Generally a lesson should contain atleast two three teaching points.

Teachers' Activities—Teacher's statements, developmental questions, demonstrations, experiments and other activities performed by the teacher in the classroom.

Students Activities—Listening, writing, watching, giving responses and other activities performed by the child in the class-room.

Black-board Summary—It should be developed with the help of students. The teacher writes the main points, thoughts, definitions, formuale, draws diagrams and gives solution of the problem.

Evaluation—After completing the lesson, the teacher evaluates the performance of the class that to what extent students have achieved the objectives of the lesson taught in the classroom. Evaluation may be written or oral. Short answer questions should be asked objective type of questions, are best for evaluation of the lesson.

Home work—It should be based on the application of acquired knowledge.

References—In the end of lesson the teacher should give reference of books, magazines and other sources from where he/ she has organized and collected the subject matter.

Planning the Units

In unit plan, the emphasis is given to the organisation of learning experiences, teaching learning materials and though processes. The central importance is given to the needs and contemporary goals of the learnes. A unit may be conceived as a series of group planned, related and unifying experiences or activities in which the child participates in order to achieve an adaptation to or control over an area of living. This learning product is an integrated combination of skills, habits, attributes, knowledge, under standings and appreciations of the child.

Unit is not a mixture of lesson plans but it is a compound form of them. It is a big Gestalt of a teaching learning situation which can be broken up into smaller constituents not less than two and not more than seven in number which are more popularly called the lesson Plans. Each lesson presents a certain fact of the Unit. Unit plan permits the application of Gestalt Psychology in that an overview of the unit may be presented by the teacher with the help of the pupils before the actual assimilation activity of the unit begin. Hence, a unit is a logical division of class-work or activities.

Definitions of Unit Plan

According to Morrison, H.C.— "A unit is a comprehensive and significant aspect of the environment of an organized science and art."

According to Preston— "A unit is as large a block of related subjects matters as can be overviewed by the learner."

According to Samford— "Unit is an outline of carefully selected subject matter which has been isolated because of its relationship to pupils' need and interests."

According to wisley— "The unit is an organized body of information and experience designed to effect significant out come for the learner."

Need and Importance. In comparision to the lesson plan, a unit presents key ideas or big ideas of mathematics in more unified and systematic manner at various levels of treatment, for the learners of different categories. A unit is designed to plan in advance or accomplish the following—

(i) It initiates new activities or experiences which are not possible during the class period.

(ii) It individualizes instruction at its best or alternatively provides for individual and group actively on certain phases mostly resting with the children.

(iii) A unit included various type of teaching activities.

(iv) It extends students experiences beyond the limits prescribed by the syllabus.

(v) It anticipates future needs e.g., illustrative material to be borrowed, purchased or developed.

(vi) It enables links to be established either with community or a specific key idea, rather than the simple statement of either topic or headings.

(vii) It provides an opportunity for teacher and pupil interaction.

(viii) It provides the basis for evaluating pupils performance.

According to James Michael (Principles and Methods of Secondary Education, Page 276); a good unit plan should possess the following characteristics—

* The suggested learning experiences should be logically related and meaningful to the learner.
* Built in mechanism to afford definite worthwhile learning outcomes.
* The learning experiences should leave no psychological gaps in the final educational outcomes.
* The structure of a unit is broad, comprehensive and organise to achieved the learning out comes.

Various Types. According to James Michael (Principles and Methods of Secondary Education, p. 275), there are two basic types of unit—

* Teaching Unit
* Resource Unit

Teaching Unit—A teaching unit is one which is intended to be actually implemented by the teacher and the pupil instructuring large segments of a courses. Hence, it is the most important type of unit for any teacher.

Resource Unit—A resource unit is one which is intended to be a general guide in assisting the teacher to enrich the teaching unit. Thus, the resource unit is more general and comprehensive than the teaching unit.

Consequently, resource unit will include such items as extensive bibliographies, suggested problem areas, methods of teaching, analysing pupil needs and suggestions for evaluating various educational outcomes.

Essential Features. A good unit should answer some questions like;

* Why? *i.e.,* objectives.
* What? *i.e.,* content or subject matter.
* How? *i.e.* methods, techniques and procedures.
* With What? *i.e.* Material needed.
* How will? *i.e.,* Evaluation process

Thus analysing the above questions. We can conclude that a unit plan should have some essential features. Some essential features of a unit plan are as follows:

* Objectives of the unit
* The content of the unit
* The materials needed
* The methods and procedures.
* The Teaching sequence
* The Evaluation
* The References
* The brief description of the above points in given below—

Objectives. Effective teaching is based upon well defined objectives. A clearcut statement of the objectives of a unit plan should be formulated at the outset. The statements should be recorded as an essential part of his plan, it will give direction to the choice of experiences proposed later on.

In a unit plan a general objectives might be, "To develop in the student an understanding of how the sum of interior angles of a triangle is equal to 180°" and how the area of circle is equal to πr^2."

The Content of the Unit. It should indicate clearly that what content is to be included in the unit? The needed detail varies with the teacher and with the situation. In general, the beginning teacher will need to anticipate in greater details then the experienced teacher. Thus the plan include additional sources that will provide not only facts, principles, generalizations, and applications but also skills, habits, and attitudes clearly.

The Material Needed. It is a essential feature of unit planning. The material needed includes the reading materials, laboratory apparatus, films, slides, chemicals and other related material. The teacher examines the material and select for his own use. In general sense the materials are the resources needed.

Methods and Procedures. The mathematics teacher should keep in mind that the methods and procedure are the vehicles for child's experiences. If the kind and quality of child's experiences are carefully studied and planned in a systematic way in advance, the results will probably be far better. So the teacher should select and employ method and procedures very carefully.

The Teaching Sequence. It is also one of the important features of a unit plan. It indicates the sequence of the teaching activities and the time relationship of the development of ideas. It is not enough to state the objectives, outline of the content and list of the procedures and materials needed. Since the teaching is going forward on a time basis, the plan should indicate what is to be done first, and the sequence of the development of the unit. Hence, while planning a unit, the methods and procedures of the study should be scheduled well in advance.

The Evaluation. In the unit plan the anticipated procedures, methods and techniques of evaluation to be used should be indicated well. If precaution is taken in the planning phase there is greater likelihood that the evaluation will be objective based.

References. At the end of the plan proper references should be given because the student can not be directed to further study related to the proper unit.

Criteria. While planning a teaching unit, the teacher should keep following points in his mind—

* It should take in to account the needs, the interests and the capabilities of the children.
* It should provide a variety of field trips, experiments, demonstrations and projects, etc.
* The material of the unit plan should consists of familiar and related topic.
* It should be related to the social and physical environment of the children.
* It should provide new experiences which the children have not experienced earlier.
* The previous knowledge, experiences and background of the pupils should be given due importance.
* It should help and satisfy some of the future needs of the children.
* It should be the result of the co-operative planing of teacher and pupils as far as possible.
* The length of unit should be such as to maintain the interests of the students.
* It should be flexible.

The Merits. There are many merits or advantages of unit plan, some of them are as follows—

* It develops scientific attitude, problem-solving, critical thinking, skills and scientific inquiry among the children.
* While keeping in mind the mental development of child, the teacher can present subject matter in a systematic, logical and effective manner.
* It is psychologically sound approach for effective teaching learning process.
* It provides opportunity to the teacher to do experiments with his over ideas in-colaboration with pupils.

* It facilitate the use of a wide range of resource such as laboratory equipments, charts, films, reference material as an integral part of the learning experiences.
* It develops the qualities like self confidence, persistence, security, etc. in the students.
* It is also flexible to deal with a wide range of learning-situations.

The Limitations. Some of the important limitations or disadvantages are as follows—

* Preparation/Planning of unit is not easy task.
* Use of guide sheets tends to make learning monotonous and stereotyped.
* There is lack of freshness.
* Overburdening of teacher with written work.
* It is time consuming also.
* Teaching becomes mechanical.

Principles Involved

1. Principle of Unit
2. Principle of Interest
3. Principle of Development
4. Principle of Dynamism
5. Principle of Organisation.

Example of Unit Plan. Name of the unit-set Theory and Operation

Class-IX — No. of sub-unit—6

Total Periods—15 — Duration of Period—35 Minute

S.No.	*Sub-Units*	*No. of Periods*
I	Set theory and operations — Basic informations and notations	02

II	Methods of representation of a set.	02
III	Kinds of sets	03
IV	Union and intersection of sets	03
V	Venn Diagram	02
VI	Exercise: solution of problems	03
	Total Periods	15

Format of Unit Plan

1. Class............ Subject..................
2. Name of the Unit................S.No. of Unit. ....
3. No. of Periods required for the unit................
4. Duration of the period...............
5. No. of Periods for evaluation/recapitalization....................
6. No. of Periods for Remedial Teaching.............

Sub-unit and topic	Teaching points	Specific objectives & Expectual Change in behaviour	Teaching-Learning Situations		Teaching AidsHome or Audio visual aids	Evaluation Assignment	
			Teacher's Activities	Student's Activities			
1.							
2.							
3.							
4.							
5.							

Design of Unit Test —To evaluate the unit, the teacher prepares a test which is called unit test. While preparing the unit test, objectives, content (sub-units) and types of questions are given due weightage. After the selection of content and determination of objectives the weightage is given to the different

aspects of the unit, 'Blue-Print' is prepared, Blue-Print presents the distribution of marks to various objectives, nature of content and types of questions. Blue-Print plays an important role in designing a unit test. Blue print represents the distribution of marks on the following three basis :

(i) Weightage to objectives

(ii) Weightage to sub-units

(iii) Weightage to forms of questions

UNIT TEST
DESIGN OF UNIT TEST

Units : Elementary Set Theory

Class IX

Time 35 Minute *Maximum marks: 20*

Weightage to Objectives

S.No.	*Objectives*	*Marks*	*Percentages (%)*
1.	Knowledge (K)	8	40%
2.	Understanding (U)	2	10%
3.	Application (A)	8	40%
4.	Skill (S)	2	10%
	Total marks	20	100%

Number and Forms of questions

S. No.	*Types of Question (Items)*	*Marks allotted to each question*	*Number of question*	*Total marks*
1.	Objective Type	1	10	10
2.	Short Answer Type	1½	4	6
3.	Essay Type	4	1	4
	Total		15	20

Weightage to Sub-Units

S.No.	*Contents*	*Marks*	*Percentage*
1.	Definitions and Notations of Sets.	2	10%
2.	Different types of the Sets.	6	30%
3.	Difference of two sets and equality of sets.	3	15%
4.	Basic operations on sets.	5	25%
5.	Venn-diagrams and its representation.	4	20%
	Total	20	100%

Thus on the basis of Blue-Print, the test is constructed. After the construction of test, the test is administered in the class. The scoring key is also prepared at the time of test construction. On the basis of Scoring key the response sheets are evaluated.

Planning for Resources

It has been observed that the role of the pupil-teacher in preplanning is to discover resources and techniques to help pupils' learning through a group attack upon real problems. In the efforts to achieve this end, pupil teachers are turning to the development of resource plans. In resource plans knowledge increases because in the preparation of resource plan number of books are considered and we get a large number of concepts which help in the development of our knowledge.

A resource plan is simply a collection of suggested learning activities and materials oraganised around a given topic to be used for teacher's pre-planning. It means when resources are added to a unit plan, it is called a resource plan. In other words, we can say to provide sources to the unit which assists teacher in preplanning is called a resource plan. Thus resource plan is a device that can given teachers the security they seek. The resource plan may be employed to provide a unified approach to some particular problem. A school may further extend the development of resource plan until they constitute an overall curriculum plan for general education.

A resource plan is developed by a group of teachers, preferably representing several subject areas, around a broad problem area. The goal-statements, the activities of child, and the material developed in the teaching unit on one specific problem will contribute constantly to the work of the group of teachers who are constructing the resource unit plan. In this way classroom ideas, activities and discoveries produced by various specific learning units flow continuously into the resource unit plan and enrich it considerably.

There are various problems which are faced by the teacher and student in the class. Some of these problems may be:

* Entering a new school
* Choosing an occupation
* Understanding and respecting other members of society.
* Getting along with people

The above problem may be removed if the teacher is also familiar with these problems. In other words it mean that a resource plan should not only be bookish but it should be related to all round development of a child.

Definitions of Resource Plan

According to Biddick—"A record of exploration made by a teacher or a group of teachers of the needs of pupils within some broad area of living, in which it is believed these needs might be appropriately met and of ways for determining whether or not they have been met."

According to Prof. Harold Alberty—"A systematic and comprehensive survey, analysis and organization of the possible resource including problems, issues, activities, bibliographies, etc. which a teacher might utilize in planning, developing and evaluating a learning unit."

It is clear from the above definitions that the resource plan is much more comprehensive than a lesson or units plan.

Blue Print of the Unit

S. No.	Objectives Types of Questions Contents	Knowledge			Understanding			Application			Skill			Total
		OT	SAT	ET	OT	SAT	ET	OT	SAT	ET	OT	SAT	ET	
1.	Definition and the Notation of the set	–	1½(1)	–	–	–	–	–	–	–	1(1)	–	–	2½(2)
2.	Different types of the sets	1(1)	–	–		1(1)	1½(1)	(1)	1	–	–	–	–	4½(4)
3.	Difference of two sets and equality of sets	1(1)	–	–	2(2)	–	–	1½(1)	–	–	–	–	–	4½(4)
4.	Basic Operations on the sets	–	–	2(½)	–	–	–	–	1½(1)	–	–	–	–	3½(1)
5.	Venn-diagram and its representation.	1(1)	–	–	1(1)	–	–	–	–	2(½)	1(1)	–	–	5(3½)
	Total	3(3)	1½	(1)2(½)	4(4)	1½	(1)	1(1)	3(2)	2(½)	2 (2)–	–		20(15)

Note— (a) Number out side the bracket indicate number of marks.

(b) Number inside the bracket indicates the number of question.

(c) Abbreviations : OT = Objective Type, SAT = Short Answer Type; Et = Essay Type Questions.

There are some ways or sources from where the teacher gets the resources for preparing the resource plan. Some of the places from where resources are taken by the teachers are as follows—

* Consulting books and literature from liberary.
* Teacher's own knowledge, experiences and memory.
* Enquiry from the other teachers.
* Resources are also available in the State Research centres. Teachers can go and find resources to make resource plan.

Criteria for Constuction and Evaluation of a Resource Plan. There are some suggested criteria for constuction and evaluation of resouce plan:

1. It should stimulate professional growth in democratic ways of learning with students.
2. It should provide the experiences to students that are necessary for reflective thinking.
3. It should be recognized for easy use by teachers.
4. It should be based on a definite philosophy of education.
5. It should be developed by several teachers representing as many subject areas as much as possible.
6. It should explore community resources that will be useful in developing the learning unit.
7. It should be based upon sound principles of learning.
8. It should be practicable under prevailing school conditions.
9. It should contain many more suggestions than any class is likely to use.
10. It should be suited to students, maturity.
11. The resource plan should recognize student's needs and interests.
12. It should include specific ways in which the students can participate in planning, developing and evaluating the work.
13. It should provide suitable socializing activities.

Though all these criteria runs the important thread of pupil-teacher planning. It is rather a vehicle for facilitating such planning. If it is used as a dynamic flexible device that grows and changes as each successive class group draws upon the suggestions it contain. It can become a stimulus to group planning by children as well as teachers.

Steps Involved in developing a Resource Plan. The following steps are involved in a resource plan —

Significance of the Area/Topic — In this step, the importance of the topic is written which is going to be taught.

Possible Learning Outcomes — In this step, objectives are written. The objectives may be of knowledge, comprehension and application, etc.

Outline of the Content — In this step, the content of the area is written.

Suggested Activity — It is the heart of the resource plan. In this step, suggested activities are organised. There are three types of suggested activities such as —

Introductory Activities — In this, after showing charts, models, pictures questions are asked to the students and the introduction is extracted by the students or with the help of children. (Less resources)

Developmental Activities — It includes observation, experiences, drill activity, group co-operation, experimentation and creativity. (maximum resources)

Concluding Activities—It involves the bringing of learning experiences closer to the knowledge of the children, (minimum resources)

Suggested Materials—Here comes the charts, models, pictures, etc or any other audio-visual aid.

Suggestion for Evaluation—In the end, evaluation is done for testing the knowledge gained by the students by asking questions to them.

Format of Resource Planning

Subject

Topic/Area

Level/STD

Possible Learning Outcomes/Objectives

S. No.	*Content Analysis/ Sub Topic*	*Suggested Activities*	*Suggested Materials*	*Suggested Evaluation*

References—In the end, write the references, means from where you have collected the resources.

Difference between a Resource Plan and A Unit Plan

Unit Plan	Resource Plan
1. It is a narrower terms	1. It is a wider term. Unit incorporates in resource unit.
2. Less number of experiences due to planning	2. Number of experiences are more due to large resources.
3. It is important as it is for the students to cover the syllabus.	3. Not much important as it is for teachers to make teaching effective.
4. It is rigid as it is needed by the curriculum.	4. It is flexible. The work can be done if we are not able to get resource.
5. It is prepared by a teacher individually.	5. It may be prepared by a group of teachers.

Importance of Resource Plan. The importance of resource plan are as follows—

1. It may be employed to provide a unified approach to some particular problems.

2. It better organises the learning experience as we can decide weekly in which topic which resource is used.
3. It makes the reference material familiar or it gives the knowledge of resources only when we use resources.
4. It works as a practical stock house for teachers.
5. It makes the teaching-learning effective.
6. It determines the work system means which sub-unit is taught and which aid is used.
7. It is a device that can give teachers the security which they seeks.

Utility of Resource Plan. The resource plan is intended to help a group of teachers to plan the ways or sources in which they themselves and their students may enrich their study of a given problem. The mathematics teachers and other subject specialist can be helpful to the pupil teachers as they work out the resource plan. The mathematics teachers usually develop a brief statement of the problem and its significance to the learners. They answer the questions that pupils were asking about the problem. That questions would remain open for additions and revision.

Then the mathematics teachers work out a list of objectives related to the problem area. This list of objectives should be based upon the pupil's own needs and interests. After preparing a list of objectives, the teacher might develop a list of learning experiences that will contribute to the solution of the problems to achieve the teacher's and pupils purposes. These learning experiences should include reading, writing, listening, speaking, observations, computing, manipulating, creating, hurraying, summarizing, and evaluating activities. There should be a list of possible learning experiences focussing around the development of the problem. The learning experiences may be categorized in the form of various activities such as:

* Initiatory or preparatory activities.
* Developmental and investigational activities.
* Evaluative activities.

Hence with such an approach to planning, a mathematics teacher can lay the foundation of a rich and real learning-experiences. The teacher of mathematics need not work alone at this task, but he/she may be a member of a team of mathematics teachers and all concerned with the same goal.

Summary

Lesson Planning in Maths

Meaning and Definitions. Lesson Plan is a kind of discipline, which has to be learnt in the training college. Lesson Planning constitutes essential learning experiences for all teachers in training because pre-planning is essential for quality teaching.

While planning some principles should be followed such as: The plan should be—

* Flexible
* Specific
* Realistic
* Linked with the previous knowledge
* Contain suitable subject-matter, etc.

Generally there are three levels of planning—

* Weekly
* Monthly
* Annual

Various Approaches to Lesson Planning

The Herbarian Approach—Five steps system.

Steps:

(a) Preparation → Presentation → Association
Recapitulation → Application → Generalization

(b) Introduction (Preparation) → Presentation → Comparision and Association

Application ← Generalization←
(evaluation)

The Project Approach—Dewey and Kilpatrick approach

Steps:

Creating the situation → Proposing and choosing the project → Planning the Project
↓
Recording of the Project ← Evaluation of the Project ← Execution of the Project.

The Evaluation Approach — (Dr. B.S. Bloom)

Formulating educational objectives and expected behavioural changes	→	Creating Learning Experiences	→	Evaluating The changes in Behaviour

Indian Approach — RCE, Mysore

Steps :

Input (EBO's)	Process (Teacher's and Student's Activities)	Output (RLO's)

Morrison's Approach—H.C. Morrison

Exploration → Presentation → Assimilation
↓
Recitation ← Organisation ←

* Characteristics of good lesson plan
* Precautions while preparing a Lesson Plan
* Merits and Demerits of Lesson Plan
* Steps involved in Lesson Planning

Unit Planning in Maths—It permits the application of Gestalt psychology. A unit may be conceived as a series of experiences and activities.

* Meaning and Definitions
* Need and importance of unit plan

* Types of Unit Plan : Teaching unit and resource unit.
* Essential Features of a Unit Plan: Objectives, the content, material needed, methods and procedures, teaching sequence, evaluation and references.
* Criteria of a good unit.
* Merits and Demerits/Limitations of unit plan.,
* Principles involved in unit planning: Principles of unit, interest.
* Development, Dynamism and organisation.
* Example of unit plan.
* Format of unit plan.

Design of Unit Test

(a) Selection of content/Unit.

(b) Determination objectives with specifications and expected behaviour changes.

(c) Preparation of Blue-Print

(i) Weightage to objectives

(ii) Weightage to content; sub-units

(iii) Weightage to forms of questions

(d) Construction of Unit test.

(e) Administration and scoring of the test.

Resource Plan in Mathematics

* Meaning and Definitions

A resource plan is simply a collection of suggested learning activities and materials organised around a given topic to be used for teacher's pre-planning. Resource plan is a device that can give teachers the security they seek. It is much more comprehensive than a lesson or unit plan.

* Some places from where resources are taken by the teachers— Books, literature, teachers' over knowledge, experiences, memory, enquiry from other teachers, etc.
* Criteria for construction and evaluation of a resource plan.
* Steps involved in developing a resource plan: Significance of Area/ topic, possible Learning out comes, out line of the content, suggested activities, suggested materials, suggestions for evaluation.
* Format of Resource Plan.
* Difference between a Resource and Unit Plan
* Utility of resource plan for a mathematics teacher.

QUESTIONS

(A) Essay Type Questions

1. What is the importance of planning in mathematics teaching? Describe the origin and various approaches to lesson planning.
2. What do you mean by unit plan? Mention its merits and demerits.
3. What are the aims of unit plan in mathematics teaching? Differentiate between Unit and lesson plan.
4. Give the importance of unit and lesson plan.
5. Why should a teacher plan his lesson before going to the classroom? Clarify.
6. Prepare a lesson plan on any topic of mathematics for a period of 35 minutes duration giving specific objectives in terms of behavioural changes.
7. What is unit test? How is it prepared? Explain.
8. Prepare a detailed lesson plan on any of the following topics, mentioning clearly the teaching points, teaching method and teaching objectives.

(i) Set theory

(ii) Compound Interest

(iii) $(a + b)^2 = a^2 + b^2 + 2ab$

(iv) Law of Indices

(v) Logarithms

9. Illustrate the various steps of lesson planning. What is the utility of lesson planning for a mathematics teacher?
10. From any branch of mathematics, selecting a unit for any class, prepare a table of questions for various teaching points, objectives, teaching aids and evaluation.
11. What do you mean by 'Resource Plan' in mathematics? What is the utility of resource plan for a mathematics teacher?
12. Define 'Resource Plan' Discuss the various steps in developing a resource plan in mathematics.
13. What is the importance of resource plan in maths teaching? What is the criteria for construction and evaluation of a Resource Plan?
14. Define the term 'Resource Plan'. What is the difference between resource and unit plan.
15. What is a 'Resource Plan'? How is it prepared? Explain.
16. Write notes on the following.

    (a) Steps and criteria for construction and evaluation of Resource Plan.

    (b) Utility of Resource Plan for a mathematics teacher.

    (c) Deference between lesson and Unit planning.

    (d) Importance of Resource Plan and deference between unit and resource plan.
17. What are the different approaches of lesson planning? Explain in detail.

18. What do you understand by the lesson-planning in maths? What precautions should be taken which preparing a lesson plan.

(B) Objective Type Questions—

1. The five steped system of lesson planning was started by—

   (a) Herbart (c) Kilpatrick
   (b) Morrison (d) None of them

2. Preparation of Daily lesson planning includes—

   (a) Determination of objectives
   (b) Selection of Content
   (c) Determination of methods
   (d) a + b + c

3. According to RCEM approach the correct order is—

   (a) Input, output, Process (c) Output Process, Input,
   (b) Process, Input, output (d) None of them

4. Essential features of a unit plan are:

   (a) Objectives of the unit (c) Teaching sequence
   (b) Content of the unit (d) All the above

5. A unit Plan should—

   (a) be flexible
   (b) provide a variety
   (c) consists of familiar topics
   (d) All the above

6. The more comprehensive Plan is—

   (a) Resource Plan (c) Lesson Plan
   (b) Unit Plan (d) All the above

(C) Underline the Correct Alternative in the Following—

(i) Lesson Plan/Unit Plan is the mathematics teacher's planning for a period.

(ii) Unit Plan/Lesson Plan helps the teacher of maths to be systematic in classroom.

(iii) Unit Plan/Resource plan is prepared by a group of mathematics teachers.

(iv) Prepration/Generalization/introduction is the first step of Herbartian approach to lesson planning.

(v) Resource unit/Teaching unit is a larger block or part of content.

17

Major Contributors

Arya Bhata

The Indian mathematician and astronomer Aryabhata (476 A.D.) is well known for his work. 'Arya Bhata' dealing will astronomy and mathematics (Quadratic equation) tables of sines and other rules of algebra and trigonometry.

He was born in 476 A.D. at Pataliputra near Patna in Bihar. He gave the idea of representing unknown quantities with letters. The digits from 1 to 25 are represented by the first 25 (वर्ग) letters, for example, ka (क) means 1 kha (ख) means 2 and so on. Similarly letter य, र, ल, व, श, ब, स, ह, represents 30, 40, 50, 60, 70, 80 etc. Where as अ, आ, इ, ई, उ, ऊ etc. represents 10^0, 10^1, 10^2 and so on.

His most famous book is known as 'Aryabhrtia.' One chapter of the book refers to mathematics while the remaining four chapters deal with Astronomy. In arithmetic, Algebra and place Geometry Aryabhata suggested humerons rules. A few important rules are enlisted Below—

1. Area of triangle $= \frac{1}{2} \times$ Base $\times$ Height
2. The value of Pi (π) $= 3.1416$
3. Area of circle πr^2
4. Sum (sn) of AP $= \frac{n}{2}[2a + (n - l)d]$

Besides this, he gave the idea of decimal system, properties of (corresponding sides are proportional). Similar triangles method of finding sum of squares and cubes of natural numbers are pythagoras theorem.

To sum up Aryabhata was really one of the greatest genius of his time in the field of mathematics and Astronomy.

Brahmagupta

The ancient Indian astronomer Brahmagupta is credited with having put forth the concept or zero for the fist time : Brahmagupta is said to have been born in the year 598 A.D. st Bhillamala (today's Bhinmal) in Gujarat, Western India. Much is known about Brahmagupta's early life, we are told that his name as a mathematician was well established when K. Vyaghramukha of the Chapa dynasty made him the court astronomer. Of his two treatises, Brahma-sputa siddhanta and Karanakhandakhadyaka, first is more famous. It was a corrected version of the old Astronomical text, Brahma siddhanta, it was in his Brahma-sputa siddhanta, for the first time ever he had formulated the rules of the operation zero, foreshadowing the decimal system numeration. With the integration of zero into the numerals it became possible to note higher numerals with limited characters.

In the earlier Roman and Babylonian systems of numeration, a large number of characters were required to denote higher numerals. Thus enumeration and computation became unwieldy. For instance, as E the Roman system of numeration, the number thirty would have to be written as X: while as per the decimal system it would 30, further the number thirty three would be XXXIII as per Roman system, would be 33 as per the decimal system. Thus it is clear how the introduction of the decimal system made possible the writing of numerals having a high value with limited characters. This also made computation easier.

Apart from developing the decimal system based on the incorporation of zero in enumeration, Brahmagupta also arrived at solution for indeterminate equations of 1 type ax 2 + 1 = y^2 and thus can be called the founder of higher branch of mathematics called numerical analysis. Brahmagupta's treatise Brahma sputa-siddhanta was translated into Arabic under the title Sind Hind.

For several centuries this translation gained a standard text of reference in the Arab world. It was from this translation of an

Indian text of mathematics that the Arab mathematics perfected the decimal system and gave the world its current system of enumeration which we call the Arab numerals, which are originally Indian numerals.

Bhaskara

Bhashara or Bhasharacharya is the most well known ancient Indian mathematician. He was born on 1114 A.D. At Bijjada Bida (Bijapur, Karnataka) in the Sahyadari hill. He was the first to declare that any number divided by zero is infinity and that the sum of any number and infinity is infinity. He is famous for his book Siddhanta Shiromani (1150 A.D.). It is divided into four sections—Leelavati (a book on arithmetic), Bijaganita (algebra), Goladnayaya (chapter on sphere—celestial globe), and Granoganita (mathematics of a planets), Leelavati contains many interesting problems and was a very popular text book. Bhaskara introduce Chakrawal, or the cyclic method, to solve algebraic expressions. Six centuries later, European mathematician like Galois, Euler and lagrange rediscovered its method and called it "Inverse cyclic". Bhaskara can also be called the founder of differential calculus. He gave an example of what is now called "differential coefficient" and the basic idea of what is now called "Rolle's theorem." Unfortunately, later Indian mathematician did not take any notice of this. Five centuries, later, Newton and Leibnitz developed this subject. As an astronomer Bhaskara is renowned for his concept of Tatakalikagati (instantaneous motion).

Shrinivasa Ramanujan Aiyanger

Ramanujan one of the Indian mathematics (1887-1920) is best known for his work on hypergeometric series and continued fraction.

Ramanujan was born in Brahmin family on December 22, 1887 at Erode (Tanjore district) Madras. He got his school education at Kumba-koram. He won a scholarship in matriculation examination. His teachers were very much impressed by his injected and special gifted abilities in mathematics.

At the age of thirteen, he could solve all problems of Loney's trigonometry without any external help and by the time he was fourteen, he got the theorems for sine and the cosine which were given by L. Euler, Besides this in 1903 he studied the synopsis of George School Bridge, related to elementary result in pure and applied mathematics.

This book opened a whole for new world him. He got the solution with his own methods.

Later, on the he joined the government college, Kumba koram. For the sake of mathematics, he took least interest in English. Due to this he was plucked in the examination and was debarred from scholarship. After this he went to Vishakhapatnam (A.P.) and then to Madras. Once again he tried to pass his university examination but due to ill health at the time of examination in (1907), he could not do so. He did not loose heart and worked independently for years together.

In 1909, he was married. For livelihood a means of earning was must. He got a job of clerk in the office of Madras port trust. Even in service here kept his interest alive in the field of mathematics.

In 1991, he started to publish some of his finding, Prof. G.H. Hardy of the university of Cambridge was greatly impressed by his talented abilities in the field of mathematics. After going through 120 theorems of Ramanujan. Professor Hardy remarked : "I had never seen anything the least like them before. A single look at them is enough to show that they could only be written down by a mathematician of the highest class."

His work thrown light on divergent series; Hypergeometric series and continued fraction, Definite integrals. Partition-functions, Ecliptic functions, the theory of numbers, fractional differentiation and highly composite numbers.

In 1914 Ramanujan went to Cambridge. His patience, memory, power of calculation and intution made him the greatest formalist of his time. Later on, in 1918 he was elected a fellow of trinity college Cambridge. He did a lot of work in a very short period of his life. Due to Tuberculosis, he died on April 26, 1920. He was simply thirty three old at that time.

"He was unquestionably one of the great masters"

Blaise Pascal

He was a French mathematician, physicist, religious philosopher, and a master of prose. He laid the foundation for the modern theory of probabilities. He formulated Pascal's law of pressure and propagated a religious doctrine that taught the experience of God through the heart rather than through reason. Pascal's theory of probability was based upon gambling for as he once said him self, "we are compelled to gamble." He said that if two players of equal skill were to leave the table before the game, their scores, the number of points which constitute the game being given, it is desired to find in what proportion they should divide the stakes. Through his studies he discovered that whenever a game is won by whoever obtained m + n points (one) player has m while other has n points the answer is simply derived from the arithmetical triangle.

P.C. Mahalanobis

He founded the Indian Statistical Research Institute in Calcutta. In 1958, he started the National Sample Surveys which gained international fame. He died in 1972 at the age of 79.

C.R. Rao.

A well know statistician, famous for his "theory of estimation" (1945). His formulae and theory include "Cramer-Rao inequality", "Fischer-Rao theorem" and "Rao-Blackwellisation."

C.R. Kaprekar

Fond of numbers. Well known for *"Kaprekar Constant"* 6174. Take any four digit number in which all digits are not alike. Arrange its digits in descending order and subtract from it the number by arranging the digits in ascending order. If this process is repeated with remainders ultimately number 6174 is obtained, which then generates itself.

Harish Chandra

Greatly developed the branch of higher mathematics known as the infinite dimensional group representation theory.

Narendra Karmarkar

Indian born Narendra Karmakar, working at Bell Labs USA, stunned the world in 1984 with his new algorithm to solve linear programming problems. This made the complex calculations much faster, and had immediate applications in airports, warehouses, communication networks etc.

The most fundamental contribution of ancient India in mathematics is the invention of decimal system of enumeration, including the invention of zero. The decimal system uses nine digits (1 to 9) and the symbol zero (for nothing) to denote all natural numbers by assigning a place value to the digits. The Arabs carried this system to Africa and Europe. The vedas and Valmiki Ramayana used this system, though the exact dates of these work are not known. Aryans came 1000 years later, around 2000 B.C. they identified various nakshatras (constellations) and named the months after them. They could count up to 10^{12}, while the Greeks count upto 10^4 and Romans up to 10^8. Pythagoras theorem can be also traced to Aryans sulbasutras. These sutras, estimated to be between 800 B.C. and 500 B.C., cover large number of geometric principles.

The concept of zero originated in ancient India. It is fundamental because, terms to identify visible or perceptible objects do not require much ingenuity. In ancient India the terms used to describe zero included Pujyam, Shunyam, Bindu the concept of a void on blank was termed as Shukla and Shubra.

It is a short-hand method of calculation and by this feature, it scores ones conventional arithmetic. In ancient India conventional mathematics is termed ganitam.

Contribution of Mathematicians

Contribution of Arya-Bhata Brahmagupta, Bhaskara-charya, Ramanujan and Pascal etc.

QUESTIONS

(A) Essay Type Items—

1. Shri Ramanujan is considered as the greatest Indian mathematician of this age. Outline his contribution to the mathematics world.
2. Discuss the contribution of Arya Bhata and Brahamagupta in the field of mathematics.
3. Write an essay on contribution of "ancient India to mathematics."
4. Discuss the historical background of mathematics. Enlist the great Indian mathematician.
5. Explain the contribution of Arya Bhata and Srinivasa Ramanujana as a great mathematician.
6. Discuss the contribution of following Indian mathematics in the development of mathematics —

   (a) Brahamagupta (b) Arya Bhata
   (c) Ramanujan
7. Write an essay on 'Algebra the other mathematics.'
8. Write short notes on the following—
   (a) Concept of zero
   (b) Development of Algebra as other mathematics
   (c) Contribution of Arya Bhata & Brahamagupta to mathematics
   (d) Historical development of mathematics in ancient India.

(B) Objective Type Items

(i) Multiple Choice Items—Select correct alternative--

1. Which of the following were formulated and applied in the drafting of mandalas for architectural purposes—

(a) arithmetic (c) rekha-ganita
(b) algebra (d) none of these

2. Algorithm, which is widely used in designing soft ware programmes for computers was derived from—

(a) Arabic mathematics (c) Christian kingdom
(b) Indian mathematics (d) Australian mathematics

3. Bhaskara's Leelavati was translated into English by—

(a) James Taylor (c) A.L. Basham
(b) Mark Taylor (d) none of these

4. Who arrived at solution for indeterminate equations of type $ax^2 + 1 = y^2$

(a) Arya Bhata (c) Brahamagupta
(b) Ramanujan (d) none of these

5. The cyclic method or chakrawal was introduced by—

(a) Brahmagupta (c) Pascal
(b) Bhaksara (d) Arya Bhata

(ii) True/False Items—

1. Aryans identified various nakshatras and named the months.
2. The concept of zero and algebra was originated in ancient India.
3. Algebra is a short-hand method of calculation.
4. The book siddhanta suramin was written by Brahamagupta.
5. The formula to calculate area of triangle and circle was given by Arya Bhata.